GERMAN
Conversational
REVIEW GRAMMAR

GERMAN *Conversational* REVIEW GRAMMAR

Walter E. Glaettli
R. Elwood Backenstoss
CENTENARY COLLEGE FOR WOMEN

AMERICAN BOOK COMPANY NEW YORK

Illustrated by Jon Nielsen
Cover motif and frontispiece: Kaiser-Wilhelm-Gedächtniskirche, Berlin

EP 10 9 8 7 6 5 4 3 2 1

Preface

German Conversational Review Grammar presents a systematic review of German grammar, along with a great deal of oral and written practice in the language. It combines lively dialogs, comprehensive yet concise explanations of structural elements, and varied exercises. The following principles guided the authors in the preparation of the text:

1. Progress in German consists in the gradual sharpening of several skills: to understand spoken German, to speak it with reasonable fluency, and to write correct German on a level with one's speaking ability. (These skills also relate to the reading skill, which is best promoted through a variety of materials and sources appropriate to particular situations and objectives.)
2. Most intermediate German courses enroll students with varied basic preparation. It is necessary and desirable, therefore, to have a thorough review of fundamentals, along with much audio-lingual and written practice.

Each lesson consists of four major sections: *Gespräch*, *Nützliche Ausdrücke*, *Grammatik*, *Übungen*.

In the *Gespräche*, the authors have made every effort to keep the language uncontrived and spontaneous. Each conversation is accompanied by its English equivalent, which allows the student to check meanings immediately, without losing the flow of speech through having to refer to footnotes or vocabularies. As much as practicable, the conversations apply the inductive technique: points of grammar, idiomatic expressions, and verb forms featured in a lesson are used in the *Gespräche* before their formal presentation and explanation in

Grammatik. Each *Gespräch* is immediately followed by a set of questions and by a sequence of directed dialog designed to extend the student's oral experience.

The *Nützliche Ausdrücke* include the most important idiomatic expressions occurring in a *Gespräch*. A subsequent exercise asks the student to use a specified number of these expressions in sentences of his own.

In *Grammatik*, grammatical principles are thoroughly reviewed. Frequency, difficulty, and importance have in general determined the order of topics. For example, the subjunctive, since it is extensively used in conversation, is presented in Lessons Thirteen and Fourteen, starting with contrary-to-fact conditions because of the more fixed usage of subjunctive II forms, and following with indirect discourse. Grammar topics are consecutively numbered throughout the book for easy reference. In line with modern linguistic methods, examples patterned closely after material in the *Gespräche* precede the explanations of the constructions involved.

The *Übungen* reinforce what the student has learned in the earlier sections of a lesson. They concentrate on thorough practice in listening and comprehending, varying patterns, substituting, and completing. The translation exercise near the end of each lesson avoids isolated sentences by following a theme suggested by the *Gespräch*. Starting with Lesson Six, each lesson has an *Aufsatz* giving a detailed topic to guide the student in the preparation of a composition.

For classes having three or four meetings a week, the following procedure is recommended for minimum completion of one lesson a week:

First day: *Gespräch*, *Fragen*, *Konversation*, *Nützliche Ausdrücke*, and the exercise based on the latter.

Second day: Review of *Grammatik* and structural exercises.

Third day: Review of the *Gespräch*, the translation exercise, and (from Lesson Six on) the *Aufsatz*.

Information about the tapes accompanying *German Conversational Review Grammar* appears inside the front cover of this book.

Contents

GERMAN
Conversational
REVIEW GRAMMAR

Present Tense;
Imperative.

Lektion 1

I. GESPRÄCH: Fahrt zum Flughafen

(Herr und Frau Lenz und ihr Sohn Otto fahren im Auto zum Flughafen von Frankfurt.)

FRAU LENZ: Wie weit ist es zum Flughafen?

OTTO: Etwa fünfunddreißig Minuten. Ich kenne den Weg sehr gut. Ich kann die Strecke sogar in zwanzig Minuten fahren.

HERR LENZ: Fahr nicht zu schnell! Du bist erst achtzehn Jahre alt, Otto. Ich lasse dich heute gern am Steuer sitzen, aber ich bitte dich, sei vorsichtig!

OTTO: Keine Angst! Hier in der Stadt fahre ich langsam. Aber wir kommen bald auf die Autobahn. Dort geht es sehr schnell.

Ride to the Airport

(Mr. and Mrs. Lenz and their son Otto are driving to the Frankfurt airport.)

MRS. LENZ: How far is it to the airport?

OTTO: About 35 minutes. I know the way very well. I can even drive it in twenty minutes.

MR. LENZ: Don't drive too fast! You're only eighteen years old, Otto. I'm glad to let you drive today, but please be careful.

OTTO: Don't worry. Here in the city I drive slowly. But we're coming to the autobahn soon. There the traffic is very fast.

HERR LENZ: Der Weg zum Flughafen führt gar nicht über die Autobahn. Ich glaube, du fährst in der falschen Richtung.

OTTO: Wenn wir durch die Stadt gehen, müssen wir bei jeder Straßenkreuzung halten. Wir machen besser einen Umweg und nehmen die Autobahn.

HERR LENZ: Es fällt mir eben ein, daß wir noch tanken müssen. Halte bei dieser Tankstelle!

TANKWART: Guten Morgen! Was wünscht der Herr?

HERR LENZ: Geben Sie mir zwanzig Liter Benzin! Bitte prüfen Sie auch den Ölstand!

TANKWART: Sehr gerne. (*Füllt den Tank und prüft den Ölstand.*) Sie brauchen einen Liter Öl. Wünschen Sie schweres oder leichtes Öl?

HERR LENZ: Mittelschwer, bitte. Wieviel schulde ich Ihnen?

TANKWART: Das Benzin ist dreizehn Mark, das Öl vier Mark fünfzig. Also siebzehn Mark fünfzig.

HERR LENZ: Hier.

TANKWART: Danke. Auf Wiedersehen!

OTTO: So. Nun sind wir auf der Autobahn. In zehn Minuten sind wir am Flughafen.

MR. LENZ: You don't take the autobahn to go to the airport. I think you're driving in the wrong direction.

OTTO: If we go through the city, we have to stop at every intersection. It's better to make a detour and take the autobahn.

MR. LENZ: It just occurs to me that we still have to get gas. Stop at this gas station.

ATTENDANT: Good morning. What would you like, sir?

MR. LENZ: Give me twenty liters of gas. Please check the oil, too.

ATTENDANT: Certainly. (*Fills the gas tank and checks the oil.*) You need a liter of oil. Do you want heavy or light oil?

MR. LENZ: Medium, please. How much do I owe you?

ATTENDANT: The gas is 13 marks, the oil 4 marks 50. That makes 17 marks 50.

MR. LENZ: Here you are.

ATTENDANT: Thank you. So long!

OTTO: Well, now we're on the autobahn. In ten minutes we'll be at the airport.

HERR LENZ:	Das Flugzeug landet um zehn Uhr zwanzig. Es dauert noch eine halbe Stunde, bis unser junger Freund aus Amerika ankommt.
FRAU LENZ:	Er ist gewiß sehr müde. Er sitzt ja schon zehn Stunden im Flugzeug.
HERR LENZ:	Das lange Sitzen ist nicht sehr angenehm. Er hat gewiß die ganze Nacht nicht geschlafen. Immerhin, der Flug von New York nach Frankfurt dauert nicht zehn, sondern nur sechs Stunden. Unser junger Freund sitzt also erst sechs Stunden im Flugzeug.
OTTO:	Da drüben seht ihr bereits den Flughafen. Der Parkplatz ist gleich beim Hauptgebäude.
HERR LENZ:	Hier ist die Einfahrt. Du hast gut gefahren, Otto.

MR. LENZ:	The plane lands at 10:20. We still have a half-hour before our young friend from America arrives.
MRS. LENZ:	He must be very tired. He has been sitting in the airplane for ten hours.
MR. LENZ:	Sitting a long time isn't very pleasant. He probably hasn't slept all night. However, the flight from New York to Frankfurt doesn't take ten but only six hours. Therefore, our young friend has been sitting in the airplane for only six hours.
OTTO:	Over there you see the airport already. The parking lot is right by the main building.
MR. LENZ:	Here is the entrance. You drove well, Otto.

Fragen

Antworten Sie auf deutsch!

1. In wieviel Minuten kann Otto die Strecke zum Flughafen fahren?
2. Was sagt Herr Lenz zum Tankwart?
3. Wieviel Benzin wünscht Herr Lenz?
4. Wo fährt Otto langsam?
5. Wie fährt man direkt zum Flughafen?
6. Was fällt dem Vater unterwegs ein?
7. Was für Öl verlangt Herr Lenz?
8. Wie lange dauert der Flug von New York nach Frankfurt?
9. Wie lange sitzt der junge Mann schon im Flugzeug?
10. Seit wann lernen Sie Deutsch?

Konversation

Fragen Sie Ihren Nachbar,

1. wer das Automobil zum Flughafen fährt! [Ihr Nachbar muß selbstverständlich jede Frage beantworten.]
2. was Herr Lenz an der Tankstelle kauft!
3. wie Herbert nach Deutschland kommt!
4. wie lange Herberts Flug dauert!
5. wie lange Herbert schon im Flugzeug sitzt!
6. wo Otto den Wagen parkt!

II. NÜTZLICHE AUSDRÜCKE

da drüben	*over there*
einfallen	*to occur (to someone)*
Es fällt mir ein.	*It occurs to me.*
erst (*adv.*)	*only, just, not until [with future idea]*
Keine Angst!	*Don't worry. Have no fear.*
Keine Umstände!	*Don't go to any trouble. Don't make any fuss.*
am Steuer sitzen	*to drive, be at the wheel*
das Steuer nehmen	*to take the wheel*
über (*plus acc.*)	*via, by way of*

III. GRAMMATIK

gehen - go

1. Present Tense

(a) **Ich gehe** *I go, I do go, I am going*

The present tense in German is equivalent to three meanings in English.

(b)

ich geh**e**	*I go*	ich antworte	*I answer*
du geh**st**[1]	*you go*	du antwort**est**	*you answer*
er geh**t**	*he goes*	er antwort**et**	*he answers*
wir geh**en**	*we go*	wir antwort**en**	*we answer*
ihr geh**t**[2]	*you go*	ihr antwort**et**	*you answer*
sie geh**en**	*they go*	sie antwort**en**	*they answer*
Sie geh**en**[3]	*you go*	Sie antwort**en**	*you answer*

The personal endings are added to the stem of the infinitive to form the present tense. Note that to facilitate pronunciation an **e** is inserted before **-st** and **-t** when the infinitive stem ends in **-t** (**antwortet** above) or **-d** (**findet**), or in **-m** or **-n** preceded by a different consonant other than **l** and **r** (**atmet, öffnet;** but **kommt, kennt, filmt, lernt**).

(c)

f**a**hren	*to drive*	du f**ä**hrst	er f**ä**hrt
l**au**fen	*to run*	du l**äu**fst	er l**äu**ft
g**e**ben	*to give*	du g**i**bst	er g**i**bt
s**e**hen	*to see*	du s**ie**hst	er s**ie**ht

Most strong verbs with stem vowel **a** or **au** change the vowel to **ä** and **äu,** respectively, and verbs with stem vowel **e** change to **i** or **ie** in the second and third persons singular of the present.

---

[1] The **du** form (familiar singular) is used when addressing a relative, close friend, child, or pet.

[2] The **ihr** form (familiar plural) is used when addressing relatives, close friends, children, or pets.

[3] The **Sie** form (singular and plural) is the conventional form of address. In subsequent verb listings, the **Sie** form of the verb will not be given because it is identical with the third person plural, except that the pronoun (**Sie**) is always capitalized.

(d) sitzen *to sit* du sitzt
passen *to fit* du paßt
essen *to eat* du ißt

Verbs with stem ending in an **s**-sound (**-s, -sp, -ß, -sch, -z**) normally add only **-t** in the **du** form to facilitate pronunciation.

(e) Review the present tense of **sein, haben,** and **werden** in the Appendix.

2. Uses of the Present Tense

(a) Ich **glaube,** du **fährst** in der falschen Richtung.
I think you're driving in the wrong direction.

The present tense is used as in English to express an action or condition at the present time.

(b) Das lange Sitzen **ist** nicht sehr angenehm.
Sitting a long time isn't very pleasant.

The present tense is used as in English for a general statement of fact not specifically limited to the present time.

(c) In zehn Minuten **sind** wir am Flughafen.
In ten minutes we'll be at the airport.
Er **kommt** morgen.
He's coming tomorrow.

The present tense is used to express future action if future time is clearly meant.

(d) **Er sitzt schon seit zehn Uhr** im Flugzeug.
He has been sitting in the airplane since ten o'clock.
Wie lange lernen Sie schon Deutsch?
How long have you been studying German?

The present tense used with a time expression like **seit, schon, schon seit, schon lange, wie lange** describes or asks about an action that began in the past and is continuing at the present time. (There are no progressive forms in German.)

3. Imperative

(a) **Fahren Sie** langsam, bitte!
Drive slowly, please.
Warten Sie bitte einen Augenblick!
Please wait a moment.

The conventional imperative (used for persons addressed by **Sie,** both singular and plural) is identical with the **Sie** form of the present tense, except that the personal pronoun follows the verb.

Note: The imperative in German is usually followed by an exclamation point.

(b) **Fahr(e)** langsam, Otto!
Drive slowly, Otto.
Komm(e) herein, Wolfgang!
Come in, Wolfgang!

The familiar singular imperative (used for persons addressed by **du**) normally ends in **-e,** but this ending is often omitted colloquially. The personal pronoun is normally omitted.

(c) **Gib** mir die Fotographie, Karl!
Give me the photo, Karl.

Strong verbs which change the stem vowel from **e** to **i** or **ie** in the present tense have the same vowel change in the familiar singular imperative.

(d) **Kommt** mit uns, Kinder!
Come with us, children.

The familiar plural imperative (used for persons addressed by **ihr**) is identical with the **ihr** form of the present, except that the personal pronoun is normally omitted.

(e) Imperative Forms of **sein** and **werden**

FAMILIAR SINGULAR	**sei!**	**werde!**
FAMILIAR PLURAL	**seid!**	**werdet!**
CONVENTIONAL	**seien Sie!**	**werden Sie!**

(f) First Person Plural Imperative

Gehen wir ins Hauptgebäude!
Let's go into the main building.
Warten wir hier!
Let's wait here.

The first person plural of the present tense, with the personal pronoun following the verb, may function as an imperative. It is usually equivalent to English *Let's* plus verb.

IV. ÜBUNGEN

A. *Setzen Sie die folgenden Sätze in die* **er**-*Form!* (*Change the following sentences to the* **er**-*form.*)

1. Ich kaufe Benzin.
2. Ich esse Eis furchtbar gerne.
3. Ich lese immer die Frankfurter Rundschau.
4. Ich sehe sie nicht.
5. Ich mache jetzt die Arbeit.
6. Ich rede immer viel.
7. Ich lasse den Wagen gewöhnlich im Parkplatz.
8. Ich schlafe immer gerne.
9. Ich vergesse diesen Namen nicht.
10. Ich warte schon seit zwei Stunden.

B. *Setzen Sie die Sätze in Übung A in die* **wir**-*Form!*

C. *Setzen Sie die folgenden Sätze in die* **du**-*Form!*

1. Er ist sehr willkommen.
2. Sie hat keine Angst.
3. Sie fährt nach Deutschland.
4. Er kauft zuviel.
5. Sie sieht den Flughafen.
6. Liest sie keine Bücher?
7. Kennt er den Weg?
8. Glaubt er das?
9. Wünscht er etwas?
10. Braucht er viel?

D. *Setzen Sie die Sätze in Übung C in die* **Sie**-*Form!*

E. *Antworten Sie mit „ja"!*

BEISPIEL: Bleiben Sie lange hier?
Ja, ich bleibe lange hier.

1. Sind Sie jetzt in der Stadt?
2. Fahren Sie immer langsam in der Stadt?
3. Kennen Sie den Weg zum Flughafen?
4. Machen Sie einen Umweg zum Flugplatz?
5. Nehmen Sie die Autobahn zum Flugplatz?
6. Brauchen Sie Öl?
7. Haben Sie genug Benzin?
8. Halten Sie bei einer Tankstelle?
9. Kaufen Sie viel Benzin?
10. Sehen Sie den Flugplatz?

F. *Antworten Sie auf deutsch, indem Sie die angegebenen Ausdrücke benutzen!* (*Answer in German, using the expressions indicated.*)

since when wait you

BEISPIEL: Seit wann warten Sie? (zwei Uhr)
Wir warten seit zwei Uhr.

1. Seit wann ist er hier? (Sonntag)
2. Wie lange sitzt er schon im Flugzeug? (sechs Stunden)
3. Lernen Sie schon lange Deutsch? (seit einem Jahr)
4. Seit wann ist er verheiratet? (Juni)
5. Fährt er schon lange Auto? (seit fünf Wochen)
6. Wie lange wohnen Sie schon hier? (erst seit zwei Monaten)
7. Kennen Sie ihn schon lange? (sehr lange)
8. Wie lange schläft er schon? (eine halbe Stunde)

G. *Setzen Sie die folgenden Imperative in die* **Sie**-*Form!*

BEISPIEL: Fülle den Tank!
Füllen Sie den Tank!

1. Wartet hier!
2. Nimm das Steuer!
3. Gib mir das Geld!

4. Laufe schnell!
5. Lauft schnell!
6. Sei ruhig!
7. Mach keine Umstände!
8. Bleib am Steuer!
9. Steigt ein!
10. Vergiß es nicht!

H. *Setzen Sie die folgenden Imperative in die* **du**-*Form!*

BEISPIEL: Helfen Sie mir!
Hilf mir!

1. Essen Sie das nicht!
2. Kommen Sie herein!
3. Seien Sie nicht so unhöflich!
4. Warten Sie hier, bitte!
5. Laufen Sie zu ihm!
6. Vergessen Sie die Geschichte!
7. Bringen Sie die Blumen, bitte!
8. Singen Sie nicht so laut!
9. Sprechen Sie langsamer!
10. Halten Sie hier, bitte!

I. *Bilden Sie Imperative!*

BEISPIEL: Wir gehen jetzt.
Gehen wir jetzt!

1. Wir fahren zum Flughafen.
2. Wir kaufen etwas Benzin.
3. Wir nehmen den Umweg nicht.
4. Wir halten bei der Tankstelle.
5. Wir sprechen nicht zu schnell.
6. Wir vergessen das Geld nicht.
7. Wir geben ihm ein Trinkgeld.
8. Wir lassen den Wagen im Parkplatz.
9. Wir bleiben nicht im Hauptgebäude.
10. Wir warten am Ausgang.

J. *Gebrauchen Sie vier der Nützlichen Ausdrücke in ganzen Sätzen! (Use four of the Useful Expressions in complete sentences.)*

K. *Sagen Sie zuerst und schreiben Sie danach auf deutsch! (Say, then write in German.)*

1. Otto is eighteen years old and lives in Frankfurt.
2. His family is meeting a young friend from America at the airport.
3. They do not take a route directly through the city; they go by way of the autobahn.
4. Suddenly the father says, "Otto, stop at the next gas station."
5. It occurs to him that they have to get gas.
6. He says to the attendant, "Fill the tank, please."
7. Now the father takes the wheel.
8. He has been driving for twenty-five years, and he drives very well.
9. Mother, do you see the airplanes?
10. We'll be at the airport in two minutes, and then we'll see our young friend.

Weak Verbs:
Simple Past, Compound Past.

Lektion 2

I. GESPRÄCH: Auf der Terrasse des Flughafens

FRAU LENZ: Unser neuer Flughafen ist wirklich schön und modern. Es ist herrlich, hier auf der Terrasse zu sitzen.

HERR LENZ: Ja, alles ist neu und sauber. Und heute haben wir schönes Wetter, obwohl es die ganze Nacht geregnet hat.

OTTO: Da drüben sind die Landebahnen. Da stehen auch zwei Flugzeuge der Lufthansa. Eins davon ist eben gelandet.

HERR LENZ: Mit der Lufthansa bin ich auch schon gereist. Otto, du darfst hier nicht rauchen! Hast du die Tafel „Rauchen verboten" nicht bemerkt?

OTTO: Verzeihung!

HERR LENZ: Hier kommt das Flugzeug. Ein Düsenflugzeug natürlich.

On the Airport Observation Deck

MRS. LENZ: Our new airport really is beautiful and up to date. It's marvelous to sit here on the observation deck.

MR. LENZ: Yes. Everything is new and clean. And the weather is fine today, although it rained all night long.

OTTO: Over there are the landing strips. And two Lufthansa planes are standing there. One of them has just landed.

MR. LENZ: I traveled by Lufthansa once. Otto, you can't smoke here! Didn't you notice the "No Smoking" sign?

OTTO: I'm sorry.

MR. LENZ: Here comes the plane. A jet, of course.

OTTO: Es rollt schon. Nun hat es gestoppt.

FRAU LENZ: Wir wollen versuchen, unseren Gast zu erkennen, wenn er aussteigt.

HERR LENZ: Das wird schwer sein. Wir haben ihn ja noch nie gesehen. Wir kennen nur seine Fotografie.

FRAU LENZ: Er gleicht seinem Vater. Ich erinnere mich sehr gut an seinen Vater. Er wohnte ein ganzes Jahr bei uns vor dem Kriege.

HERR LENZ: Ja, da warst du noch ein junges Mädchen, und deine Mutter führte eine Pension für Studenten in Heidelberg. Du hast mir oft davon erzählt.

FRAU LENZ: Nach dem Kriege hat Herbert uns auch einmal besucht. Wir wohnten damals in Berlin.

HERR LENZ: Stimmt. Ich erinnere mich jetzt. Er machte schon damals Pläne für seinen Sohn und hoffte, ihn eines Tages nach Deutschland zu schicken.

FRAU LENZ: Weißt du noch, wie ich gelacht habe, als er das sagte? Der Sohn war ja erst drei Jahre alt.

HERR LENZ: Und heute ist er einundzwanzig.

OTTO: It's already rolling. Now it has stopped.

MRS. LENZ: We'll try to recognize our guest when he gets out.

MR. LENZ: That will be difficult. We have never seen him. We know only his photograph.

MRS. LENZ: He looks like his father. I remember his father very well. He lived with us for a whole year before the war.

MR. LENZ: Yes, you were still a girl then, and you mother ran a boarding-house for students in Heidelberg. You've told me about it often.

MRS. LENZ: Herbert also visited us once after the war. We were living in Berlin then.

MR. LENZ: That's right. I remember now. He was already making plans for his son at that time, and he hoped to send him to Germany some day.

MRS. LENZ: Do you remember how I laughed when he said that? His son was only three years old.

MR. LENZ: And today he's twenty-one.

OTTO: Jetzt steigen die Leute aus. — Kannst du ihn erkennen, Mutter?

FRAU LENZ: Noch nicht. Wir müssen warten, bis die Leute näher kommen. — Dort! Ich glaube, ich habe ihn erkannt. (*Sie winkt.*) Es ist der junge Mann mit der blauen Reisetasche.

HERR LENZ: Das glaube ich nicht. Herbert Senior hatte schwarze Haare. Der junge Mann, der da kommt, ist ja blond.

FRAU LENZ: Doch, das ist er! Siehst du, er hat uns gewinkt.

HERR LENZ: Tatsächlich. (*Er winkt auch.*) Jetzt geht er zur Paßkontrolle und zum Zoll. Wir können erst mit ihm sprechen, wenn er den Zoll passiert hat.

OTTO: Now people are getting out. — Can you recognize him, mother?

MRS. LENZ: Not yet. We must wait until they come closer. — There! I believe I've recognized him. (*She waves.*) It's the young man with the blue traveling bag.

MR. LENZ: I don't think so. Herbert senior had black hair. The young man coming there is blond.

MRS. LENZ: Yes, it's he. You see, he waved to us.

MR. LENZ: You're right. (*He, too, waves.*) Now he's going to have his passport checked and go through customs. We won't be able to talk with him until he has gone through customs.

FRAU LENZ: Dauert das lange?

HERR LENZ: Wahrscheinlich nicht. Ich glaube nicht, daß er viel zu verzollen hat.

FRAU LENZ: Also gehen wir in die Halle hinunter, um unseren Gast zu begrüßen.

HERR LENZ: Gut. Wo hast du das Geschenk, das du ihm geben wolltest?

FRAU LENZ: Meine Güte! Die Blumen! Ich habe sie zu Hause ins Wasser gestellt.

OTTO: Beruhige dich! Ich habe eben ein Päckchen Zigaretten gekauft, ein Geschenk für unseren Gast, damit er sofort sieht, ob ihm unsere deutschen Zigaretten schmecken.

MRS. LENZ: Does that take long?

MR. LENZ: Probably not. I don't think he has much to declare.

MRS. LENZ: Then let's go to the lobby to greet our guest.

MR. LENZ: Fine. Where do you have the gift you wanted to give him?

MRS. LENZ: Good heavens! The flowers! I put them in water at home.

OTTO: Don't worry! I've just bought a pack of cigarettes, a gift for our guest, so that he can see at once if our German cigarettes are to his taste.

Fragen

Antworten Sie auf deutsch!

1. Wie findet Frau Lenz den neuen Flughafen?
2. Wie ist das Wetter?
3. Mit was für einem Flugzeug ist Herbert Junior geflogen?
4. Wie alt ist Herbert?
5. Bei wem wohnte Herberts Vater vor dem Kriege?
6. Wann hat Herbert Senior Herrn und Frau Lenz einmal besucht?
7. Welche Pläne machte er damals für seinen Sohn?
8. Warum hat Frau Lenz damals gelacht?
9. Was hat Frau Lenz als Geschenk für Herbert Junior gekauft?
10. Warum gibt Otto Herbert Zigaretten?
11. Sind Sie schon einmal nach Deutschland gereist?
12. Sind Sie schon mit der Lufthansa gereist?

Konversation

Fragen Sie Ihren Nachbar,

1. wie das Wetter ist! [Ihr Nachbar muß selbstverständlich jede Frage beanworten.]
2. wie viele Flugzeuge gelandet sind!
3. was für ein Flugzeug Otto gesehen hat!
4. wohin Herbert nach der Landung gehen muß!
5. wo die Familie auf Herbert wartet!
6. was Frau Lenz vergessen hat!

II. NÜTZLICHE AUSDRÜCKE

bei (*plus dat.*)	*at the home of*
eben	*just* (*with reference to time*)
finden	*to find*
Wie finden Sie (*plus acc.*)?	*What do you think of . . .?*
zu Hause	(*at*) *home*
nach Hause	*home* (*action directed toward home*)
noch nicht	*not yet*

passieren	*to pass, go by*; (*with auxiliary* **sein**) *to occur, happen*
Was ist passiert?	*What has happened?*
Das stimmt.	*That's right.*
Das stimmt nicht.	*That's not right.*

III. GRAMMATIK

4. Simple Past of Weak Verbs

(a) ich machte

The simple past in German may be equivalent to four meanings in English: *I made, I did make, I was making, I used to make.*

(b) Forms of the Simple Past

ich mach**te**	*I made*	ich antwort**ete**	*I answered*
du mach**test**	*you made*	du antwort**etest**	*you answered*
er mach**te**	*he made*	er antwort**ete**	*he answered*
wir mach**ten**	*we made*	wir antwort**eten**	*we answered*
ihr mach**tet**	*you made*	ihr antwort**etet**	*you answered*
sie mach**ten**	*they made*	sie antwort**eten**	*they answered*

To form the simple past of weak verbs, the personal endings are added to the infinitive stem. Observe the characteristic **-t-** of the simple past at the beginning of personal endings. To facilitate pronunciation, an **e** is inserted before the personal endings when the stem ends in **-t** (**antwortete**) or **-d** (**landete**) or in **-m** or **-n** preceded by a different consonant other than **l** and **r** (**atmete, öffnete;** but **filmte, lernte**).

5. Past Participle of Weak Verbs

(a) Formation of Past Participle

1.

INFINITIVE		PAST PARTICIPLE	
machen	*to make*	**gemacht**	*made*
antworten	*to answer*	**geantwortet**	*answered*
öffnen	*to open*	**geöffnet**	*opened*
lernen	*to learn*	**gelernt**	*learned*

The past participle of weak verbs adds the prefix **ge-** and the suffix **-t** to the stem of the infinitive. To facilitate pronunciation, an **e** is inserted before the **t** when the infinitive stem ends in **-d** or **-t** or in **-m** or **-n** preceded by a different consonant other than **l** or **r.**

2.

INFINITIVE		PAST PARTICIPLE	
besuchen	*to visit*	**besucht**	*visited*
erzählen	*to relate*	**erzählt**	*related*
passieren	*to occur*	**passiert**	*occurred*

Verbs with inseparable prefixes and verbs with infinitive ending in **-ieren** do not add **ge-** in the past participle.

6. Compound Past of Weak Verbs

(a) The compound past in German is generally equivalent to an English past or present perfect: *I made, I have made.* We will discuss its uses and those of the simple past in Section 7.

(b) Forms of the Compound Past

ich **habe gemacht**	*I made, have made*
du **hast gemacht**	*you made, have made*
er **hat gemacht**	*he made, has made*
wir **haben gemacht**	*we made, have made*
ihr **habt gemacht**	*you made, have made*
sie **haben gemacht**	*they made, have made*

The compound past of most verbs consists of the present tense of **haben** plus past participle.

Note: The past participle is at the end of a main clause: Er hat es **gemacht.** *He (has) made it.*

(c) Compound Past with **sein**

1.

ich **bin gereist**	*I traveled, have traveled*
du **bist gereist**	*you traveled, have traveled*
er **ist gereist**	*he traveled, has traveled*
wir **sind gereist**	*we traveled, have traveled*
ihr **seid gereist**	*you traveled, have traveled*
sie **sind gereist**	*they traveled, have traveled*

Intransitive verbs denoting change of place or condition form their compound past with the present tense of **sein** plus past participle.

2. While most intransitive verbs showing change of place or condition are strong verbs, a number of common weak verbs belong to this category:

begegnen	*to meet*
folgen	*to follow*
landen	*to land*
marschieren	*to march*
reisen	*to travel*
rennen	*to run*
wandern	*to wander*

7. Uses of the Compound Past and Simple Past

(a) Compound Past

Ich **habe** die Blumen zu Hause ins Wasser **gestellt.**
I put the flowers in water at home.
Es **hat** die ganze Nacht **geregnet.**
It rained all night long.
Wir **sind** damals nicht mit dem Flugzeug **gereist.**
At that time we did not travel by plane.

The compound past is the normal German past tense in conversation and informal writing. Its chief function is to express completed past actions or isolated events. Note that an English simple past is often equivalent to a German compound past.

(b) Simple Past

Da **warst** du noch ein junges Mädchen, und deine Mutter **führte** eine Pension.
You were still a girl then, and your mother ran a boardinghouse.
Der Sohn **war** damals erst drei Jahre alt.
His son was only three years old then.
Wir **mußten** lange auf ihn warten.
We had to wait a long time for him.
Ich habe gelacht, als er das **sagte.**
I laughed when he said that.

The simple past is used primarily to narrate or describe related events and situations, occurring chiefly in literature and other formal contexts. It is rarely used in conversation, except with **haben** and **sein,** the modal auxiliaries (**dürfen, können, mögen, müssen, sollen, wollen**), and in dependent time clauses, especially after **als.**[1]

8. Idiomatic Use of the Simple Past

Er **war seit 1924** in Berlin wohnhaft.
He had been living in Berlin since 1924.
Wir **warteten schon seit zwei Uhr.**
We had been waiting since two o'clock.

The simple past used with the time expressions **seit, schon, schon seit, wie lange** describes or asks about an action that began in the past and was still in progress at a later time in the past.

9. Past Perfect Tense

(a)

ich **hatte gemacht**	*I had made*
du **hattest gemacht**	*you had made*
er **hatte gemacht**	*he had made*
wir **hatten gemacht**	*we had made*
ihr **hattet gemacht**	*you had made*
sie **hatten gemacht**	*they had made*
ich **war gereist**	*I had traveled*
du **warst gereist**	*you had traveled*
er **war gereist**	*he had traveled*
wir **waren gereist**	*we had traveled*
ihr **wart gereist**	*you had traveled*
sie **waren gereist**	*they had traveled*

The past perfect consists of the simple past of **haben** or **sein** plus past participle.

(b) Er **hatte** es schon **vergessen.**
He had already forgotten it.

---

[1] There are also regional differences. Northern Germans often prefer the simple past in conversation.

Er **war** sehr krank **gewesen,** aber man merkte es nicht mehr.
He had been very ill, but one didn't notice it anymore.

The past perfect is used as in English to describe an action that occurred before another action in past time.

10. Irregular Weak Verbs

INFINITIVE		SIMPLE PAST	PAST PARTICIPLE
brennen	*to burn*	**brannte**	**gebrannt**
rennen	*to run*	**rannte**	**ist gerannt**
nennen	*to name*	**nannte**	**genannt**
kennen	*to know*	**kannte**	**gekannt**
senden	*to send*	**sandte**	**gesandt**
wenden	*to turn*	**wandte**	**gewandt**
bringen	*to bring*	**brachte**	**gebracht**
denken	*to think*	**dachte**	**gedacht**

Irregular weak verbs change their stem vowel in the simple past and past participle.

IV. ÜBUNGEN

A. *Setzen Sie die folgenden Sätze in das Perfekt (compound past)!*

1. Ich erkenne ihn.
2. Ich reise mit der Lufthansa.
3. Ich antworte zu schnell.
4. Ich denke immer an Sie.
5. Ich sage gar nichts.
6. Wir bringen Blumen.
7. Wir kaufen Zigaretten.
8. Wir studieren Deutsch.
9. Wir verkaufen unser Haus.
10. Wir kennen ihn nicht.
11. Er lacht nie.
12. Er denkt an seine Mutter.
13. Er lernt es nicht.
14. Er spielt nicht gern.
15. Er hört es oft.
16. Sie wohnen nicht hier.
17. Sie reden zuviel.
18. Sie öffnen die Tür.
19. Sie warten schon lange.
20. Sie arbeiten zu wenig.

B. *Setzen Sie die Sätze in Übung A in das Plusquamperfekt (past perfect)!*

C. *Antworten Sie mit „ja“!*

1. Haben Sie in Heidelberg gewohnt?
2. Sind Sie nach Deutschland gereist?

3. Haben Sie Zigaretten gekauft?
4. Haben Sie lange gewartet?
5. Sind Sie Ihrem Freund begegnet?
6. Haben Sie das Mädchen erkannt?
7. Ist das Düsenflugzeug gelandet?
8. Hat Herberts Vater in Berlin gewohnt?
9. Hat er einen Freund besucht?
10. Ist er mit der Lufthansa gereist?
11. Hat er oft davon erzählt?
12. Hat er lange gewartet?

D. *Antworten Sie dem Beispiel entsprechend!*

BEISPIEL: Wohnte er in Berlin?
Ja, er hat in Berlin gewohnt.

1. Besuchte er seinen Freund?
2. Rauchte er deutsche Zigaretten?
3. Kannte er das Mädchen?
4. Lebte er in Hamburg?
5. Öffnete sie das Fenster?
6. Dachte er an uns?
7. Arbeitete er jeden Tag?
8. Studierte sie Englisch?
9. Erzählte er es?
10. Warteten wir lange?

E. *Beantworten Sie die Fragen, indem Sie die angegebenen Ausdrücke gebrauchen!*

BEISPIEL: Was hatte er gekauft? (Benzin)
Er hatte Benzin gekauft.

1. Wo hatte Otto gewohnt? (in Berlin)
2. Wo hatte er Englisch gelernt? (in Amerika)
3. Wie oft war er nach England gereist? (jedes Jahr)
4. Was hatte er immer geraucht? (Zigaretten)
5. Wann war das Flugzeug gelandet? (um zehn Uhr)
6. Wo waren Sie ihm begegnet? (am Flughafen)
7. Wo hatten Sie ihn begrüßt? (in der Halle)

8. Wie lange hatten Sie gewartet? (eine Stunde)
9. Was hatten Sie ihm gebracht? (Blumen)
10. Wie lange hatten Sie mit ihm geredet? (fünf Minuten)

F. *Ergänzen Sie die passenden Formen von* **haben** *oder* **sein!** (*Supply the correct forms of* **haben** *or* **sein.**)

1. Wir ______ vorigen Monat nach Frankreich gereist.
2. Wer ______ Herbert zuerst erkannt?
3. Zwei Flugzeuge ______ eben gelandet.
4. Was ______ er gefragt?
5. Bis jetzt ______ nichts passiert.
6. Herbert Senior ______ bei uns in Heidelberg gelebt.
7. Er ______ zu uns gekommen, als wir in Berlin wohnten.
8. Ach, wie ______ wir nur gelacht!
9. Sie ______ durch einen großen Wald gewandert.
10. Sie ______ aber keine Furcht gehabt.

G. *Ergänzen Sie die korrekte Form des angegebenen Verbs!*

1. (sein) Er ______ seit zwei Uhr im Flugzeug und fühlt sich etwas müde.
2. (arbeiten) Er ______ seit Juni in Spanien, aber er spricht nur Englisch.
3. (sein) Seine Mutter ______ schon lange tot, als wir ihn besuchten.
4. (haben) Er ______ seit zwei Monaten einen Reisepaß.
5. (studieren) Er ______ erst kurze Zeit in Heidelberg, als wir ihn kennenlernten.
6. (sein) Er ______ seit sechs Jahren verheiratet und hat einen Sohn von drei Jahren.
7. (wohnen) Sie ______ schon lange bei ihren Verwandten, aber wir haben es bisher nicht gewußt.
8. (sein) Dort ist mein Onkel. Er ______ seit Samstag auf Besuch bei uns.
9. (rauchen) Ich ______ schon lange nur deutsche Zigaretten.
10. (lernen) Sie ______ erst seit September Deutsch, aber sie spricht schon ganz gut.

H. *Gebrauchen Sie vier der Nützlichen Ausdrücke in ganzen Sätzen!*

I. *Sagen Sie zuerst und schreiben Sie danach auf deutsch!*

1. Mother, have you ever seen Herbert?
2. Yes, Otto, I saw him when he was three years old.
3. I have not seen him for eighteen years, but I know him very well.
4. Before the war his father lived at our house in Heidelberg.
5. He was a student in Heidelberg, and my mother ran a boardinghouse for students.
6. After the war we saw him often in Berlin.
7. He had traveled to Berlin for the American government.
8. He had been there for two months before we knew he was living in Berlin.
9. He visited us frequently because we were old friends.
10. But he stayed only six months, and then he went to Austria.

Strong Verbs:
Simple Past, Compound Past;
Word Order.

Lektion 3

I. GESPRÄCH: Auf der Bank

FRAU HARTUNG:	Guten Tag, Frau Lenz.
FRAU LENZ:	Guten Tag, Frau Hartung. Heiß heute, nicht wahr?
FRAU HARTUNG:	Ja. Ich bin eben zum Laden gegangen und habe ein paar Flaschen Mineralwasser gekauft.
FRAU LENZ:	Darf ich Ihnen einen jungen Freund aus Amerika vorstellen. Herr Becker, aus New York.
HERBERT:	Es freut mich sehr.
FRAU HARTUNG:	Es freut mich auch, Sie kennenzulernen. Sind Sie schon lange in Frankfurt?

At the Bank

MRS. HARTUNG:	Hello, Mrs. Lenz.
MRS. LENZ:	Hello, Mrs. Hartung. Hot today, isn't it?
MRS. HARTUNG:	Yes, I've just gone to the store and bought several bottles of mineral water.
MRS. LENZ:	May I introduce a young friend from America to you. Mr. Becker, from New York.
HERBERT:	How do you do?
MRS. HARTUNG:	How do you do? Have you been in Frankfurt long?

FRAU LENZ: Herr Becker ist erst vor wenigen Stunden angekommen. Wir haben ihn heute morgen am Flughafen empfangen.

FRAU HARTUNG: Ach, Sie sind über den Atlantik geflogen? Ich hoffe, Sie sind gut gereist, Herr Becker.

FRAU LENZ: Ja, denken Sie nur, er hat die ganze Nacht geschlafen. Er ist von der Reise gar nicht müde geworden.

FRAU HARTUNG: Und wie lange haben Sie vor, in Frankfurt zu bleiben?

FRAU LENZ: Herr Becker wohnt bei uns. Er bleibt den ganzen Sommer in Deutschland.

FRAU HARTUNG: Spricht Herr Becker denn kein Deutsch?

HERBERT: Doch. Aber noch nicht sehr geläufig.

FRAU LENZ: Und jetzt gehen wir zur Bank, denn Herr Becker will einen Reisescheck einlösen. Er hat gar kein deutsches Geld mitgebracht.

FRAU HARTUNG: Auf Wiedersehen, Frau Lenz. Auf Wiedersehen, Herr Becker. Ich wünsche Ihnen einen schönen Aufenthalt in Deutschland.

HERBERT: Danke. Auf Wiedersehen.

MRS. LENZ: Mr. Becker arrived just a few hours ago. We met him at the airport this morning.

MRS. HARTUNG: Oh, you flew over the Atlantic? I hope you had a good trip, Mr. Becker.

MRS. LENZ: Yes. Just think, he slept the whole night through. He didn't get at all tired from the trip.

MRS. HARTUNG: And how long are you planning to stay in Frankfurt?

MRS. LENZ: Mr. Becker is staying with us. He'll spend the whole summer in Germany.

MRS. HARTUNG: Well, doesn't Mr. Becker speak any German?

HERBERT: Oh yes. But not very fluently yet.

MRS. LENZ: And now we're going to the bank, because Mr. Becker wants to cash a travelers check. He didn't bring any German money with him. Good-by, Mrs. Hartung.

MRS. HARTUNG: Good-by, Mrs. Lenz. Good-by, Mr. Becker. I wish you a pleasant stay in Germany.

HERBERT: Thank you. Good-by.

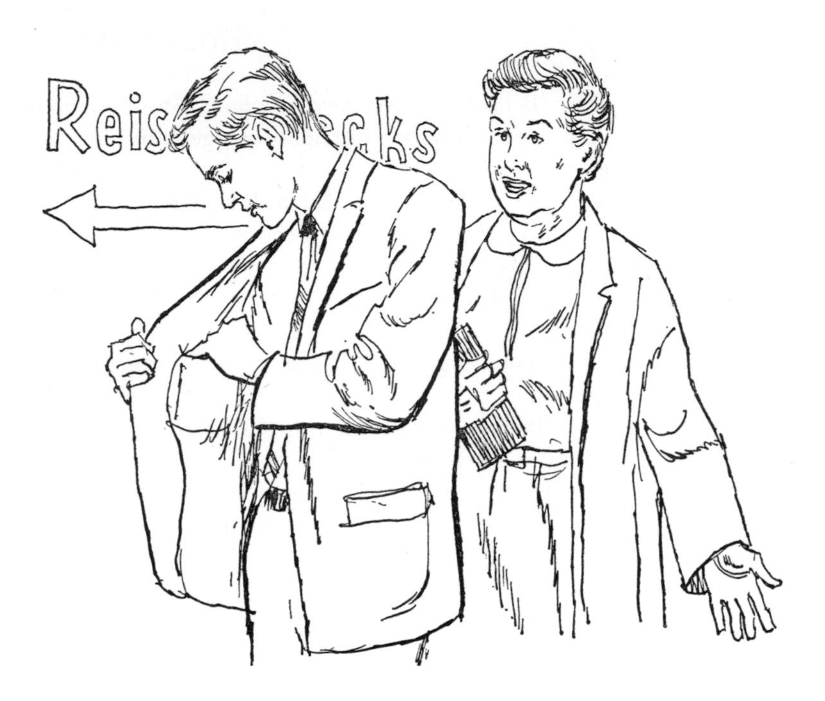

(Auf der Bank.)

FRAU LENZ: Hier sind wir endlich. Es ist der dritte Schalter rechts.

HERBERT: Bitte, sprechen Sie für mich, Frau Lenz. Ich mache bestimmt zu viele Fehler.

FRAU LENZ: Keineswegs, Herbert. Jetzt müssen Sie es versuchen. Ich habe schon genug für Sie gesprochen.

HERBERT: (*Tritt an den Schalter.*) Kann ich hier einen amerikanischen Reisescheck einlösen?

(At the bank.)

MRS. LENZ: Here we are at last. It's the third window on the right.

HERBERT: Please speak for me, Mrs. Lenz. I'll certainly make too many mistakes.

MRS. LENZ: Not at all, Herbert. Now you must try it. I have already talked enough for you.

HERBERT: (*Steps up to the window.*) Can I cash an American travelers check here?

BANKBEAMTER: Jawohl. Wir geben Ihnen deutsches Geld dafür.

HERBERT: Wie viele Mark bekomme ich für einen Dollar?

BANKBEAMTER: Gestern stand der Kurs auf DM 4,15 (vier Mark fünfzehn). Heute steht er auf DM 4,13 (vier Mark dreizehn). Darf ich Ihren Reisepaß sehen?

HERBERT: Meinen Reisepaß? Den habe ich zu Hause gelassen.

BANKBEAMTER: Dann tut es mir leid. Ich kann Ihren Scheck nicht einlösen, bevor ich Ihre Ausweispapiere gesehen habe.

FRAU LENZ: Oh, wie dumm von mir! Herbert, ich vergesse immer alles. Heute morgen vergaß ich die Blumen, und nun habe ich vergessen, Ihnen zu sagen, daß Sie auf der Bank den Reisepaß brauchen.

HERBERT: Das macht nichts aus. (*Zum Bankbeamten.*) Können Sie mir diese Dollarnoten in deutsches Geld umwechseln?

BANKBEAMTER: Gewiß. Zwanzig Dollar, das macht DM 82,60.

HERBERT: (*Zählt das Geld nach.*) Stimmt. Ich danke Ihnen. Auf Wiedersehen.

FRAU LENZ: Sehen Sie, es ist ganz gut gegangen.

BANK CLERK: Certainly. We'll give you German money for it.

HERBERT: How many marks do I get for a dollar?

BANK CLERK: Yesterday the exchange was at four marks fifteen. Today it's at four marks thirteen. May I see your passport?

HERBERT: My passport? I left it at home.

BANK CLERK: Then I'm sorry. I cannot cash your check until I have seen your identity papers.

MRS. LENZ: Oh, how stupid of me. Herbert, I always forget everything. This morning I forgot the flowers, and now I've forgotten to tell you that you need your passport at the bank.

HERBERT: Oh that doesn't make any difference. (*To the bank clerk.*) Can you change these dollar bills into German money?

BANK CLERK: Certainly. Twenty dollars. That makes eighty-two marks sixty.

HERBERT: (*Counts the money.*) Correct. Thank you. Good-by.

MRS. LENZ: You see, it went pretty well.

Fragen

Antworten Sie auf deutsch!

1. Wem sind Frau Lenz und Herbert auf der Straße begegnet?
2. Was sagt man, wenn man einen Freund vorstellt?
3. Wie sagt man auf deutsch „How do you do?"?
4. Wie ist Herbert über den Atlantik gereist?
5. Warum ist Herbert von der Reise nicht müde?
6. Wie lange haben Sie vor, Deutsch zu lernen?
7. Was für Geld hat Herbert mitgebracht, Dollars oder Mark?
8. Wie spricht Herbert Deutsch?
9. Wo findet Herbert den richtigen Bankbeamten?
10. Was will Herbert auf der Bank tun?
11. Warum will er Geld umwechseln?
12. Wo hat er seinen Reisepaß gelassen?
13. Was hat Frau Lenz vergessen?
14. Was kann Herbert ohne seinen Reisepaß nicht tun?

Konversation

Fragen Sie Ihren Nachbar,

1. wie das Wetter heute ist! [Ihr Nachbar muß selbstverständlich jede Frage beanworten.]
2. wem Frau Lenz und Herbert auf der Straße begegnet sind!
3. ob Herbert gut gereist ist!
4. wo Herbert in Deutschland wohnt!
5. warum Herbert nicht müde ist!
6. warum Herbert auf die Bank gegangen ist!

II. NÜTZLICHE AUSDRÜCKE

etwas vor haben — *to have something in mind, have a plan*

vorstellen — *to present, introduce*

  Darf ich (Ihnen meinen Freund) vorstellen? — *May I introduce (my friend to you)?*

Es freut mich (sehr). — *How do you do? I'm delighted.*

gut gehen	*to work out well, go well, be appropriate*
die Hand geben	*to shake hands*
Er gibt ihr die Hand.	*He's shaking hands with her.*
Es tut mir leid.	*I'm sorry.*
Das macht nichts (aus).	*That makes no difference. That doesn't matter.*
nicht wahr?	*isn't it? don't you? hasn't she? etc.*
Heiß heute, nicht wahr?	*Hot today, isn't it?*

III. GRAMMATIK

11. Simple Past of Strong Verbs

(a)

ich **schrieb**	*I wrote*	wir **schrieben**	*we wrote*
du **schriebst**	*you wrote*	ihr **schriebt**	*you wrote*
er **schrieb**	*he wrote*	sie **schrieben**	*they wrote*

The simple past of strong verbs has a vowel different from that of the infinitive. It does not add the **-t-** characteristic of the simple past of weak verbs, and the **ich** and **er** forms have no endings. The change of vowel is called ablaut.

(b) Review the simple past of **haben, sein,** and **werden** in the Appendix.

12. Past Participle of Strong Verbs

(a)

INFINITIVE		PAST PARTICIPLE	
schreiben	*to write*	**geschrieben**	*written*
fliegen	*to fly*	**geflogen**	*flown*

The past participles of many strong verbs also have ablaut. Past participles of strong verbs take the prefix **ge-** and the suffix **-en.**

(b)

INFINITIVE		PAST PARTICIPLE	
versprechen	*to promise*	**versprochen**	*promised*
erscheinen	*to appear*	**erschienen**	*appeared*

Verbs with inseparable prefixes do not add **ge-** to the past participle.

13. Compound Past and Past Perfect

(a)

COMPOUND PAST:	ich **habe geschrieben**	*I wrote, have written*
	ich **bin geflogen**	*I flew, have flown*
PAST PERFECT:	ich **hatte geschrieben**	*I had written*
	ich **war geflogen**	*I had flown*

The compound past and the past perfect are formed like those of weak verbs by using **haben** or **sein** with the past participle.

(b) Common strong verbs conjugated with **sein** (Note that these are intransitive verbs indicating change of place or condition)

einschlafen	*to fall asleep*
fahren	*to ride, drive*[1]
fallen	*to fall*
gehen	*to go*
geschehen	*to happen*
kommen	*to come*
laufen	*to run*
springen	*to jump*
sinken	*to sink*
sterben	*to die*
wachsen	*to grow*
werden	*to become*

(c) Two intransitive verbs which do *not* indicate change of place or condition are conjugated with **sein: sein** (*to be*) and **bleiben** (*to stay, remain*).

14. Principal Parts of Verbs

INFINITIVE		SIMPLE PAST	PAST PARTICIPLE
machen	*to make*	**machte**	**gemacht**
besuchen	*to visit*	**besuchte**	**besucht**

---

[1] A number of intransitive verbs, among them **fahren,** may also be used transitively with a direct object. Compare:

(Intransitive) Er **ist** heute nicht in die Stadt **gefahren.**
He didn't drive to town today.
(Transitive) Er **hat** seinen Freund in die Stadt **gefahren.**
He drove his friend to town.

INFINITIVE		SIMPLE PAST	PAST PARTICIPLE	3RD PERS. SING. PRESENT
schreiben	*to write*	**schrieb**	**geschrieben**	
versprechen	*to promise*	**versprach**	**versprochen**	**er verspricht**
springen	*to jump*	**sprang**	**ist gesprungen**	

The principal parts of all verbs consist of the infinitive, the simple past, and the past participle. From these principal parts other tenses are derived.

The **er**-form of the present tense is listed if stem-vowel changes occur in the **du**-form and **er**-form of the present tense.

Verbs conjugated with **sein** are indicated by **ist** before the past participle.

15. Irregularities in Principal Parts of Strong Verbs

The following common strong verbs have irregularities in certain forms. These are printed in bold type.[1]

INFINITIVE		SIMPLE PAST	PAST PARTICIPLE	3RD PERS. SING. PRESENT
bitten	*to beg*	**bat**	**gebeten**	
erschrecken	*to be frightened*	**erschrak**	ist erschrocken	
essen	*to eat*	aß	**gegessen**	er ißt
gehen	*to go*	**ging**	ist **gegangen**	
gleiten	*to glide*	**glitt**	ist **geglitten**	
greifen	*to seize*	**griff**	**gegriffen**	
kommen	*to come*	**kam**	ist gekommen	
leiden	*to suffer*	**litt**	**gelitten**	
nehmen	*to take*	nahm	**genommen**	er **nimmt**
reiten	*to ride*	**ritt**	ist **geritten**	
schneiden	*to cut*	**schnitt**	**geschnitten**	
sitzen	*to sit*	**saß**	**gesessen**	
stehen	*to stand*	**stand**	**gestanden**	
treten	*to step*	trat	ist getreten	er **tritt**
tun	*to do*	**tat**	**getan**	
verstehen	*to understand*	**verstand**	**verstanden**	
ziehen	*to pull*	**zog**	**gezogen**	

[1] For a more complete list of strong verbs, with their principal parts, see the Appendix.

16. Word Order

(a) Normal Word Order: Main Clause

Frau Lenz und Herbert gehen jetzt zur Bank.
Mrs. Lenz and Herbert are going to the bank now.
Sie müssen es jetzt **versuchen.**
You must try it now.
Ich habe schon genug für Sie **gesprochen.**
I have already talked enough for you.

In normal word order, the subject and its modifiers stand first, the finite verb second, and the remaining parts of the clause third. (An infinitive or past participle stands at the end of the main clause.)

(b) Inverted Word Order: Main Clause

Am Vormittag **gehen Frau Lenz und Herbert** zur Bank. (1)
In the morning Mrs. Lenz and Herbert will go to the bank.
Meinen Reisepaß **habe ich** zu Hause **gelassen.** (2)
I've left my passport at home.
Daß er aus Amerika kommt, **habe ich** nicht **gewußt.** (3)
I didn't know that he comes from America.

If, for emphasis or variety of style, an element other than the subject stands first, the subject *follows* the verb. Such an element may be an adverb or adverbial phrase (example 1), an object (example 2), or a whole dependent clause (example 3).

Note: The finite verb always stands in second position in a main clause.

(c) Dependent Word Order: Dependent Clause

Als wir zur Bank **gingen,** sind wir Frau Hartung begegnet.
When we went to the bank, we met Mrs. Hartung.
Er ist nicht müde, **da er** die ganze Nacht **geschlafen hat.**
He isn't tired because he slept all night.
Ich weiß, **daß ich** Deutsch **sprechen muß.**
I know that I must speak German.

In dependent clauses (introduced by subordinating conjunctions), the finite verb stands *at the end of the clause.*[1] The past participle or the infinitive immediately precedes the finite verb (**geschlafen hat, sprechen muß**).

(d) Interrogative Word Order: Questions

Haben Sie Ihre Ausweispapiere? (1)
Do you have your identity papers?
Warum geht Otto zur Bank? (2)
Why is Otto going to the bank?
Was für Geld hat Otto mitgebracht? (3)
What kind of money did Otto bring with him?

In questions the subject follows the verb. A question may begin with a verb (example 1) or with an interrogative word or phrase (examples 2 and 3). Note that such interrogative word order is similar to English.

Note: As in English, a statement may be turned into a question by raising the voice at the end of the statement:

Herr Becker spricht kein Deutsch?
Mr. Becker doesn't speak any German?

17. Coordinating and Subordinating Conjunctions

(a) Coordinating Conjunctions

Er ist müde, **aber er ist nicht unglücklich.**
He is tired, but he is not unhappy.
Er ist müde, **denn er hat viel gearbeitet.**
He is tired because he has worked a lot.

The coordinating conjunctions **aber, allein, denn, oder, sondern, und** join main clauses and cause no change in word order.

[1] In German, all dependent clauses are set off by commas.

(b) Subordinating Conjunctions

Some of the most common subordinating conjunctions are:

als	*when, as, than* (in comparisons)
als ob	*as if*
als wenn	*as if*
bis	*until*
bevor	*before*
da	*because, since* (causal)
damit	*so that, in order that*
daß	*that*
ehe	*before*
falls	*in case*
indem	*while*
nachdem	*after*
ob	*whether*
obgleich, obschon, obwohl	*although*
ohne daß	*without*
seitdem	*since* (time)
sobald	*as soon as*
so lange	*as long as*
so oft	*as often as*
während	*while*
weil	*because*
wenn	*when, if*
wenn . . . auch, auch wenn	*even if*

Subordinating conjunctions require dependent word order.

(c) Omission of **daß**

Ich glaube, **daß Sie** den Reisepaß **brauchen.**
Ich glaube, **Sie brauchen** den Reisepaß.
I believe (that) you need your passport.

The subordinating conjunction **daß** is frequently omitted. A clause from which **daß** is omitted follows the normal word order of a main clause.

IV. ÜBUNGEN

A. *Setzen Sie die folgenden Sätze in das Perfekt!*

1. Ich beginne meine Arbeit.
2. Ich nehme das nächste Flugzeug.

3. Ich schreibe einen Brief.
4. Ich esse nicht gern allein.
5. Ich laufe ins Haus.
6. Ich gehe auf die Bank.
7. Ich trinke ein Glas Wasser.
8. Ich komme zu spät.
9. Ich schließe die Tür.
10. Ich erfahre etwas Neues.
11. Wir vergessen es nicht.
12. Wir sehen die Stadt.
13. Wir bleiben nicht lang.
14. Wir geben ihm die Hand.
15. Wir fliegen nie.
16. Wir verlieren alles.
17. Wir singen ein Lied.
18. Wir sitzen auf der Terrasse.
19. Wir schwimmen über den See.
20. Wir verstehen es nicht.
21. Er findet eine Dollarnote.
22. Er reitet gern im Sommer.
23. Er trägt einen Hut.
24. Er leidet sehr.
25. Er lügt nie.
26. Er liest ein Buch.
27. Er trifft eine Freundin.
28. Er gewinnt das Spiel.
29. Er liegt im Bett.
30. Er steht am Schalter.
31. Sie lesen den Brief.
32. Sie ziehen durch die Stadt.
33. Sie sprechen zu schnell.
34. Sie sehen es nicht.
35. Sie essen zuviel.
36. Sie schlafen die ganze Nacht.
37. Sie helfen uns nicht.
38. Sie tun es nicht.
39. Sie rufen uns.
40. Sie vergessen die Geschichte.

B. *Setzen Sie die Sätze in Übung A in das Plusquamperfekt!*

C. *Ergänzen Sie die korrekten Formen von* **haben** *oder* **sein!**

1. Er ______ nach Hamburg gefahren.
2. Er ______ seinen alten Wagen nicht mehr gefahren.
3. Wir ______ nur ein paar Minuten geblieben.
4. Das Kind ______ endlich eingeschlafen.
5. Es ______ die ganze Nacht geschlafen.
6. Er ______ die Paßkontrolle schon passiert.
7. Gar nichts ______ passiert.
8. Sie ______ immer sehr nett zu uns gewesen.
9. Der Arzt ______ das Kind schnell geheilt.
10. Die Wunde ______ von selbst geheilt.

D. *Verbinden Sie die folgenden Sätze mit der angegebenen Konjunktion!*

1. (und) Sie gehen zur Bank. Sie begegnen einer Freundin von Frau Lenz.
2. (aber) Herbert wünscht, einen Reisescheck einzulösen. Er hat seine Ausweispapiere zu Hause gelassen.
3. (oder) Er kann seine Dollars in deutsches Geld umwechseln. Er kann morgen mit Ausweispapieren zurückkommen.
4. (sondern) Er hat kein deutsches Geld. Er hat nur amerikanisches Geld.
5. (und) Der Bankbeamte stellt Herbert eine Frage. Herbert antwortet auf deutsch.
6. (aber) Seine Reiseschecks kann er ohne Reisepaß nicht einlösen. Dollarnoten kann er umwechseln.
7. (denn) Sie gehen jetzt zur Bank. Herbert will Geld umwechseln.

E. *Ändern Sie die folgenden Sätze, indem Sie mit dem Nebensatz anfangen!* (*Change the following sentences by beginning with the dependent clause.*)

BEISPIEL: Er trägt nie einen Hut, wenn er zur Schule geht.
Wenn er zur Schule geht, trägt er nie einen Hut.

1. Man ist nicht immer glücklich, auch wenn man viel Geld hat.
2. Er muß zur Bank gehen, weil er kein deutsches Geld hat.
3. Sie müssen morgen zurückkommen, falls Sie Ihren Reisepaß nicht mitgebracht haben.
4. Er ist nicht müde, da er gut geschlafen hat.
5. Die Zeit verging schnell, während wir mit Frau Hartung plauderten.
6. Wir wissen alle, daß Herbert gut Deutsch spricht.
7. Ich weiß nicht, wie es passiert ist.
8. Otto ist bescheiden, obgleich er schon ziemlich gut Deutsch spricht.

F. *Ändern Sie die folgenden Sätze, indem Sie jeden Satz mit dem angegebenen Satzteil beginnen!*

BEISPIEL: Er hat *gestern* zehn Briefe geschrieben.
Gestern hat er zehn Briefe geschrieben.

1. Ich bin *eben* zum Laden gegangen.
2. Ich habe *ein paar Flaschen Mineralwasser* gekauft.
3. Herr Becker ist *vor wenigen Stunden* angekommen.
4. Wir haben Herrn Becker *heute* am Flughafen empfangen.
5. Er hat *die ganze Nacht* geschlafen.
6. Er hat *kein deutsches Geld* mitgebracht.
7. Er will *in Deutschland* nur Deutsch sprechen.
8. Wir geben Ihnen deutsches Geld *dafür*.
9. Ich habe *meinen Reisepaß* zu Hause gelassen.
10. Ich kann *diese Dollarnoten* in deutsches Geld umwechseln.

G. *Verbinden Sie die folgenden Sätze mit der angegebenen Konjunktion!*

1. (obgleich) Er ist nicht müde. Er hat gar nicht geschlafen.
2. (weil) Er ist zu uns gekommen. Wir kennen seinen Vater.
3. (sobald) Wir haben ihn erkannt. Er ist aus dem Flugzeug ausgestiegen.
4. (bevor) Er lernte lange Deutsch. Er konnte fließend sprechen.
5. (weil) Er spricht nicht viel. Er ist ein bescheidener junger Mann.
6. (wenn) Wir sprechen nur Deutsch. Wir sind in Deutschland.
7. (daß) Ist es wahr? Er hat kein Geld.
8. (da) Er hat kein deutsches Geld. Er ist erst heute morgen angekommen.
9. (als) Herbert winkte. Er sah die Familie Lenz.
10. (weil) Das macht nichts. Ich kann morgen wiederkommen.

H. *Gebrauchen Sie vier der Nützlichen Ausdrücke in ganzen Sätzen!*

I. *Sagen Sie zuerst und schreiben Sie danach auf deutsch!*

1. When Mrs. Lenz met her friend on the street, she shook hands with her.
2. One always does that in Germany.
3. She was going to the bank with Herbert because he had no German money.
4. He had just arrived from America, and he had only travelers checks and dollars.
5. Although Herbert had said, "How do you do?" in German, Mrs. Hartung asked, "Don't you speak any German?"

6. Herbert replied, "I have been studying German for two years, but I arrived in Frankfurt only this morning."
7. He needs time before he can speak fluently.
8. Mrs. Lenz forgot to tell me that I need my passport.
9. With the passport I can exchange a travelers check for German money.
10. Everything went well, didn't it?

Modal Auxiliaries.

Lektion 4

I. GESPRÄCH: Im Kino

OTTO: Herbert, wollen Sie heute abend mit mir ins Kino?
HERBERT: Gerne. Ich wollte zwar noch einige Briefe schreiben, aber wenn Sie mich einladen, will ich gerne mit Ihnen gehen.
OTTO: (*etwas verlegen.*) Es ist leider keine Einladung. Ich möchte Sie ja nur fragen, ob Sie Lust haben, mit mir zu kommen.
HERBERT: Natürlich habe ich Lust. Ich hoffe sogar, für Sie bezahlen zu dürfen.
OTTO: Nein, das brauchen Sie nicht.
HERBERT: Warum nicht?
OTTO: Weil Sie mich nicht eingeladen haben.
HERBERT: Na, schön. Wie Sie wollen. — Was haben Sie vor?

At the Movies

OTTO: Herbert, do you want to go to the movies with me this evening?
HERBERT: Yes, I'd like to. I did want to write a few more letters, but if you invite me, I'll be glad to go with you.
OTTO: (*somewhat embarrassed.*) Unfortunately it's not an invitation. I would just like to ask you if you'd like to come with me.
HERBERT: Of course, I'd like to. I even hope that I may pay for you.
OTTO: No. You don't need to do that.
HERBERT: Why not?
OTTO: Because you didn't invite me.
HERBERT: Well, all right. As you wish. — What do you have in mind?

OTTO: Gleich hier an der Ecke ist ein Kino. Da läuft ein Film mit John Wayne. Paßt Ihnen das auch?

HERBERT: Eigentlich kann ich in Amerika genug amerikanische Filme sehen.

OTTO: Mögen Sie amerikanische Filme nicht?

HERBERT: Oh doch! Aber hier in Deutschland sehe ich lieber deutsche Filme.

OTTO: Dann gehen wir ins Odeon. Dort spielt ein Film mit Curt Jürgens.

HERBERT: Gut. Das paßt mir. Filme mit Jürgens gefallen mir immer.

OTTO: Haben Sie ihn schon spielen sehen?

HERBERT: Gewiß. Jürgens ist auch in Amerika ziemlich gut bekannt. Er spielt oft in amerikanischen Filmen, sogar im Fernsehen. Aber da spricht er natürlich immer Englisch.

OTTO: Der Film im Odeon ist deutsch. Er heißt „Der Mann ohne Gewissen".

HERBERT: Der Titel klingt gut. Wieviel kostet das Kino?

OTTO: Ich nehme gewöhnlich einen Platz für drei Mark. Aber wenn Sie ganz vorne sitzen wollen, dann kostet es nur zwei Mark. In der Mitte kostet es drei Mark, und hinten auf den besten Plätzen DM 4,50 (vier Mark fünfzig).

OTTO: Right here at the corner is a movie. They're showing a film with John Wayne. Does that suit you, too?

HERBERT: Actually, I can see enough American films in America.

OTTO: Don't you like American films?

HERBERT: Oh, yes. But here in Germany I prefer to see German movies.

OTTO: Then we'll go to the Odeon. There's a film with Curt Jürgens there.

HERBERT: Good. That suits me. I always like films with Jürgens.

OTTO: Have you already seen him?

HERBERT: Yes indeed. Jürgens is rather well known in America, too. He often plays in American films, even on television. But there he always speaks English, of course.

OTTO: The film at the Odeon is German. It's called "The Man Without a Conscience."

HERBERT: The title sounds good. How much does the movie cost?

OTTO: I usually get a seat for three marks. But if you want to sit way up front, it costs only two marks. It costs three marks in the middle, and four marks fifty in the best seats in the back.

HERBERT: Das habe ich nicht gewußt. Bei uns in Amerika müssen wir im allgemeinen für alle Plätze gleich viel bezahlen. Nur für Kinder kostet es weniger.

OTTO: Kinder? Kinder dürfen doch nicht ins Kino!

HERBERT: In Amerika schon. Gehen hier in Deutschland nur die Erwachsenen?

OTTO: Meistens nur die Erwachsenen. Ich habe früher selten ins Kino gehen dürfen, und nur zu Kindervorstellungen oder vielleicht einmal mit meinen Eltern.

HERBERT: Warum denn?

OTTO: Das weiß ich auch nicht recht. Ich glaube, es ist überall in Europa so. — Na, kommen Sie! Wir müssen uns beeilen, denn die Vorstellung beginnt um acht.

HERBERT: I didn't know that. In America we generally have to pay the same amount for all seats. Only for children does it cost less.

OTTO: Children? But children can't go to the movies.

HERBERT: In America they can. Do only adults go here in Germany?

OTTO: Generally only adults. I was rarely allowed to go to the movies years ago, and only to children's showings or perhaps occasionally with my parents.

HERBERT: Why?

OTTO: I don't really know that either. I believe it's that way everywhere in Europe. Well, come on. We have to hurry, because the show starts at eight.

Fragen

Antworten Sie auf deutsch!

1. Was hat Otto heute abend vor?
2. Warum ist Otto etwas verlegen?
3. Was für einen Film möchte Otto sehen?
4. Warum will Herbert lieber einen deutschen Film sehen?
5. Wie heißt der Film, der im Odeon läuft?
6. Welchen deutschen Schauspieler hat Herbert schon oft spielen sehen?
7. Wieviel kosten die besten Plätze in einem deutschen Kino?
8. Was für einen Platz nimmt Otto gewöhnlich?
9. Warum durfte Otto früher nur selten ins Kino gehen?
10. Um wieviel Uhr beginnt die Vorstellung im Odeon?

Konversation

Fragen Sie Ihren Nachbar,

1. ob er heute abend etwas vor hat! [Ihr Nachbar muß selbstverständlich jede Frage beanworten.]
2. wie oft er ins Kino geht!
3. ob er im Kino lieber vorne oder hinten sitzt!
4. ob er schon deutsche Filme gesehen hat!
5. welche deutschen Filmschauspieler er kennt!
6. welche Filme ihm besser gefallen, deutsche oder amerikanische!

II. NÜTZLICHE AUSDRÜCKE

bei uns (in Amerika), (in Deutschland)	*where I come from; in my country*
gefallen (*plus dat.*)	*to please*
Das gefällt mir.	*I like that.*
gern(e)	*gladly*
Er spricht gern(e) Deutsch.	*He likes to speak German.*
lieber	*preferably*
Er wohnt lieber in Frankfurt.	*He prefers to live in Frankfurt.*
gleich hier	*right here*

gleich viel	*exactly as much*
laufen	*to run*
Dort läuft ein deutscher Film.	*There's a German film showing there.*
Lust haben	*to feel like, want to*
Ich habe keine Lust, ins Kino zu gehen.	*I don't feel like going to the movies.*
na	*well*
nicht recht wissen	*not to be too sure*
schön	*all right, good, fine, O.K.*

III. GRAMMATIK

18. Modal Auxiliaries

(a)

dürfen		**können**	
ich **darf**	*I may*	ich **kann**	*I can*
du **darfst**	*you may*	du **kannst**	*you can*
er **darf**	*he may*	er **kann**	*he can*
wir **dürfen**	*we may*	wir **können**	*we can*
ihr **dürft**	*you may*	ihr **könnt**	*you can*
sie **dürfen**	*they may*	sie **können**	*they can*

mögen		**müssen**	
ich **mag**	*I like*	ich **muß**	*I must*
du **magst**	*you like*	du **mußt**	*you must*
er **mag**	*he likes*	er **muß**	*he must*
wir **mögen**	*we like*	wir **müssen**	*we must*
ihr **mögt**	*you like*	ihr **müßt**	*you must*
sie **mögen**	*they like*	sie **müssen**	*they must*

sollen		**wollen**	
ich **soll**	*I am supposed to*	ich **will**	*I want to*
du **sollst**	*you are supposed to*	du **willst**	*you want to*
er **soll**	*he is supposed to*	er **will**	*he wants to*
wir **sollen**	*we are supposed to*	wir **wollen**	*we want to*
ihr **sollt**	*you are supposed to*	ihr **wollt**	*you want to*
sie **sollen**	*they are supposed to*	sie **wollen**	*they want to*

In the present tense, first and third person singular forms of modal auxiliaries have no endings.

(b) Simple Past

	dürfen
ich **durfte**	*I was allowed to*
du **durftest**	*you were allowed to*
er **durfte**	*he was allowed to*
wir **durften**	*we were allowed to*
ihr **durftet**	*you were allowed to*
sie **durften**	*they were allowed to*

The simple past of all modal auxiliaries is formed like that of regular weak verbs:

ich **konnte,** etc.	*I could*, etc.
ich **mochte,** etc.	*I liked to*, etc.
ich **mußte,** etc.	*I had to*, etc.
ich **sollte,** etc.	*I was supposed to*, etc.
ich **wollte,** etc.	*I wanted to*, etc.

(c) Compound Past and Past Perfect

COMPOUND PAST:	ich **habe gedurft,** etc.	*I was allowed to*, etc.
PAST PERFECT:	ich **hatte gedurft,** etc.	*I had been allowed to*, etc.

The compound past and past perfect of modal auxiliaries are formed with **haben** and the past participle: **gedurft, gekonnt, gemocht, gemußt, gesollt, gewollt.**

(d) **Wissen**

The present tense of **wissen** follows the pattern of modal auxiliaries:

ich **weiß**	*I know*
du **weißt**	*you know*
er **weiß**	*he knows*
wir **wissen**	*we know*
ihr **wißt**	*you know*
sie **wissen**	*they know*

SIMPLE PAST: ich **wußte,** etc. *I knew*, etc.
COMPOUND PAST: ich **habe gewußt,** etc. *I knew, have known*, etc.

19. Meanings of Modal Auxiliaries

Modal auxiliaries express various manners ("modes") of activity, such as: permission, ability, possibility, desire, compulsion, obligation.

(a) Ich **darf** ins Kino gehen.
I am allowed to (I may) go to the movies.
Sie **dürfen** hier **nicht** rauchen.
You must not (You can't) smoke here.

Dürfen denotes permission:

may, to be permitted to, to be allowed to;
must not, cannot (in negative present).

(b) Ich **kann** es bezahlen.
I can pay for it.
Meinetwegen **kann** er kommen.
As far as I'm concerned, he may come.
Das **kann** wahr sein.
That may be true.
Herbert **kann** Deutsch.
Herbert knows German.
Können Sie deutsche Bücher lesen?
Do you know how to read German books?

Können denotes ability or possibility:

can, be able to;
may (permission, possibility);
to know (a subject or skill), *know how to.*

(c) **Mögen** Sie amerikanische Filme nicht?
Don't you like American films?
Ich **mag** es **nicht tun.**
I don't like to do it.
Das **mag** sein.
That may be.

Mögen expresses liking or possibility:

to like, care for (plus direct object), *like to* (plus infinitive);
may (possibility).

(d) Ich **muß** jetzt Deutsch sprechen.
I must (have to) speak German now.
Wie alt ist er? Ich weiß es nicht genau, aber er **muß** achtzehn sein.
How old is he? I don't know exactly, but he must be eighteen.

Müssen denotes compulsion, necessity, conjecture, probability:

must, to have to[1] (compulsion);
must (conjecture or probability).

(e) Der Bankbeamte sagt, ich **soll** morgen zurückkommen.
The bank clerk says I am (supposed) to come back tomorrow.
Wie **soll** ich das machen?
How shall I (am I to) do that?
Er **sollte** deutlicher sprechen.
He should (ought to) speak more clearly.
Er **soll** sehr reich sein.
He is said to be very rich.

Sollen expresses moral compulsion or expectation:

to be supposed to; to be to;
shall, should; ought to;
to be said to.

(f) Ich **will** eine Tasse Tee.
I want a cup of tea.
Ich **will** noch einige Briefe **schreiben.**
I want to write a few more letters.
Ich **wollte** eben gehen.
I was just about to go.
Er **will** sehr einflußreich sein.
He claims to be very influential.

Wollen denotes will, desire, intention:

to want (plus direct object), *want to* (plus infinitive);
to be about to, intend to;
to claim.

---

[1] In the negative, **brauchen** often replaces **müssen** when the meaning is *need not, don't have to;* **brauchen** requires a dependent infinitive with **zu:**

Sie **brauchen nicht zu kommen,** wenn Sie nicht wollen.
You need not (don't have to) come, if you don't want to.

20. Uses of Modal Auxiliaries

(a) With Dependent Infinitive

Ich **will** einen deutschen Film **sehen.**
I want to see a German film.

The dependent infinitive of a modal stands at the end of a main clause.

Ich wußte nicht, daß er mich **sprechen wollte.**
I didn't know that he wanted to talk to me.

In a dependent clause the finite verb stands last; the dependent infinitive immediately precedes the finite verb. (See Lektion 3, paragraph 16c.)

(b) Omission of Infinitive of Motion

Wollen Sie heute abend mit mir ins Kino?
Do you want to go to the movies with me tonight?
Ich **darf** nicht hinein.
I'm not allowed to go in.

The infinitive of a verb of motion is usually omitted after a modal auxiliary if the meaning is clear from the context.

(c) With Direct Object

Ich habe **es** gekonnt.
I was able to (do it).
Das dürfen Sie nicht.
You can't do that.

Contrary to English, German modal auxiliaries may take a direct object.

21. The "Double Infinitive"

(a) 1. Das **habe** ich **gedurft.**
I was allowed to (do that).
Er **hat** es **gemußt.**
He had to (do it).

2. Ich **habe** ins Kino **gehen dürfen.**
I was allowed to go to the movies.
Er **hat** es **tun müssen.**
He had to do it.

1. The regular form of the past participle is used when the modal auxiliary has no dependent infinitive.

2. An alternate form of the past participle, identical with the infinitive, is used when the modal auxiliary has a dependent infinitive. This construction is commonly called a "double infinitive." A double infinitive stands last in any clause.

(b) Marlene Dietrich **habe** ich öfter **gesehen.**
I have often seen Marlene Dietrich.
Marlene Dietrich **habe** ich öfter **spielen sehen.**
I have often seen Marlene Dietrich act.

Caruso **habe** ich nie **gehört.**
I have never heard Caruso.
Caruso **habe** ich nie **singen hören.**
I have never heard Caruso sing.

The verbs **sehen, hören, helfen, heißen,** and **lassen** commonly use the double-infinitive construction when they have a dependent infinitive.

(c) Double Infinitive in Dependent Word Order

Ich weiß nicht, warum er nicht ins Kino **hat gehen dürfen.**
I don't know why he wasn't allowed to go to the movies.
Er hat mich eingeladen, weil er nicht allein **hat gehen wollen.**
He invited me because he didn't want to go alone.[1]

When the double-infinitive construction occurs in a dependent clause, the finite form of the verb stands immediately before the double infinitive.

22. Kennen, wissen, können

(a) Ich **kenne** den Weg zum Flughafen.
I know the way to the airport. (I am familiar with it; I have driven it before.)
Ich **kenne** Curt Jürgens.
I know Curt Jürgens. (I am personally acquainted with him.)

---

[1] Conversational German prefers the simple past instead of the compound past of modal auxiliaries, especially in dependent clauses, to avoid an awkward sequence of verbs:

Er hat mich eingeladen, weil er nicht allein **gehen wollte.**
He invited me because he didn't want to go alone.

Kennen means *to know* in the sense of being acquainted with a person or thing. It can never be followed by a clause.

(b) Ich **weiß,** wie man zum Flughafen fährt.
I know how to drive to the airport. (I know which streets to take.)
Ich **weiß,** daß Curt Jürgens ein bekannter Filmschauspieler ist.
I know that Curt Jürgens is a well-known film actor. (I know this fact.)

Wissen means *to know* in the sense of knowing facts. Its direct object is frequently a clause.

(c) Er **kann** Deutsch.
He knows German.
Sie **kann** Auto fahren.
She knows how to drive.
Die **können** ihre Sache.
They know their business. (They know what they're doing.)

Können means *to know* in the sense of knowing how, mastering a subject or a skill.

IV. ÜBUNGEN

A. *Ergänzen Sie in den folgenden Sätzen die korrekte Form des angegebenen Verbes im Präsens!*

1. (dürfen) Ich ______ noch nicht gehen.
2. (können) Ich ______ alles verstehen.
3. (mögen) Ich ______ es nicht essen.
4. (müssen) Ich ______ viel arbeiten.
5. (sollen) Du ______ ihn treffen.
6. (wollen) Du ______ ins Kino gehen.
7. (dürfen) Du ______ schneller fahren.
8. (können) Du ______ mit ihm spielen.
9. (mögen) Wir ______ nicht ins Theater gehen.
10. (müssen) Wir ______ später wiederkommen.
11. (sollen) Wir ______ um acht Uhr dort sein.
12. (wollen) Wir ______ ihm helfen.
13. (dürfen) ______ er hier bleiben?
14. (können) ______ er Klavier spielen?
15. (müssen) ______ er so viel studieren?

16. (wollen) ______ er es allein tun?
17. (sehen) Wir ______ ihn kommen.
18. (hören) ______ du sie singen?
19. (lassen) Er ______ sich die Haare schneiden.
20. (hören) Ich ______ sie lachen.

B. *Setzen Sie die Sätze in Übung A in das Imperfekt!*

C. *Setzen Sie die Sätze in Übung A in das Perfekt!*

D. *Setzen Sie die folgenden Sätze in das Imperfekt!*

1. Otto hat ins Kino gehen dürfen.
2. Herbert hat einen deutschen Film sehen wollen.
3. In Deutschland hat er keinen amerikanischen Film sehen mögen.
4. Er hat in Amerika genug amerikanische Filme sehen können.
5. Er hat für Otto bezahlen wollen.
6. Das hat er aber nicht gedurft.
7. Herbert hat noch viele Briefe schreiben sollen.
8. Deswegen hat Otto allein ins Kino gehen müssen.
9. Das hat er nicht besonders gemocht.
10. Otto hat einmal Charlie Chaplin spielen sehen.

E. *Antworten Sie mit „ja" und ersetzen Sie das Imperfekt durch das Perfekt!*

BEISPIEL: Wollte er länger in Deutschland bleiben?
Ja, er hat länger in Deutschland bleiben wollen.

1. Wollte Herbert für Otto bezahlen?
2. Durfte Herbert den ganzen Sommer in Deutschland bleiben?
3. Mußten Sie zu Hause bleiben?
4. Sollten Sie ihn heute morgen sehen?
5. Konnten Sie mit ihm sprechen?
6. Wollte er ins Kino gehen?
7. Durfte er Otto einladen?
8. Mußten Sie es ihm sagen?
9. Mochte er einen deutschen Film sehen?
10. Konnten Sie einen guten Platz bekommen?

F. *Antworten Sie mit „ja" und ersetzen Sie das Imperfekt durch das Perfekt!*

BEISPIEL: Wollte er mitfahren?
Ja, das hat er gewollt.

1. Konnte er singen?
2. Wollte er ins Kino gehen?
3. Durften die Kinder ins Kino gehen?
4. Mußten Sie viel bezahlen?
5. Wollten Sie ihn einladen?
6. Mußten Sie früh zu Hause sein?
7. Durfte Herbert nach Berlin fahren?
8. Mußte Herbert auf der Bank Deutsch sprechen?
9. Konnte Herbert seine Reiseschecks einlösen?
10. Wollten Sie eine lange Reise machen?

G. *Beginnen Sie die folgenden Sätze mit* **Ich weiß, daß . . .** *und gebrauchen Sie das Imperfekt!*

BEISPIEL: Er hat es tun wollen.
Ich weiß, daß er es tun wollte.

1. Es hat früher so sein müssen.
2. Sie hat es bezahlen können.
3. Herbert hat einen deutschen Film sehen wollen.
4. Er hat die Sache schnell vergessen wollen.
5. Herbert hat seine Briefe schreiben wollen.
6. Sie haben ihm seine Handschuhe suchen helfen.
7. Du hast die Tür öffnen sollen.
8. Er hat kein Fleisch essen dürfen.
9. Sie hat ihre Tante immer gern singen hören.
10. Er hat es ihr nicht sagen mögen.

H. *Gebrauchen Sie vier der Nützlichen Ausdrücke in ganzen Sätzen!*

I. *Sagen Sie zuerst und schreiben Sie danach auf deutsch!*

1. Yes, Herbert, I'm free this evening. What do you have in mind?
2. I don't like to write letters, and I don't have to write these letters now.

3. I can go to the movies with you, if you want to.
4. Is there a German film at the Winterhaus?
5. I must learn to speak German fluently, and my father says I can't see American movies now.
6. In my class I was supposed to speak only German, and now I want to see a German film.
7. A film with Maximilian Schell is playing at the Winterhaus.
8. Do you like him?
9. Do you know his films?
10. I have never seen him act, but I know he can act very well.

Inseparable and Separable Verbs.

Lektion 5

I. GESPRÄCH: Am Stammtisch

OTTO: Hat Ihnen der Film gefallen?

HERBERT: Oh ja. Leider habe ich nicht alles verstanden. Die deutschen Schauspieler sprechen furchtbar schnell. Es ist mir einfach unmöglich, alles zu verstehen.

OTTO: Genau das Gleiche kann ich von Ihren amerikanischen Filmen sagen. Es entgeht mir auch immer die Hälfte.

HERBERT: Otto, ich habe Durst. Können wir irgendwo etwas trinken?

OTTO: Hier ist ein Lokal. Da gehe ich oft hin, wenn ich aus dem Kino komme.

HERBERT: Nehmen wir ein Glas Bier! Ich lade Sie ein.
(*Sie treten ein und bestellen zwei Glas Bier.*)

At the Club Table

OTTO: Did you like the movie?

HERBERT: Oh yes. Unfortunately I didn't understand everything. German actors speak terribly fast. It's simply impossible for me to understand everything.

OTTO: I can say exactly the same thing about your American movies. I always miss half, too.

HERBERT: Otto, I'm thirsty. Can we drink something somewhere?

OTTO: Here is a place. I often go there when I come from the movies.

HERBERT: Let's have a glass of beer. Be my guest.
(*They enter and order two glasses of beer.*)

HERBERT: Viel Rauch und Biergeruch — so habe ich mir ein deutsches Wirtshaus immer vorgestellt.

OTTO: Auch die Bierkrüge und die dicke Kellnerin?

HERBERT: Auch die. Aber alles sieht sehr neu aus.

OTTO: Ja, wissen Sie, dies ist kein altes Lokal. Das Gebäude existiert erst seit dem Wiederaufbau.

(*Die Kellnerin bringt das Bier. Sie stoßen an.*)

OTTO: Also, Prost!

HERBERT: Prost! — Mein Bier ist nicht recht kalt.

OTTO: Allzu kaltes Bier ist ungesund, sagt man hier. — Warum schauen Sie den Tisch an?

HERBERT: Ich versuche eben, diese Inschrift in der Tischplatte zu entziffern. Ist dies ein Stammtisch?

OTTO: Ja, der Tisch gehört einem Turnverein. Hinter Ihnen an der Wand hängt eine Fahne, die auch dem Verein gehört.

HERBERT: Dann dürfen wir doch hier nicht sitzen!

OTTO: Oh doch. Der Tisch ist nur an gewissen Abenden reserviert. Heute nicht. Dort drüben in der Ecke sehen Sie noch einen anderen runden Tisch.

HERBERT: Dort, wo die Männer Karten spielen?

HERBERT: A lot of smoke and the smell of beer — that's the way I have always imagined a German tavern.

OTTO: The beer mugs and the fat waitress, too?

HERBERT: Them, too. — But everything looks very new.

OTTO: Yes, you know, this place isn't old. The building has been in existence only since rebuilding started.

(*The waitress brings the beer. They clink glasses.*)

OTTO: Well, here's to you!

HERBERT: Here's to you! — My beer isn't very cold.

OTTO: Beer that's too cold is not healthy, they say here. — Why are you looking at the table?

HERBERT: I'm just trying to decipher this inscription in the tabletop. Is this a club table?

OTTO: Yes, this table belongs to an athletic club. On the wall behind you hangs a banner that also belongs to the club.

HERBERT: Well, then we can't sit here.

OTTO: Oh yes, we can. The table is reserved only on certain evenings. Not today. Over there in the corner you see another round table.

HERBERT: There, where the men are playing cards?

OTTO: Ja, das ist auch ein Stammtisch. Der gehört einer Verbindung und ist immer reserviert.

HERBERT: Einer Verbindung? Einem Studentenverein? Aber das sind doch keine Studenten, die dort Karten spielen! Das sind Männer von fünfzig, sechzig Jahren!

OTTO: Die waren früher Studenten. Jetzt sind sie „alte Herren", aber sie kommen immer noch am Stammtisch zusammen. Mein Vater hat auch ein Lokal, wo er jeden Mittwoch hingeht und mit alten Freunden zusammenkommt.

HERBERT: Otto! Da kommen ein paar junge Leute. Sie schauen uns an.

OTTO: Ah, das sind Freunde von mir. Wir kriegen Gesellschaft.

OTTO: Yes, that's also a club table. It belongs to a fraternity and is always reserved.

HERBERT: A fraternity? A student club? But those aren't students playing cards over there. Those are men fifty, sixty years old.

OTTO: They were students once. Now they're "old grads," but they still get together at the club table. My father also has a place where he goes every Wednesday and gets together with old friends.

HERBERT: Otto. Some young people are coming in. They're looking at us.

OTTO: Oh, those are friends of mine. We're getting company.

Fragen

Antworten Sie auf deutsch!

1. Wie hat Herbert der Film gefallen?
2. Warum kann Herbert in einem deutschen Film nicht alles verstehen?
3. Wo geht Otto oft hin, wenn er aus dem Kino kommt?
4. Was bestellen Herbert und Otto im Wirtshaus?
5. Warum sieht das Lokal sehr neu aus?
6. Was versucht Herbert, auf der Tischplatte zu entziffern?
7. Was hängt an der Wand hinter Herbert?
8. Was ist eine Verbindung?
9. Wo kommen die „alten Herren" immer zusammen?
10. Was tun die jungen Leute, die in die Gaststube hereinkommen?

Konversation

Fragen Sie Ihren Nachbar,

1. ob er in einem deutschen Film alles verstehen kann! [Ihr Nachbar muß selbstverständlich jede Frage beantworten.]
2. ob er kaltes Bier ungesund findet!
3. ob er schon an einem Stammtisch gesessen hat!
4. wem die Fahne hinter Herbert gehört!
5. was die „alten Herren" am Stammtisch tun!
6. an welchen Abenden Ottos Vater zum Stammtisch geht!

II. NÜTZLICHE AUSDRÜCKE

die Absicht haben (*plus infinitive with* **zu**)	*to intend*
Durst haben	*to be thirsty*
Hunger haben	*to be hungry*
entgehen	*to miss, fail to understand*
es entgeht mir = ich verstehe nicht	
früher	*formerly, once*

immer noch	*still*
leider	*unfortunately, I'm sorry to say*
etwas im Sinn haben	*to have something in mind*
teil-nehmen an (*plus dative*)	*to take part in, participate in*

III. GRAMMATIK

23. Verbs with Prefixes

Many German verbs consist of a prefix and a basic verb, whose meaning is usually changed by the prefix:

gehen	*to go*
begehen	*to commit*
entgehen	*to escape*
mitgehen	*to go along*
hinaufgehen	*to go up*

Some prefixes are inseparable (always attached to the verb); others are separable (separated from the verb in certain situations).

24. Verbs with Inseparable Prefixes

INFINITIVE		SIMPLE PAST	PART PARTICIPLE
bemerken	*to notice*	**bemerkte**	**bemerkt**
entgehen	*to escape*	**entging**	ist **entgangen**
gehören	*to belong*	**gehörte**	**gehört**
verstehen	*to understand*	**verstand**	**verstanden**

The inseparable prefixes, occurring in both strong and weak verbs, are **be-, emp-, ent-, er-, ge-, miß-, ver-, wider-, zer-.** Verbs with inseparable prefixes always have the stress on the stem of the verb.

The past participle of a verb with inseparable prefix never adds the prefix **ge-.**[1]

[1] Note, for example, that the past participle of **gefallen** is identical with the past participle of **fallen: gefallen.**

Inseparable prefixes cannot be used by themselves (hence "inseparable") and have no independent meanings of their own.[1] Notice, however, how they may affect the meaning of a basic verb: **stehen** *to stand*, **bestehen** *to undergo*, **entstehen** *to begin*, **gestehen** *to admit*, **verstehen** *to understand*, **widerstehen** *to resist.*

25. Verbs with Separable Prefixes

zurụ̈ck-kommen[2]	*to come back*
he̲im-kehren	*to return home*
ạn-sehen	*to look at*
mịt-nehmen	*to take along*
lo̱s-lassen	*to set free*
kẹnnen-lernen	*to become acquainted with, meet*

Verbs with separable prefixes consist usually of an adverb (**zurück, heim,** etc.) or a preposition (**an, mit,** etc.) and a simple verb; adjectives (**los,** etc.) and infinitives (**kennen,** etc.) may also occur as separable prefixes.

Verbs with separable prefixes are always stressed on the prefix. The meaning of a verb with separable prefix is usually a literal combination of the prefix and the stem verb.

26. Position of Separable Prefixes

(a) Separated from Verb

1. Er **sieht** die Tischplatte sehr genau **an.**
   He looks very carefully at the table surface.
   Er **kam** mit Frau Lenz **zurück.**
   He came back with Mrs. Lenz.

---

[1] The adjective **voll** is an exception. Though it has independent meaning of its own, it functions also as an inseparable prefix in a few verbs, such as **vollbringen** *to accomplish*, **vollenden** *to complete*, **vollstrecken** *to execute*.

[2] The hyphen is here inserted between the prefix and the verb stem merely to indicate that the prefix is separable. The hyphen is not part of the verb.

Note also that German does not have printed stress marks. To point out a stressed syllable in German, we are using a dot (ụ̈) under a short vowel and a dash (o̱) under a long vowel and a diphthong.

A separable prefix is separated from the verb in the present tense and simple past and stands at the end of a main clause.

2. **Kommen** Sie sofort **zurück!**
Come back at once!
Schau mich nicht so **an!**
Don't look at me like that!

A separable prefix is separated from the verb in an imperative construction and stands at the end of the clause.

(b) Attached to Verb

1. Ich bemerke, daß er die Tischplatte sehr genau **ansieht.**
I notice that he is looking very carefully at the table surface.
Ich sah, daß er mit Frau Lenz **zurückkam.**
I saw that he was coming back with Mrs. Lenz.

A separable prefix is attached to the verb in dependent clauses in the present and simple past.

2. Er hatte die Absicht, mit seinen Freunden **zusammenzukommen.**
He had the intention of getting together with his friends.
Herbert hatte im Sinn, Otto ins Kino **einzuladen.**
Herbert had in mind inviting Otto to the movies.

The preposition **zu,** if used, is inserted between the prefix and the verb.

3. Er ist mit seinen Freunden **zusammengekommen.**
He got together with his friends.
Sie waren nicht **aufgestanden.**
They had not got up.

The syllable **-ge-** of the past participle is inserted between the prefix and the verb.

27. Variable Prefixes

The prefixes **durch, hinter, über, um, unter, wieder** may be either inseparable or separable.

INSEPARABLE		SEPARABLE	
durchschauen	*to see through*	**durch-fallen**	*to fail (an exam)*
überraschen	*to surprise*	**über-ziehen**	*to pull over*
umarmen	*to embrace*	**um-drehen**	*to turn around*
unternehmen	*to undertake*	**unter-bringen**	*to house*
wiederholen	*to repeat*	**wieder-holen**	*to get again*

Ich **umarmte** das Kind. *I embraced the child.*	Ich **drehte** den Ring **um.** *I turned the ring around.*
Er **hat** etwas Neues **unternommen.** *He undertook something new.*	Er **hat** seine Gäste im Hinterhause **untergebracht.** *He housed his guests in the rear building.*
Sie **wiederholte** die Aufgabe. *She repeated the lesson.*	Sie **holte** das Buch **wieder.** *She got the book again.*

The stress is on the stem verb if the variable prefix is inseparable and on the prefix if it is separable. Note that the meaning of an inseparable verb is usually figurative, while the meaning of a separable verb is usually literal.

IV. ÜBUNGEN

A. *Setzen Sie die folgenden Sätze ins Perfekt!*

1. Heute morgen empfangen wir einen Gast aus Amerika.
2. Ich entziffere mit Schwierigkeit Ihre Briefe.
3. Ich verstehe nicht immer alles.
4. Wegen des großen Lärms entgeht mir viel.
5. Der Stammtisch gehört einem Verein.
6. Das Wirtshaus gefällt den „alten Herren".
7. Sie bestellen eine Tasse Kaffee.
8. Die Kellnerin entfernt die leeren Tassen.
9. Wir erwarten Freunde im Lokal.
10. Herbert bemerkt Ottos Freunde zuerst.

B. *Setzen Sie die folgenden Sätze ins Präsens!*

1. Haben Sie alles verstanden?
2. Ist Ihnen viel entgangen?
3. Herbert hat zwei Glas Bier bestellt.
4. Was hat Herbert versucht?

5. Otto hat die Inschrift entziffert.
6. Otto hat Herberts Frage beantwortet.
7. Der Tisch hat einem Turnverein gehört.
8. Otto hat seinen amerikanischen Freund am Flughafen empfangen.
9. Zuerst hat Herbert die Kellnerin nicht bemerkt.
10. Haben Sie Ihre Freunde begrüßt?

C. *Setzen Sie die Sätze in Übung B ins Imperfekt!*

D. *Setzen Sie die folgenden Sätze ins Perfekt!*

1. Er reist heute nachmittag ab.
2. Sie treten in die Gaststube ein.
3. Die „alten Herren" nehmen an allen Festlichkeiten teil.
4. Warum kommt er gerade um acht Uhr zurück?
5. Der Soldat schlägt seine Feinde tot.
6. Ich lerne jeden Tag mehr junge Deutsche kennen.
7. Manchmal gehe ich mit ihnen spazieren.
8. Wir leeren unsere Tassen aus.
9. Sie bauen alles wieder auf.
10. Die jungen Leute schauen im Lokal umher.

E. *Setzen Sie die folgenden Sätze ins Präsens!*

1. Haben Sie mich ins Kino eingeladen?
2. Wir sind vor dem Kino stehengeblieben.
3. Sie sind ins Kino eingetreten.
4. Herbert hat sich angestrengt, alles zu verstehen.
5. Wie hat sich Herbert ein deutsches Wirtshaus vorgestellt?
6. Alles hat sehr neu ausgesehen.
7. Herbert hat die Tischplatte genau angesehen.
8. Man hatte eine Fahne aufgehängt.
9. Die „alten Herren" sind öfter zusammengekommen.
10. Sie sind sehr zeitig angekommen.

F. *Setzen Sie die Sätze in Übung E ins Imperfekt!*

G. *Verbinden Sie die folgenden Sätze, indem Sie mit der angegebenen Konjunktion aus dem zweiten Satz einen Nebensatz machen!*

BEISPIEL: Ich trinke Tee. Ich bin durstig. (wenn)
Ich trinke Tee, wenn ich durstig bin.

1. Man sagt „Guten Tag!“ Man begrüßt einen Freund. (wenn)
2. Wir wurden neugierig. Die neuen Gäste schauten uns an. (als)
3. In Deutschland gibt man sich immer die Hand. Man begegnet einem Freund auf der Straße. (wenn)
4. Er geht in ein Lokal. Er kommt mit anderen „alten Herren“ zusammen. (wo)
5. Herbert wollte für Otto bezahlen. Otto hat es nicht erlaubt. (aber)
6. Man sagt „Wie bitte?“ Man versteht etwas nicht. (wenn)
7. Ich war nicht überrascht. Ich hatte mir ein Wirtshaus immer so vorgestellt. (denn)
8. Wir sprachen nur so miteinander. Sie trat ein. (als)
9. Die Kellnerin brachte uns drei Tassen Tee. Wir hatten sie nicht bestellt. (obwohl)
10. Das Zimmer gefiel mir gut. Es sah sehr gemütlich aus. (weil)

H. *Bilden Sie Sätze, indem Sie* **Ich hatte die Absicht** *mit den folgenden Satzteilen verbinden:*

BEISPIEL: heute fortfahren
Ich hatte die Absicht, heute fortzufahren.

1. Ihnen einen Freund vorstellen
2. hinausgehen
3. meine Freunde einladen
4. sie nur kurz anschauen
5. an dem Kartenspiel teilnehmen
6. mit Ihnen zusammenkommen
7. mir das Buch ansehen
8. früh aufstehen
9. schnell heraussteigen
10. mitfahren

I. *Bilden Sie Sätze, indem Sie den ersten Satzteil mit dem zweiten verbinden:*

BEISPIEL: Ich hatte im Sinn   für Sie bezahlen
Ich hatte im Sinn, für Sie zu bezahlen.

1. Ich hatte vor	eine Tasse Kaffee bestellen
2. Er hatte mir empfohlen	die Aufgabe wiederholen
3. Er hat ihnen befohlen	die Stadt verlassen
4. Er hatte im Sinn	die Inschrift entziffern
5. Ich hatte die Absicht	meine Freunde besuchen
6. Wir beschlossen	dem Kinde helfen
7. Ich habe ihm versprochen	seine Tochter begleiten
8. Wir hatten vor	es noch einmal versuchen
9. Wir hatten im Sinn	Sie überraschen
10. Sie hat mir versprochen	ihn heute empfangen

J. *Gebrauchen Sie vier der Nützlichen Ausdrücke in ganzen Sätzen!*

K. *Sagen Sie zuerst und schreiben Sie danach auf deutsch!*

1. After they had seen the movie, Otto and Herbert went into a restaurant.
2. Herbert had not understood everything in the movie.
3. He invited Otto to drink something with him, because he was thirsty.
4. After they had ordered something, they looked at the people in the restaurant.
5. Herbert could not decipher the inscription in the tabletop because it was very old.
6. The table belonged to an athletic club, and this surprised Herbert.
7. Herbert noticed a flag on the wall; it belonged to a fraternity.
8. Some of the "old grads" had come together at another table, where they were playing cards.
9. Other students began to come into the place, and Otto presented them to Herbert.
10. After Herbert had met them, they discussed German fraternities.

Relative Pronouns;
Idiomatic Use of Modals.

Lektion 6

I. GESPRÄCH: Eine Gesellschaft

FRAU LENZ: Herbert, Frau Hartung hat mich eben angerufen. Sie möchte uns auf heute Nachmittag zum Tee einladen.

HERBERT: Frau Hartung? Ist das nicht die Dame, die ich neulich auf dem Weg zur Bank kennengelernt habe?

FRAU LENZ: Ja. Hätten Sie Lust zu kommen? Frau Hartung möchte Sie gern mit ihrer Familie bekanntmachen.

HERBERT: Gerne. Ich bin heute nachmittag frei.

FRAU LENZ: Guten Tag, Frau Hartung.

FRAU HARTUNG: Ach, Frau Lenz. Bitte treten Sie ein! Und Herr Becker. Wie nett von Ihnen, daß Sie gekommen sind!

A Party

MRS. LENZ: Herbert, Mrs. Hartung has just phoned me. She would like to invite us for tea this afternoon.

HERBERT: Mrs. Hartung? Isn't that the lady I met recently on the way to the bank?

MRS. LENZ: Yes. Would you like to come? Mrs. Hartung would like you to meet her family.

HERBERT: Gladly. I'm free this afternoon.

MRS. LENZ: Good afternoon, Mrs. Hartung.

MRS. HARTUNG: Oh, Mrs. Lenz. Please come in. And Mr. Becker. How nice of you to have come.

HERBERT: Guten Tag, Frau Hartung. Es war sehr nett von Ihnen, mich einzuladen.

FRAU HARTUNG: Darf ich Sie gleich ins Eßzimmer bitten? — Hier ist Frau Lenz, die ihr alle kennt. Und dies ist Herr Becker, von dem ich euch erzählt habe. Darf ich vorstellen? Meine Schwägerin — meine Schwester — mein Mann — und meine Tochter Ilse.

HERBERT: (*gibt allen die Hand.*) Sehr angenehm.

FRAU HARTUNG: Nun, setzen wir uns zu Tisch! — Herr Becker, bitte nehmen Sie hier zwischen mir und meiner Tochter Platz! Was trinken Sie? Tee oder Kaffee?

HERBERT: Kaffee, wenn ich bitten darf.

ILSE: Herr Becker, Sie müssen uns ihre Eindrücke schildern. Ich möchte hören, was ein Ausländer, der zum ersten Mal in Frankfurt ist, von unserer Stadt hält.

HERBERT: Die Stadt ist sehr schön. Alles, was ich bis jetzt gesehen habe, hat mir sehr gut gefallen. — Dürfte ich um den Zucker bitten?

FRAU HARTUNG: Bitte schön. Und hier ist das Gebäck, Apfelkuchen und Torte. Sie müssen von beiden ein Stück versuchen.

HERBERT: Hello, Mrs. Hartung. It was very nice of you to invite me.

MRS. HARTUNG: May I ask you to go into the dining room right away? Here is Mrs. Lenz, whom you all know. And this is Mr. Becker, about whom I have told you. May I introduce? My sister-in-law — my sister — my husband — and my daughter Ilse.

HERBERT: (*shakes hands with everybody.*) How do you do?

MRS. HARTUNG: Well, let's sit down at the table. Mr. Becker, please sit here between me and my daughter. What will you drink — tea or coffee?

HERBERT: Coffee, if I may.

ILSE HARTUNG: Mr. Becker, you must describe your impressions to us. I'd like to hear what a foreigner who is in Frankfurt for the first time thinks about our city.

HERBERT: The city is very beautiful. Everything I've seen up to now I've liked very much. — May I have the sugar?

MRS. HARTUNG: Certainly. And here is pastry: apple cake and torte. You must try a piece of each.

HERBERT: Vielen Dank. Die Torte ist ausgezeichnet.

HERR HARTUNG: Herr Becker, könnten Sie uns etwas über die politische Lage in Amerika sagen? Die Dinge, von denen wir hier in den Zeitungen lesen, sind oft schwer zu verstehen.

HERBERT: Leider ist Politik ein Gebiet, mit dem ich mich nur selten befasse. Ich bin da gar kein Spezialist. Ich bin Mathematikstudent.

ILSE: Wirklich? Ich studiere auch Mathematik, jedenfalls als Nebenfach. Mein Hauptfach ist Chemie.

HERBERT: Das begreife ich. Wer Chemie studiert, muß auch Mathematik studieren.

FRAU HARTUNG: Herr Becker, nehmen Sie bitte noch eine Tasse Kaffee! Und erzählen Sie uns doch etwas von Ihren Eindrücken! Über Mathematik können Sie mit Ilse ein andermal sprechen.

HERBERT: Thank you very much. The torte is excellent.

MR. HARTUNG: Mr. Becker, could you tell us something about the political situation in America? The things we read about in the newspapers are often hard to understand.

HERBERT: Unfortunately, policitics is a subject with which I seldom concern myself. I'm not at all a specialist in that. I'm a mathematics student.

ILSE HARTUNG: Really? I'm also studying math, at least as a minor. My major is chemistry.

HERBERT: I can understand that. Whoever studies chemistry must also study math.

MRS. HARTUNG: Mr. Becker, please have another cup of coffee. And do tell us something of your impressions. You can talk with Ilse about mathematics some other time.

Fragen

Antworten Sie auf deutsch!

1. Wer hat Frau Lenz eben angerufen?
2. Was für eine Einladung hat Frau Lenz von Frau Hartung bekommen?
3. Wer ist Frau Hartung?
4. In welches Zimmer bittet Frau Hartung ihre Gäste?
5. Wer sind die Leute, die Herbert im Eßzimmer kennenlernt?
6. Wo nimmt Herbert Platz?
7. Was wünscht Ilse Hartung von Herbert zu hören?
8. Wie findet Herbert die Torte?
9. Warum ist Herbert kein Spezialist in der Politik?
10. Was studiert Ilse Hartung auf der Universität?

Konversation

Fragen Sie Ihren Nachbar,

1. ob er heute Nachmittag frei ist! [Ihr Nachbar muß selbstverständlich jede Frage beantworten.]
2. ob er gerne Apfelkuchen ißt!
3. ob er sich oft mit Politik befaßt!
4. wie viele Personen bei Frau Hartung eingeladen waren!
5. wie Frau Hartungs Tochter heißt!
6. was Ilse Hartung als Nebenfach studiert!

II. NÜTZLICHE AUSDRÜCKE

bekannt-machen — *to introduce (a person or fact)*
bitten — *to ask, beg*
  um etwas bitten — *to ask for something*
denken an (*plus accusative*) — *to think about, concentrate one's thoughts on*
  Denken Sie an ihn? — *Are you thinking of him?*
halten von (*plus dative*) — *to think of, have an opinion about*
  Was halten Sie von ihm? — *What do you think of him?*
auf heute Nachmittag — *(for) this afternoon*

Platz nehmen	*to sit down, take a seat*
Sehr angenehm.	*How do you do? (in response to an introduction)*
Würden Sie so gut sein, . . . (*plus infinitive with* **zu**)	*Would you be so kind . . .; Would you, please . . .*

III. GRAMMATIK

28. Relative Pronouns

	SINGULAR			PLURAL
	Masc.	Fem.	Neut.	ALL GENDERS
NOM.	**der**	**die**	**das**	**die**
GEN.	**dessen**	**deren**	**dessen**	**deren**
DAT.	**dem**	**der**	**dem**	**denen**
ACC.	**den**	**die**	**das**	**die**

The relative pronoun in general conversational use has forms identical with the definite article in all cases except the genitive singular and plural and the dative plural.

See the Appendix for forms of **welcher,** which may also be used as relative pronouns in all cases except the genitive. Forms of **welcher** are not common in conversation.

29. Uses of Relative Pronouns

(a) Without Preposition

As Subject:

Das sind keine Studenten, **die** dort sitzen.
Those aren't students sitting there.

Showing Possession:

Ist das die Dame, **deren** Tochter so schön gesungen hat?
Is that the lady whose daughter sang so beautifully?

As Indirect Object:

Dort ist der Mann, **dem** ich die Zeitung gegeben habe.
There is the man to whom I gave the newspaper.

As Direct Object:

Hier ist Frau Lenz, **die** Ihr alle kennt.
Here is Mrs. Lenz, whom you all know.

The relative pronoun introduces a dependent relative clause. The finite verb stands at the end of the clause, and the clause is set off by commas.

The gender and number of the relative pronoun are determined by its antecedent. Its case is determined by its function in the relative clause. (This usage is essentially the same in English, but in German the relative pronoun has distinct forms for each gender and case. It is, therefore, easy to see its relationship and function.)

Note that the relative pronoun may never be omitted in German:

Ist Frau Lenz die Dame, **die** ich gestern kennengelernt habe?
Is Mrs. Lenz the lady I met yesterday?
Da steht der Mann, **dem** ich es gegeben habe.
There's the man I gave it to.

(b) With Preposition

Der Tisch, **auf den** ich das Gebäck legen wollte, war zu klein.
The table on which I wanted to put the pastry was too small.
Die Politik ist ein Gebiet, **mit dem** ich mich selten befasse.
Politics is a subject I seldom concern myself with.

A relative pronoun used as object of a preposition always stands directly with the preposition. It may not be separated from it, as in English. Note that the relative pronoun must take the case form required by the preposition (dative or accusative).[1]

---

[1] A **wo**-compound may be substituted for a preposition plus relative pronoun referring to a thing (**womit, wovon, wozu**). **Wor-** is used if the preposition begins with a vowel (**woran, worauf, worin**). **Wo**-compounds in relative clauses are generally not preferred in conversation. They are more common in formal writing:

Der Tisch, **worauf** sie das Gebäck legen wollte, war zu klein.
Die Politik ist ein Gebiet, **womit** er sich nur selten befaßt.

30. Was as Relative Pronoun

(a) Das ist alles, **was** sie mir gesagt haben.
That's all they said to me.
Das ist das Schönste, **was** ich je gesehen habe.
That's the most beautiful thing I have ever seen.
Das erste, **was** wir tun müssen, ist fleißig studieren.
The first thing we must do is to study diligently.

Was is used as a relative pronoun after a general or indefinite antecedent, such as **alles, einiges, das einzige, etwas, nichts, manches, viel(es), allerhand, allerlei, wenig, genug;** after a neuter noun-adjective, such as **das Beste, das Gute, das Schönste;** after an ordinal number, such as **das erste.**

(b) Er trinkt zuviel Kaffee, **was** ich nie tue.
He drinks too much coffee, (something) which I never do.
Er ist gestern angekommen, **was** mich sehr gefreut hat.
He arrived yesterday, (a fact) which pleased me very much.

Was is used as a relative pronoun when a whole clause is the antecedent.

31. Wer and Was as Indefinite Relative Pronouns

Wer Chemie studiert, muß auch Mathematik studieren.
Whoever studies chemistry must also study mathematics.
Wer zuletzt lacht, lacht am besten.
He who laughs last laughs best.
Wir dürfen einladen, **wen** wir wollen.
We may invite whomever we want.
Was auf dem Tisch liegt, sollte genügen.
What is on the table should be enough.
Was Sie hier sagen, stimmt nicht.
What you are saying here isn't right.

Wer and **was** are used as relative pronouns whenever there is no antecedent. **Wer** occurs in the following forms: **wer** (nominative singular), **wem** (dative singular) and **wen** (accusative singular). **Was** occurs only as nominative and accusative singular. The English equivalents are usually *he who, whoever, what, that which.*

32. Expressions of Politeness

Sie möchte uns einladen.
She would like to invite us.
Möchten Sie Tee oder Kaffee?
Would you like tea or coffee?
Dürfte ich um ein Stück Kuchen bitten?
May I have a piece of cake?
Könnten Sie uns etwas über die politische Lage sagen?
Could you tell us something about the political situation?
Hätten Sie Lust zu kommen?
Would you like to come?
Würden Sie so gut sein, mir den Zucker zu reichen?
Would you be so good as to pass me the sugar?

The subjunctive forms **dürfte, hätte, könnte, möchte, würde** are frequently used in set expressions of polite request and response.

IV. ÜBUNGEN

A. *Verbinden Sie den zweiten Satz als Relativsatz mit dem ersten Satz!*

BEISPIEL: Hier ist der Brief. Ich habe ihn eben erhalten.
Hier ist der Brief, den ich eben erhalten habe.

1. Dort ist Herr Köller. Sie haben ihn gestern kennengelernt.
2. Herr Köller ist unser Nachbar. Ihm gehört das Haus an der Ecke.
3. Er ist ein netter Mensch. Alle Leute haben ihn gern.
4. Herr Köller hat einen Sohn. Der Sohn studiert Mathematik.
5. Mathematik ist ein Fach. Ich liebe das Fach nicht.
6. Unser Nachbar hat einen Hund. Er heißt Rex.
7. Gertrud ist ein braves Kind. Es arbeitet immer fleißig.
8. Sie ist eine fleißige Schülerin. Ihre Zeugnisse sind immer gut.
9. Ich kenne ein Mädchen. Sie sollten es auch kennenlernen.
10. Sie hat einen Bruder. Der Bruder geht noch nicht zur Schule.
11. Es sind Kinder. Man kann sie nur loben.
12. Kennen Sie die Dame dort? Sie spricht eben mit meinem Vater.
13. Das ist meine Tante. Ich habe sie Ihnen bereits vorgestellt.

14. Gefällt Ihnen das Kleid? Sie trägt es heute.
15. Meine Tante ist eine neugierige Person. Man muß ihr immer alles erzählen.
16. Aber sie ist die beste Köchin. Ich kenne sie.

B. *Verbinden Sie den zweiten Satz als Relativsatz mit dem ersten Satz!*

BEISPIEL: Wo ist der Mann? Er ist mit ihm gekommen.
Wo ist der Mann, mit dem er gekommen ist?

1. Hier ist das Buch. Ich dachte eben an das Buch.
2. Wie heißt der Roman? Sie haben mir von dem Roman erzählt.
3. Der Architekt hat sehr gute Pläne. Wir sind mit seinen Plänen ganz zufrieden.
4. Er hat eine Weltanschauung. Man muß vor ihr Respekt haben.
5. Ist dies das Haus? Sie wohnen in dem Haus.
6. Herr Müller ist ein netter Mensch. Mit ihm kann man sich gut amüsieren.
7. Seine Mutter ist eine gebildete Frau. Man hört viel Gutes von ihr.
8. Er ist ein guter Freund. Alle gehen gerne zu ihm.
9. Er ist ein ausgezeichneter Arzt. Man redet viel über ihn.
10. Ich kenne die jungen Damen. Er interessiert sich für sie.

C. *Wiederholen Sie die Sätze 1 bis 5 in Übung B, indem Sie statt des Relativpronomens eine Form mit* **wo-** *gebrauchen!*

D. *Verbinden Sie die beiden Sätze in jeder Gruppe, indem Sie den ersten Satz in einen Relativsatz mit* **wer** *oder* **was** *umändern!*

BEISPIEL: Er lacht zuletzt. Er lacht am besten.
Wer zuletzt lacht, lacht am besten.

Es scheint billig zu sein. Es kostet manchmal viel.
Was billig zu sein scheint, kostet manchmal viel.

1. Er will nicht hören. Er muß fühlen.
2. Es ist sehr teuer. Es ist nicht immer gut.

3. Er hat das gesagt. Er kennt die Angelegenheit nicht.
4. Es ist unpraktisch. Es kann sehr teuer sein.
5. Er ist nicht blind. Er kann das einsehen.
6. Man kann es nicht sehen. Es kann sehr wichtig sein.
7. Er hat Freunde. Er hat das größte Glück.
8. Es steht in der Zeitung. Es stimmt nicht immer.
9. Er ist eingeladen. Er muß pünktlich ankommen.
10. Sie haben etwas gesagt. Es gefällt mir nicht.

E. *Verbinden Sie die beiden Sätze in jeder Gruppe, indem Sie den zweiten Satz in einen Relativsatz mit* **was** *umändern!*

BEISPIEL: Sie ist eine fleißige Studentin. Das freut mich sehr.
Sie ist eine fleißige Studentin, was mich sehr freut.

1. Er hat verschiedenes gesagt. Es hat mir nicht gefallen.
2. Er hat immer zwei Pläne gehabt. Das war nicht nötig.
3. Sie hat uns zum Tee eingeladen. Sie tut es nur selten.
4. Die Kinder machten einen großen Lärm. Es war jedoch verboten.
5. Ich mußte zwei Stunden stehen. Es war nicht angenehm.
6. Sie haben mir viel geholfen. Ich schätze es sehr.
7. Ich arbeite viel im Garten. Das ist sehr gesund für mich.
8. Sie hat die ganze Nacht geschlafen. Das hat ihr wohl getan.

F. *Sagen Sie auf deutsch!*

1. Would you like a cup of tea?
2. May I ask for a cup of tea?
3. Would you like to go to the movies?
4. I should like to say something.
5. Could you help us?
6. Would you, please, speak louder?
7. She would like to go with us.
8. I would not say that.
9. May I say something?
10. Could you come with us?

G. *Gebrauchen Sie sechs der Nützlichen Ausdrücke in ganzen Sätzen!*

H. *Sagen Sie zuerst und schreiben Sie danach auf deutsch!*

1. Herbert is going to a party to which Mrs. Hartung has invited him.
2. Mrs. Hartung is the lady with whom he spoke on the way to the bank.
3. She has a daughter who is studying mathematics.
4. Mrs. Hartung introduces Herbert to the people who are already sitting in the living room.
5. Then she asks them to go into the dining room.
6. There she serves an apple cake her sister-in-law made.
7. Because Ilse is studying chemistry, Herbert intends to talk with her.
8. But Mrs. Hartung says, "Wouldn't you like to talk with Ilse some other time?"
9. Herbert, who would rather talk with Ilse now, doesn't think much of Mrs. Hartung's suggestion.
10. He talks with Mr. Hartung, who wants to hear something about politics in America.

Aufsatz

Sie sind bei einem Freund in Deutschland zum Abendessen eingeladen. Ihr Freund stellt Sie seinen Eltern vor. Der Vater Ihres Freundes interessiert sich für viele Dinge und stellt Ihnen viele Fragen. Schreiben Sie diese Fragen und Ihre Antworten in der Form eines Gespräches nieder! Der Vater Ihres Freundes möchte zum Beispiel wissen:
(1) wie Sie von Amerika nach Europa gereist sind;
(2) wie lange Sie schon in Deutschland sind und wie lange Sie vorhaben zu bleiben;
(3) aus welcher Stadt Sie kommen, und ob dies eine große oder kleine Stadt ist;
(4) ob Sie Brüder und Schwestern haben, und wie alt sie sind;
(5) wozu Sie nach Deutschland gekommen sind;
(6) welches Ihre ersten Eindrücke von Deutschland sind.

Definite and Indefinite Articles;
Der- and Ein-Words;
Nouns: Plural, Inflection, Formation.

Lektion 7

I. GESPRÄCH: In der Stadt

ILSE: Es ist aber nett von Ihnen, daß Sie mich begleiten wollen. Ich muß ein paar Einkäufe machen, aber ich befürchte, daß Einkaufen nicht sehr interessant für einen Mann ist.

HERBERT: Ich muß auch in einen Laden. Können Sie mir ein gutes Fotogeschäft empfehlen? Ich möchte zwei Filme entwickeln lassen.

ILSE: Fotogeschäfte gibt es viele. Hier sind wir am Goetheplatz. Gehen wir diese Straße hinauf!

HERBERT: Was für ein Verkehr! Da sind ja fast mehr Autos als Fußgänger. Der Schutzmann dort hat die Hände voll.

Downtown

ILSE: It's certainly nice of you to want to accompany me. I have to make a few purchases, but I'm afraid that shopping isn't very interesting for a man.

HERBERT: I have to go to a store, too. Can you recommend a good camera shop to me? I'd like to have two rolls of film developed.

ILSE: There are a lot of camera shops. Here we're at the Goetheplatz. Let's go up this street.

HERBERT: What traffic! There are almost more cars than pedestrians. The policeman there has his hands full.

ILSE: Frankfurt hat über 600 000 Einwohner. Und hier sind wir fast genau im Mittelpunkt der Stadt.

HERBERT: Die Häuser — ich meine diese hohen Gebäude — sind sehr modern.

ILSE: Gewiß. Der ganze Stadtteil hier ist neu.

HERBERT: Was mir besonders auffällt, sind die vielen Bücherläden. Sehen Sie mal dieses Schaufenster an! Bücher aus allen Ländern, auch sehr gute Farbdrucke. Dort sehe ich Goethes Werke ausgestellt. Zwanzig Bände!

ILSE: Wissen Sie auch, daß Goethe aus Frankfurt war. Das Goethehaus steht gleich da unten rechts.

HERBERT: Ja, das weiß ich. Herr Lenz hat es mir bereits gezeigt. Ich kann mir nur nicht recht erklären, warum der Dichter hier mitten in einem Geschäftsviertel leben wollte.

ILSE: Frankfurt has over 600,000 inhabitants. And here we're almost exactly in the center of the city.

HERBERT: The houses — I mean those tall buildings — are all modern.

ILSE: Certainly. This whole section of the city is new.

HERBERT: What strikes me particularly are the many bookstores. Just look at this (show) window. Books from all countries, also very good color prints. There I see Goethe's works displayed. Twenty volumes!

ILSE: Do you know, by the way, that Goethe was from Frankfurt? The Goethe House is right down there on the right.

HERBERT: Yes, I know that. Mr. Lenz has already shown it to me. Only I can't quite understand why the poet wanted to live here in the middle of a business district.

ILSE: Na, im 18. Jahrhundert gab es hier wahrscheinlich noch keine Warenhäuser. — Da drüben in diesem Hochhaus arbeitet mein Bruder. Er ist Rechtsanwalt, wissen Sie.

HERBERT: Nein, das habe ich nicht gewußt. Ist er hoch oben?

ILSE: Im fünften Stock. — Warten Sie! An dieser Ecke will ich meinen ersten Einkauf machen.

HERBERT: Hier? Aha, ein Herrenartikelgeschäft — Anzüge, Schuhe und Hüte . . . Natürlich, Sie wollen ein Geschenk für jemand kaufen.

ILSE: Ein Geburtstagsgeschenk für meinen Vater. Ich dachte zuerst an ein Paar Handschuhe. Aber das geht nicht gut jetzt im Sommer.

HERBERT: Vielleicht ein Halstuch? Nein, das ist auch für den Winter. Eine Krawatte oder ein paar Taschentücher?

ILSE: Ja, so etwas. Wollen Sie mir beim Aussuchen helfen?

HERBERT: Lieber nicht. Ich bringe inzwischen meine Filme zum Entwickeln. Dann treffe ich Sie hier wieder.

ILSE: Well, in the eighteenth century there probably weren't any stores here yet. My brother works over there in that skyscraper. He's a lawyer, you know.

HERBERT: No, I didn't know that. Is he up high?

ILSE: On the sixth floor. Wait. I want to make my first purchase on this corner.

HERBERT: Here? Oh, a men's-wear store — suits, shoes, and hats. . . . Of course, you want to buy a present for somebody.

ILSE: A birthday present for my father. At first I was thinking of a pair of gloves. But that isn't appropriate now in the summer.

HERBERT: Perhaps a scarf? No, that's also for winter. A tie or some handkerchiefs?

ILSE: Yes, something like that. Would you like to help me in the selection?

HERBERT: I'd rather not. I'll take my rolls of film for developing in the meantime. Then I'll meet you here again.

Fragen

Antworten Sie auf deutsch!

1. Was muß Ilse in der Stadt tun?
2. Wohin muß Herbert?
3. Warum sucht Herbert ein Fotogeschäft?
4. Wie ist der Verkehr am Goetheplatz?
5. Was sagt Herbert über den Schutzmann?
6. Wie viele Einwohner hat Frankfurt?
7. Wie findet Herbert die Häuser?
8. Warum sehen die Häuser so modern aus?
9. Was fällt Herbert besonders auf?
10. Wo arbeitet Ilses Bruder?
11. Was für ein Geschenk will Ilse kaufen?
12. Warum kauft Ilse kein Halstuch?

Konversation

Fragen Sie Ihren Nachbar,

1. ob er es interessant findet, Einkäufe zu machen! [Ihr Nachbar muß selbstverständlich jede Frage beantworten.]
2. was für Geschäfte er gerne besucht!
3. ob der Verkehr in seiner Heimatstadt groß ist!
4. wo man Filme entwickeln lassen kann!
5. welche deutschen Dichter er gelesen hat!
6. ob man gewöhnlich in einem Geschäftsviertel oder in einem Wohnviertel wohnt!
7. wie viele Krawatten er besitzt!

II. NÜTZLICHE AUSDRÜCKE

auf-fallen	*to be conspicuous*
es fällt mir auf	*it strikes me*
aus	*out of; from*
Er ist aus Frankfurt.	*He comes from Frankfurt.*

der Einkauf	*purchase*
Einkäufe machen	*to shop, go shopping*
es gibt (*plus acc.*)	*there is, there are*
die Hände voll haben	*to have one's hands full*
etwas tun lassen	*to have something done*
Er läßt zwei Filme entwickeln.	*He's having two rolls of film developed.*
was für ein	*what kind of (a), what a*
In was für einem Viertel wohnt er?	*In what kind of section does he live?*
Was für ein schöner Tag!	*What a beautiful day!*
der Stock	*story, floor*
im ersten Stock	*on the second floor*
die Treppe	*staircase*
eine Treppe hoch	*on the second floor*
zwei Treppen hoch	*on the third floor*

III. GRAMMATIK

33. Forms of the Definite Article

	SINGULAR			PLURAL
	MASC.	FEM.	NEUT.	
NOM.	**der**	**die**	**das**	**die**
GEN.	**des**	**der**	**des**	**der**
DAT.	**dem**	**der**	**dem**	**den**
ACC.	**den**	**die**	**das**	**die**

34. Uses of the Definite Article

In general, the definite article is used as in English, but observe the following differences:

(a) **Der Sonntag** ist ein Ruhetag.[1]
Sunday is a day of rest.

---

[1] Days of the week used without definite article refer to specific days:

Sonntag ist ein Ruhetag. (*Next*) *Sunday is a day of rest.*

Die schönste Jahreszeit ist **der Frühling.**
The most beautiful season is spring.
Es ist kalt **im Januar.**
It is cold in January.

The definite article is required with days of the week, months, and seasons.

(b) Nehmen Sie **den Hut** ab!
Take off your hat!
Steck es in **die Tasche!**
Put it in your pocket!

The definite article is used with parts of the body and articles of clothing when ownership is clear.

(c) Er fährt oft **in die Schweiz** (**in die Türkei**).
He often goes to Switzerland (to Turkey).
But:
Jetzt wohnt er **in Deutschland** (**in Amerika**).
Now he lives in Germany (in America).

The definite article is required with feminine names of countries.

(d) Sie geht gerne **in die Kirche** (**in die Schule**).
She likes to go to church (to school).
Er reiste **mit dem Flugzeug** (**mit dem Dampfer**) (**mit dem Zug**).
He traveled by plane (by steamer) (by train).
Was wünschen Sie **zum Frühstück** (**zum Mittagessen**) (**zum Abendessen**)?
What would you like for breakfast (for lunch) (for supper)?

The definite article is usually required in prepositional phrases.

(e) **Der Mensch** ist empfindlich.
Man is sensitive.
Das Leben ist schwer.
Life is difficult.

The definite article is required with generic nouns and abstract nouns.

35. Forms of the Indefinite Article

	SINGULAR			PLURAL
	MASC.	FEM.	NEUT.	
NOM.	**ein**	**eine**	**ein**	**keine**
GEN.	**eines**	**einer**	**eines**	**keiner**
DAT.	**einem**	**einer**	**einem**	**keinen**
ACC.	**einen**	**eine**	**ein**	**keine**

Note that the endings of the indefinite article are like those of the definite article, except in the nominative masculine singular and the nominative and accusative neuter singular, where the indefinite article has no ending.

36. Uses of the Indefinite Article

In general the indefinite article is used as in English, but observe the following differences:

(a) Mein Vater ist **Arzt,** mein Bruder ist **Rechtsanwalt.**
My father is a doctor, my brother is a lawyer.
Herbert ist **Amerikaner.** Sein Großvater war **Deutscher.**
Herbert is an American. His grandfather was a German.

The indefinite article is omitted before unmodified predicate nouns denoting profession, rank, or nationality.[1]

(b) Ich habe **Kopfweh.**
I have a headache.
Er hat **Zahnweh.**
He has a toothache.

The indefinite article is omitted in certain idiomatic phrases describing physical pain or an ache.

(c) Wir haben sie **als kleines Mädchen** gekannt.
We knew her as a little girl.

---

[1] If the predicate is modified by an adjective, the article is not omitted:

Sein Vater war **ein bekannter Arzt.**
His father was a well-known physician.

Er stellte sich **als Geschäftsmann** vor.
He introduced himself as a businessman.

The indefinite article is omitted after **als** meaning *as.*

37. Der-Words

dieser	*this, that*	**mancher**	*many a, (pl.) some*
jener	*that*	**solcher**	*such*
jeder	*each, every*	**welcher**	*which*

Der-words are so called because they have forms like **der,** except that in the nominative and accusative neuter singular the ending is **-es:**

	SINGULAR			PLURAL
	MASC.	FEM.	NEUT.	
NOM.	**dieser**	**diese**	**dieses**	**diese**
GEN.	**dieses**	**dieser**	**dieses**	**dieser**
DAT.	**diesem**	**dieser**	**diesem**	**diesen**
ACC.	**diesen**	**diese**	**dieses**	**diese**

Note:

1. **Jener** is rare except in direct comparison with **dieser:**

   Dieses Buch ist größer als **jenes** Buch.
   This book is bigger than that book.

2. English *that* without direct comparison is equivalent to German **dieser:**

   Diese Idee ist neu.[1]
   That idea is new.

3. **Solcher** is rare in the singular, except with abstract nouns:

   Solche Schönheit findet man selten.[2]
   Such beauty one seldom finds.

---

[1] The idea of "that" is often reinforced by **da:**

Dieser Mann **da** wartet auf Sie.
That man is waiting for you.

[2] In other contexts, **solcher** is usually replaced by **so ein:**

So ein Buch liest man nicht.
One doesn't read such a book.

38. Ein-Words

Ein-words are so called because they have forms like **ein:**

	SINGULAR			PLURAL
	MASC.	FEM.	NEUT.	
NOM.	**kein**	**keine**	**kein**	**keine**
GEN.	**keines**	**keiner**	**keines**	**keiner**
DAT.	**keinem**	**keiner**	**keinem**	**keinen**
ACC.	**keinen**	**keine**	**kein**	**keine**

The **ein**-words are **kein** and the possessive adjectives:

kein	*not a, no*
mein	*my*
dein	*your* (familiar singular)
sein	*his, its* (masculine singular)
ihr	*her, its* (feminine singular)
sein	*its, his, her* (neuter singular)
unser	*our*
euer	*your* (familiar plural)
ihr	*their*
Ihr	*your* (conventional)

39. Plural of Nouns

Contrary to English, there is no general rule for forming the plural of German nouns. It is, therefore, best to commit the plural of each noun to your memory as you learn it. To help you, most German nouns may be divided into several classes, each of which has a particular plural pattern for nouns in this class:

(a) CLASS 1: Nouns adding no ending to form the plural

NOM. SING.		NOM. PLURAL
der **Mantel**	*overcoat*	die **Mäntel**
der **Laden**	*store*	die **Läden**
der **Dichter**	*poet*	die **Dichter**
das **Wasser**	*water*	die **Wasser**
das **Gebäude**	*building*	die **Gebäude**
das **Gebirge**	*mountain*	die **Gebirge**
das **Mädchen**	*girl*	die **Mädchen**
das **Fräulein**	*miss*	die **Fräulein**

Nouns in Class 1 are polysyllabic and include:

1. masculine and neuter nouns ending in **-el, -en, -er;**
2. neuter nouns beginning with **Ge-** and ending in **-e;**
3. all diminutives (always neuter!) with the endings **-chen** or **-lein.**

The umlaut is added in the plural of some masculines, but never in neuters.

Note: Two feminine nouns belong to Class 1:

NOM. SING.		NOM. PLURAL
die **Mutter**	*mother*	die **Mütter**
die **Tochter**	*daughter*	die **Töchter**

(b) CLASS 2: Nouns adding **-e** to form the plural

NOM. SING.		NOM. PLURAL
der **Brief**	*letter*	die **Briefe**
der **Hut**	*hat*	die **Hüte**
der **König**	*king*	die **Könige**
der **Offizier**	*officer*	die **Offiziere**
die **Hand**	*hand*	die **Hände**
das **Haar**	*hair*	die **Haare**
das **Erlebnis**	*experience*	die **Erlebnisse**
das **Geschenk**	*gift*	die **Geschenke**
das **Paket**	*parcel*	die **Pakete**

Nouns in Class 2 include:

1. most monosyllabic masculine and feminine nouns and some monosyllabic neuter nouns;
2. masculine nouns ending in **-ich, -ig, -ling,** and some masculine nouns of non-Germanic origin usually stressed on the last syllable;
3. feminine and neuter nouns ending in **-nis, -sal;**
4. polysyllabic neuter nouns with the prefix **Ge-** and some neuter nouns of non-Germanic origin with the stress on the last syllable.

The umlaut is added in the plural of most masculines, all feminines, but never in neuters.

(c) CLASS 3: Nouns adding **-er** to form the plural

NOM. SING.		NOM. PLURAL
der **Mann**	*man*	die **Männer**
der **Wald**	*forest*	die **Wälder**
das **Bild**	*picture*	die **Bilder**
das **Buch**	*book*	die **Bücher**
das **Wort**	*word*	die **Wörter**
der **Irrtum**	*error*	die **Irrtümer**

Nouns in Class 3 include:

1. a few monosyllabic masculine nouns;
2. most monosyllabic neuter nouns;
3. nouns ending in **-tum;**
4. no feminine nouns.

The umlaut is added in the plural wherever possible.

40. Case Endings of Nouns

(a)

NOM. SING.		GEN. SING.
der Mann	*man*	**des Mann(e)s**
das Glas	*glass*	**des Glases**
das Wasser	*water*	**des Wassers**

The genitive singular of most masculine and neuter nouns ends in **-s** or **-es.**[1] A small group of masculine nouns forms the genitive and all other inflected cases in **-(e)n.** These we will review in Lektion 8 (page 102).

(b)

NOM. SING.		DAT. SING.
das Kind	*child*	**mit dem Kind(e)**
der Tag	*day*	**seit dem Tag(e)**
der Teller	*plate*	**auf dem Teller**

In the dative singular, an **-e** may be added to masculine and neuter monosyllabic nouns.

[1] The genitive ending is normally **-es** for monosyllabic nouns and nouns ending in an **s** sound. The genitive ending of polysyllabic masculine and neuter nouns *not* stressed on the last syllable is usually **-s.** Most other genitive masculine and neuter nouns may end in **-s** or **-es,** depending on sentence rhythm.

(c)

	NOM. PLURAL		DAT. PLURAL
	die Länder	*countries*	**aus allen Ländern**
	die Jahre	*years*	**seit vielen Jahren**

In the dative plural, an **-n** is added, unless the plural ends in **-n** or **-s** (den **Krawatten,** den **Autos**).

(d) Feminine nouns have no case endings in the singular.

41. Formation of Nouns

(a) Infinitive as Noun

das Entwickeln *developing, to develop*
das Aussuchen *choosing, selection*

An infinitive (capitalized!) may be used as a neuter noun.

(b) Derivative Nouns, Class 1

1. **spielen** *to play* — **der Spieler** *player*
malen *to paint* — **der Maler** *painter*

Many nouns ending in **-er** are derived from verbs and denote the person performing the action indicated by the verb. Such nouns are masculine. The equivalent feminine nouns have the additional ending **-in: die Spielerin, die Malerin.**

2. **die Musik** *music* — **der Musiker** *musician*
die Arbeit *work* — **der Arbeiter** *worker*
die Schweiz *Switzerland* — **der Schweizer** *Swiss*
(das) **Holland** *Holland* — **der Holländer** *Dutchman*

Many nouns ending in **-er** are derived from other nouns and denote a profession or nationality. The equivalent feminine nouns have the additional ending **-in: die Musikerin, die Arbeiterin, die Schweizerin, die Holländerin.**

3. **das Kind** *child* — **das Kindchen** *little child*
die Frau *woman* — **das Fräulein** *young lady*

Nouns with the diminutive ending **-chen** or **-lein** are always neuter and take umlaut if possible.

(c) Derivative Nouns, Class 2

1. **laufen** *to run* — **der Lauf** *running, course*
   fallen *to fall* — **der Fall** *fall, case*
   sitzen *to sit* — **der Sitz** *seat*

   Many monosyllabic masculine nouns are formed from the infinitive stems of verbs.

2. **gehen** *to go* — **der Gang** *going, trip*
   klingen *to sound* — **der Klang** *sound*
   reiten *to ride* — **der Ritt** *ride*

   Many monosyllabic masculine nouns are formed from ablaut forms of verbs.

(d) Derivative Nouns, Class 3

der König	*king*	**das Königtum**	*kingdom*
das Alter	*age*	**das Altertum**	*antiquity*
der Christ	*Christian*	**das Christentum**	*Christianity*
eigen	*one's own*	**das Eigentum**	*property*

Nouns with the suffix **-tum** are derived from adjectives or other nouns and are usually neuter.[1]

(e) Compound Nouns

das Hochhaus (*skyscraper*): from **hoch** (*high*), **das Haus** (*house*).
der Bücherladen (*bookstore*): from **Bücher** (*books*), **der Laden** (*store*).
der Geburtstag (*birthday*): from **die Geburt** (*birth*), **der Tag** (*day*).
der Ausgang (*exit*): from **aus** (*out*), **der Gang** (*going*).
das Schaufenster (*show window*): from **schauen** (*to view*), **das Fenster** (*window*).

Compound nouns may be a combination of a noun plus adjective, noun, preposition, adverb, or verb form.

The gender of a compound noun is that of the last component.

[1] Two masculine nouns with the suffix **-tum** are **der Irrtum** (*error*), derived from **sich irren** (*to err*), and **der Reichtum** (*wealth*), derived from **reich** (*rich*).

In some compound nouns, **-(e)s** or **-n** is added to the first part of the compound:

die Jahreszeit (*season*): from **das Jahr** (*year*), **die Zeit** (*time*).
der Sonnenaufgang (*sunrise*): from **die Sonne** (*sun*), **der Aufgang** (*rising*).

IV. ÜBUNGEN

A. *Ergänzen Sie, wenn nötig, die korrekte Form des Artikels!*

1. ______ Schweiz ist eine Republik.
2. Er hat mich zu ______ Abendessen eingeladen.
3. Mein kleiner Bruder geht noch in ______ Schule.
4. In ______ Sommer gehen wir oft schwimmen.
5. Haben Sie ______ Kopfweh?
6. Maries Vater ist ______ Professor.
7. In ______ Juli ist das Wetter sehr heiß.
8. Hast du ihn als ______ Kind gekannt?
9. Er schloß ______ Augen und schlief ein.

B. *Verwenden Sie das angegebene Substantiv als Genitivobjekt!*

BEISPIEL: Die Farben sind schön. (das Buch)
Die Farben des Buches sind schön.

1. Der Geruch verbreitet sich im ganzen Haus. (der Kuchen)
2. Der Bruder ist schon angekommen. (das Mädchen)
3. Die Hitze war sehr unangenehm. (der Sommer)
4. Der fünfte Stock war leer. (das Gebäude)
5. Das Büro ist drei Treppen hoch. (der Rechtsanwalt)
6. Die Arbeit scheint sehr leicht zu sein. (der Schutzmann)
7. Die Farben gefielen uns nicht. (das Bild)
8. Wir sind noch lange nicht am Ende. (das Jahrhundert)
9. Der Höhepunkt war noch nicht gekommen. (der Film)
10. Die Vorderseite war ganz neu. (das Haus)

C. *Bilden Sie Sätze, indem Sie das angegebene Substantiv in den Dativ setzen!*

1. Er kam aus (der Wald).
2. Er blieb vor (das Haus) stehen.

3. Er sprach mit (der Lehrer).
4. Das Buch lag in (das Schaufenster).
5. Der Brief war von (der Anwalt).
6. Er wohnte auf (das Land).
7. Er stand vor (der Laden).
8. Er wußte nichts von (das Buch).
9. Die Zeitung liegt auf (der Tisch).
10. Der Hund saß neben (der Ofen).
11. Sie lebte immer in (die Stadt).
12. Das Bild hängt an (die Wand).

D. *Setzen Sie das erste Substantiv und das Verb in den Plural!*

BEISPIEL: Das Geschenk ist für meinen Bruder.
Die Geschenke sind für meinen Bruder.

1. Das Büchlein hat nicht viel gekostet.
2. Der Bruder besitzt ein Boot.
3. Das Schaufenster war voller Bücher.
4. Das Gebäude schien neu zu sein.
5. Der Laden ist an der Ecke.
6. Der Schuh war zu eng.
7. Der Wagen hat im Parkplatz gestanden.
8. Das Geschenk war sehr willkommen.
9. Die Nacht war kühl.
10. Dieses Hochhaus ist sehr berühmt.
11. Der Mann durfte nicht hinein.
12. Das Kind hat den Weg verloren.
13. Das Dorf liegt im Tal.
14. Das Buch hat unter dem Tisch gelegen.
15. Das Ei hat ganz gut geschmeckt.

E. *Setzen Sie die Substantive in den Plural!*

BEISPIEL: Sie hat das Geschenk vergessen.
Sie hat die Geschenke vergessen.

1. Ich habe den Redner gut gehört.
2. Wer hat den Arbeiter gesehen?
3. Hat er das Gemälde verkauft?

4. Wir wollen Ihren Bruder einladen.
5. Sie ging durch den Garten.
6. Er hat die Stadt besucht.
7. Wir haben das Fotogeschäft nicht gefunden.
8. Herbert mußte seinen Film entwickeln lassen.
9. Ich habe den Tag nie vergessen.
10. Sie hat ihr Paket selbst getragen.
11. Ilse wollte das Taschentuch kaufen.
12. Hat Herbert das Bild gekauft?
13. Haben Sie dieses Lied schon gehört?
14. Er wollte den Mann etwas fragen.
15. Ich habe das Glas fallen lassen.

F. *Setzen Sie die Substantive (wenn nötig, auch die Verben) in den Singular! (Vergessen Sie die Artikel nicht!)*

1. Ich muß Einkäufe machen.
2. An dieser Ecke sind Bücherläden.
3. Hier sieht man selten Hochhäuser.
4. Er kauft sich Anzüge.
5. Ich habe keine Taschentücher bei mir.
6. Kennen Sie die Städte?
7. Sie geht gerne in die Gärten.
8. Die Stadtteile sind ganz neu.
9. Er brachte uns Geschenke.
10. Wir brauchen die Wörterbücher.

G. *Setzen Sie die Dativsubstantive in den Plural:*

BEISPIEL: Ich habe es dem Lehrer gegeben.
Ich habe es den Lehrern gegeben.

1. Er ist dem Mann lange gefolgt.
2. Er hat mit dem Bruder gesprochen.
3. Die Leute liefen aus dem Haus.
4. Das Geld gehörte dem Schüler.
5. Auf dem Berge sah man viele Häuser.
6. Mit dem Lied hat er großen Erfolg gehabt.
7. Er hat die Blumen auf dem Hügel gefunden.
8. Auf dem Schreibtisch liegen Zeitungen.

9. Auf dem Dach sah man viel Moos.
10. In der Stadt findet man schöne Schulen.

H. *Bilden Sie Substantive!*

BEISPIEL: das Haus, hoch
das Hochhaus

1. der Freund, die Bücher
2. der Schlüssel, das Haus
3. das Haus, das Land
4. der Aufbau, wieder
5. der Brief, die Liebe (add -s-)
6. der Gang, aus
7. die Zeit, das Jahr (add -es-)
8. die Hitze, der Mittag (add -s-)
9. die Feier, der Geburtstag (add -s-)
10. der Schein, die Sonne (add -n-)
11. das Spiel, die Kinder

I. *Gebrauchen Sie sechs der Nützlichen Ausdrücke in ganzen Sätzen!*

J. *Sagen Sie zuerst und schreiben Sie danach auf deutsch!*

1. Ilse had to do some shopping, and she invited Herbert to go along.
2. He had two films and wanted to take them to a camera shop for developing.
3. They saw almost more cars than people.
4. The tall buildings have eight or more stories. In Germany they don't call these buildings skyscrapers.[1]
5. Ilse was looking for leather gloves or scarves as a birthday present for her father.
6. In the summer one cannot find these articles in the stores.
7. Ties and handkerchiefs she did see, and she bought two handkerchiefs and three ties.

---

[1] Germans use **das Hochhaus** for buildings of eight or more stories. **Der Wolkenkratzer** (*skyscraper*) is reserved for tall American buildings, particularly those in New York.

8. The tall buildings are all very modern, because they have been in existence only since the war.
9. In the show windows of the bookstores Herbert saw many books and color prints.
10. After Herbert had selected a few books, they found several camera shops, where Herbert had the films developed.

Aufsatz

Sie gehen in die Stadt, um ein paar Einkäufe zu machen. Am Eingang zu einem Warenhaus treffen Sie eine Freundin, die ebenfalls Einkäufe macht. Schreiben Sie einen kurzen Aufsatz, in dem Sie Ihre Erlebnisse in der Stadt erzählen! Erwähnen Sie unter anderem:
(1) den Verkehr in den Straßen;
(2) die Gebäude und Läden;
(3) die Auslagen in den Schaufenstern;
(4) das Gespräch mit Ihrer Freundin (die verschiedenen Einkäufe, die Sie und Ihre Freundin machen wollen; ob es Geschenke sind usw.);
(5) warum Sie gern oder ungern Einkäufe machen!

Nouns: Plural (continued).

Lektion 8

I. GESPRÄCH: In einer Konditorei

HERBERT: Hier ist ein hübsches Restaurant. Darf ich Sie zu einer Erfrischung einladen?

ILSE: Eine Tasse Kaffee nehme ich gerne. Setzen wir uns in den Garten! Bei diesem warmen Wetter bleibe ich am liebsten im Freien.

HERBERT: Einverstanden. Die Gartenwirtschaften in Deutschland gefallen mir. In Amerika kennen wir das kaum.

ILSE: Dies ist eine Konditorei. Man bekommt hier nur alkoholfreie Getränke, sowie Gebäck und Süßigkeiten.

HERBERT: Die Deutschen trinken gerne Kaffee — das habe ich bereits gemerkt. Und man ißt auch gerne Kuchen dabei, nicht wahr?

In a Café

HERBERT: Here is a nice restaurant. May I invite you to some refreshment?

ILSE: I'd like a cup of coffee. Let's sit in the garden. In this warm weather I prefer to stay outdoors.

HERBERT: I agree. I like the open-air restaurants in Germany. We rarely have them in America.

ILSE: This is a café and pastry shop. Here you get only nonalcoholic beverages, as well as pastry and sweets.

HERBERT: Germans like to drink coffee. I've already noticed that. And they like to eat cake with it, don't they?

ILSE: Nein, bitte, Herr Becker, ich habe augenblicklich gar keinen Hunger.

HERBERT: Schön. (*Zum Kellner.*) Zwei Kaffee, bitte!

ILSE: Herr Becker, wo haben Sie eigentlich Deutsch gelernt? Sie sprechen die deutsche Sprache wirklich fließend.

HERBERT: In der Schule und auf der Universität. Allerdings auch zu Hause. Mein Großvater stammt aus Köln, und mein Vater spricht drei Sprachen. Er hat mir oft bei den Schulaufgaben geholfen.

ILSE: Da haben Sie Glück gehabt. Ich hatte es nicht so leicht. Ich mußte auf dem Gymnasium sieben Jahre Englisch lernen, aber mir hat niemand geholfen.

HERBERT: Und jetzt studieren Sie Chemie?

ILSE: No, thank you, Mr. Becker. At the moment I'm not at all hungry.

HERBERT: All right. (*To the waiter.*) Two coffees, please.

ILSE: Mr. Becker, where did you learn German? You speak the German language really fluently.

HERBERT: In school and at the university. And especially at home. My grandfather comes from Cologne, and my father speaks three languages. He often helped me with my homework.

ILSE: You were lucky. I didn't have it so easy. I had to study English in the Gymnasium for seven years, but nobody helped me.

HERBERT: And now you're studying chemistry?

ILSE: Ja. Ich bin im zweiten Semester. Nächste Woche beginnen meine Semesterprüfungen.

HERBERT: Nächste Woche? Ist das Semester denn noch nicht zu Ende? Es ist ja schon Juli.

ILSE: Nein. Das Frühjahrssemester endet erst Mitte Juli.

HERBERT: Ich habe noch eine Frage. Mein Deutschprofessor in Amerika hat uns erzählt, daß es auf den deutschen Universitäten gar keine Zwischenexamen, sondern nur Endprüfungen gibt. Und nun sprechen Sie von Semesterprüfungen.

ILSE: Ihr Professor hatte die gute alte Zeit im Sinn. Da konnte ein Student jahrelang ins Kolleg gehen, ohne ins Examen zu steigen. Heute ist das nicht mehr so. Es gibt Zwischenexamen in fast allen Fächern, besonders in den Naturwissenschaften.

HERBERT: Gefällt Ihnen das Studium?

ILSE: Sehr gut. Die Naturwissenschaften und die Mathematik habe ich immer geliebt.

HERBERT: Auf welchen Beruf bereiten Sie sich denn vor?

ILSE: Das weiß ich nocht nicht genau. Vielleicht auf Laborantin oder Drogistin oder so etwas.

ILSE: Yes. I'm in the second semester. Next week my semester exams begin.

HERBERT: Next week? Isn't the semester over yet? It's already July.

ILSE: No. The spring semester doesn't end until the middle of July.

HERBERT: I have another question. My German professor in America told us that there are no periodic examinations in German universities, but only final (comprehensive) examinations. And now you're speaking of semester exams.

ILSE: Your professor had the good old times in mind. Then a student could go to lectures for years without coming up for an examination. Today that's not the same anymore. There are periodic examinations in almost all subjects, especially in the natural sciences.

HERBERT: Do you like studying?

ILSE: Very much. I've always liked the natural sciences and mathematics.

HERBERT: What profession are you preparing for?

ILSE: I don't know exactly yet. Perhaps lab assistant or pharmacist or something like that.

Fragen

Antworten Sie auf deutsch!

1. Wohin gehen Herbert und Ilse?
2. Wohin setzen sie sich?
3. Was bekommt man in einer Konditorei?
4. Warum will Ilse keinen Kuchen essen?
5. Was bestellen Herbert und Ilse?
6. Wo hat Herbert Deutsch gelernt?
7. Wer hat ihm dabei geholfen?
8. Woher stammt Herberts Großvater?
9. Wann endet das Frühjahrssemester in Deutschland?
10. Welche Fächer hat Ilse immer geliebt?

Konversation

Fragen Sie Ihren Nachbar,

1. ob es in Amerika viele Gartenwirtschaften gibt! [Ihr Nachbar muß selbstverständlich jede Frage beantworten.]
2. in welcher Jahreszeit die Amerikaner gerne im Freien essen!
3. was eine Konditorei ist!
4. wann das amerikanische Frühjahrssemester endet!
5. welche Sprachen er sprechen kann!
6. woher seine Eltern stammen!
7. wie viele Semesterprüfungen er ablegen muß!
8. was er davon hält, nur Endprüfungen ablegen zu müssen!

II. NÜTZLICHE AUSDRÜCKE

ein Examen (eine Prüfung) ab-legen	*to take an examination*
ein Examen (eine Prüfung) be-stehen	*to pass an examination*
durch-fallen	*to fail an examination*
am Ende	*finally, at the end*
zu Ende	*over, at an end*
im Freien	*in the open air, outdoors*

Glück haben	*to be lucky*
jemand bei etwas helfen	*to help someone with something*
leicht	*light, easy*
es leicht haben	*to have it easy*
auf der Universität	*at the university*
Er studiert auf der Universität.	*He's a student at the University.*
an der Universität	*at the university*
Er ist Professor an der Universität Heidelberg.	*He's a professor at the University of Heidelberg.*

III. GRAMMATIK

42. Plural of Nouns (continued)

(a) CLASS 4: Nouns adding **-(e)n** to form the plural

NOM. SING.		NOM. PLURAL
der **Löwe**	*lion*	die **Löwen**
der **Mensch**	*human being, man*	die **Menschen**
der **Satellit**	*satellite*	die **Satelliten**
die **Antwort**	*answer*	die **Antworten**
die **Schule**	*school*	die **Schulen**
die **Woche**	*week*	die **Wochen**
die **Frau**	*woman*	die **Frauen**

Nouns in Class 4 include:

1. masculine nouns ending in **-e** and denoting male beings;
2. a few monosyllabic masculine nouns;
3. most masculine nouns of non-Germanic origin with the stress on the last syllable;
4. polysyllabic feminine nouns (except **die Mutter** and **die Tochter**);
5. a few monosyllabic feminine nouns not in Class 2;
6. No neuter nouns.

The umlaut is never added in the plural of Class 4 nouns.

Masculine nouns in Class 4 end in **-(e)n** in all cases except the nominative singular:

	SINGULAR		PLURAL
NOM.	der Student	*student*	die Studen**ten**
GEN.	des Studen**ten**		der Studen**ten**
DAT.	dem Studen**ten**		den Studen**ten**
ACC.	den Studen**ten**		die Studen**ten**

Note:

1. **Herr** (*gentleman, Mr.*) adds **-n** in the singular and **-en** in the plural:

	SINGULAR		PLURAL
NOM.	der **Herr**	*gentleman*	die **Herren**
GEN.	des **Herrn**		der **Herren**
DAT.	dem **Herrn**		den **Herren**
ACC.	den **Herrn**		die **Herren**

2. Feminine nouns ending in **-in** double the **n** before adding **-en** in the plural:

SINGULAR		PLURAL
die **Lehrerin**	*teacher*	die **Lehrerinnen**
die **Studentin**	*student*	die **Studentinnen**

43. Mixed Nouns

Mixed nouns add **-s** in the genitive singular and **-(e)n** to form the plural:

NOM. SING.		GEN. SING.	NOM. PLURAL
der **Nachbar**	*neighbor*	des **Nachbars**	die **Nachbarn**
der **Vetter**	*cousin*	des **Vetters**	die **Vettern**
das **Ende**	*end*	des **Endes**	die **Enden**
das **Auge**	*eye*	des **Auges**	die **Augen**
der **Professor**	*professor*	des **Professors**	die **Professoren**

Mixed nouns include:

1. a few masculine and neuter nouns;
2. masculine nouns of non-Germanic origin ending in **-or.**

44. Nouns with Irregular Forms

(a) The following masculine nouns add **-ns** in the genitive singular and **-n** in all other singular and plural forms:[1]

der **Funke**	*spark*	der **Glaube**	*belief*
der **Friede**	*peace*	der **Name**	*name*
der **Gedanke**	*thought*	der **Wille**	*will*

	SINGULAR	PLURAL
NOM.	der Glaube	die Glaube**n**
GEN.	des Glaube**ns**	der Glaube**n**
DAT.	dem Glaube**n**	den Glaube**n**
ACC.	den Glaube**n**	die Glaube**n**

Note that **das Herz** (*heart*) has a similar pattern of endings:

	SINGULAR		PLURAL
NOM.	das Herz	*heart*	die Herz**en**
GEN.	des Herz**ens**		der Herz**en**
DAT.	dem Herz**en**		den Herz**en**
ACC.	das Herz		die Herz**en**

(b) A group of nouns of non-Germanic origin that have come into the language rather recently add **-s** in the genitive singular and **-s** throughout the plural. Some of the most common are:

das **Auto**	*auto*	das **Kino**	*movie*
der **Bankier**	*banker*	der **Portier**	*doorman*
das **Büro**	*office*	das **Radio**	*radio*
das **Hotel**	*hotel*	das **Restaurant**	*restaurant*

	SINGULAR		PLURAL
NOM.	der Bankier	*banker*	die Bankier**s**
GEN.	des Bankier**s**		der Bankier**s**
DAT.	dem Bankier		den Bankier**s**
ACC.	den Bankier		die Bankier**s**

Note: These nouns do not end in **-n** in the dative plural.

[1] These nouns actually belong to Class 1 but normally drop the final **n** in the nominative singular.

IV. ÜBUNGEN

A. *Verwenden Sie das angegebene Substantiv als Genitivobjekt!*

BEISPIEL: Ich wußte den Namen nicht. (die Frau)
Ich wußte den Namen der Frau nicht.

1. Kennen Sie die Mutter? (die Studentin)
2. Die Bedeutung war mir unklar. (der Name)
3. Das Schaufenster war voller Süßigkeiten. (die Konditorei)
4. Das Hauptfach ist Naturwissenschaft. (der Student)
5. Der Sohn ist Musiker. (der Nachbar)
6. Er vergißt das Ende. (die Geschichte)
7. Die Frau ist eine Prinzessin. (ein Prinz)
8. Der Anfang war ziemlich komisch. (die Tragödie)
9. Die Fenster waren offen. (das Auto)
10. Die Kinder waren alle fleißige Schüler. (die Familie)

B. *Setzen Sie das erste Substantiv und das Verb in den Plural!*

BEISPIEL: Die Frau geht in die Kirche.
Die Frauen gehen in die Kirche.

1. Der Herr hat mit den Kindern gesprochen.
2. Der Bankier war sehr höflich.
3. Die Rose hatte einen herrlichen Duft.
4. Die Erfrischung war sehr willkommen.
5. Die Laborantin war sehr hübsch.
6. Der Student hat laut gelacht.
7. Der Professor war schon im Klassenzimmer.
8. Der Laborant war tüchtig.

C. *Setzen Sie die Substantive (wenn nötig, auch die Verben) in den Singular!*

1. Wo haben Sie die Studentinnen getroffen?
2. Haben Sie seine Ideen interessant gefunden?
3. Kennen Sie die Professoren?
4. Wann sind die Vettern angekommen?
5. Haben die Nachbarn ein großes Haus?
6. Wo sind die Frauen?

7. Finden Sie die Prüfungen schwierig?
8. Die Namen sind mir entgangen.
9. Seine Gedanken sind oberflächlich.
10. Ihre Antworten habe ich nicht verstanden.

D. *Verwenden Sie das angegebene Substantiv als Genitivobjekt!*

BEISPIEL: Dort steht das Haus. (mein Freund)
Dort steht das Haus meines Freundes.

1. Kennen Sie den Autor? (dieses Buch)
2. Ich habe den Inhalt vergessen. (seine Rede)
3. Das Ende ist noch nicht geschrieben. (diese Geschichte)
4. Wo ist das Haus? (Ihr Bruder)
5. Er kann den Titel nennen. (jede Oper)
6. Was ist der Zweck? (diese Versammlung)
7. Ich erinnere mich nicht an den Namen. (ihr Bruder)
8. Die Arbeit muß sehr genau sein. (eine Laborantin)
9. Die Mitglieder sind alle jung. (unsere Verbindung)
10. Das Ziel ist unklar. (sein Studium)

E. *Setzen Sie die Substantive in den Singular!*

1. Seine Söhne sind verheiratet.
2. Unsere Töchter wohnen in Berlin.
3. Diese Filme sind zu entwickeln.
4. Meine Bücher sind zu Hause.
5. Welche Häuser gefallen ihr nicht?
6. Manche Studenten sind arm.
7. Sie wollten diese Männer nicht sehen.
8. Er hat meine Geschenke gerne angenommen.
9. Wo haben Sie Ihre Bücher gelassen?
10. Welche Bilder hat sie mitgebracht?

F. *Setzen Sie die Dativobjekte in den Singular!*

1. Sie sind mit ihren Kindern gekommen.
2. Er hat von seinen Onkeln Geld bekommen.
3. Er versteht nichts von diesen Verbindungen.
4. Wir haben mit unseren Freunden lange geredet.

5. In unseren Schulen kann man alles lernen.
6. Bist du mit deinen Filmen nicht zufrieden?
7. Aus welchen Stadtteilen kommen sie?
8. In diesen Schaufenstern ist viel Schönes zu sehen.
9. In manchen Gartenwirtschaften findet man ein kleines Orchester.
10. Sie gibt ihren Freundinnen immer schöne Geschenke.

G. *Gebrauchen Sie sechs der Nützlichen Ausdrücke in ganzen Sätzen!*

H. *Sagen Sie zuerst und schreiben Sie danach auf deutsch:*

1. Formerly there weren't any periodic examinations at the universities in Germany.
2. The students didn't have to go to lectures if they didn't want to.
3. If the lectures weren't interesting, the students simply didn't attend them.
4. Sometimes these students went to the libraries or studied in their rooms.
5. Many a student went to a tavern, where the fraternities had their special tables.
6. Here they got together with their friends and talked.
7. What they did in the taverns made no difference to the officials at the university.
8. The parents whose sons and daughters were wasting their time instead of studying were not happy about it.
9. Often they did not know what their children were doing.
10. Such students usually failed at the end of their three years at the university.
11. Nowadays students must take semester examinations and final examinations.

Aufsatz

Sie sitzen mit einer Freundin im Garten einer deutschen Konditorei. Es ist ein heißer Sommertag, aber im Schatten der Bäume ist es angenehm kühl. Sie trinken beide Kaffee und beobachten die Leute an den anderen Tischen. Beschreiben Sie Ihre Beobachtungen in einem kurzen Aufsatz! Schreiben Sie, zum Beispiel:

(1) über das Wetter im Sommer;
(2) was man in einer Gartenwirtschaft angenehm findet;
(3) was man in einer Konditorei essen und trinken kann;
(4) zu welcher Tageszeit man gewöhnlich in eine Konditorei geht;
(5) warum man in einer Konditorei gewöhnlich mehr Frauen als Männer sieht;
(6) warum es in Amerika nur wenige Gartenwirtschaften gibt!

Adjectives and Adverbs.

Lektion 9

I. GESPRÄCH: Fernsehen

HERR LENZ: Wollen Sie heute abend noch ausgehen?

HERBERT: Ich hatte es vor. Aber es regnet, und wenn es so weiterregnet, bleibe ich lieber zu Hause.

HERR LENZ: Das ist nur ein kleines Gewitter. In einer Stunde oder so hört es wieder auf. — Nun, wenn Sie hier bleiben, können wir vielleicht etwas Radio hören.

OTTO: Es gibt auch ein paar gute Sendungen im Fernsehen.

HERBERT: Das ist ein guter Gedanke. Wenn Herr Lenz nichts dagegen hat . . .

HERR LENZ: Keineswegs. Ich will nur zuerst die Nachrichten im Rundfunk hören. Nachher könnt ihr den Fernsehapparat anstellen.

Television

MR. LENZ: Do you still want to go out this evening?

HERBERT: I was planning to. But it's raining, and if it keeps on raining like this, I prefer to stay home.

MR. LENZ: This is only a small storm. In an hour or so it will stop. — Well, if you stay here, perhaps we can listen to some radio.

OTTO: There are also some good programs on television.

HERBERT: That's a good idea. If Mr. Lenz doesn't mind . . .

MR. LENZ: Not at all. I only want to listen first to the news on radio. After that you can turn on the TV set.

OTTO: Hier. Ich habe deine Station schon eingestellt. Aber was ist denn los? So einen schlechten Empfang haben wir noch nie gehabt.

HERR LENZ: Das Gewitter! Es kracht wie ein Maschinengewehr. (*Er dreht am Knopf.*) So. Nun ist es etwas besser.

OTTO: (*spricht leise zu Herbert.*) Da ist das Heft mit den Fernsehprogrammen der Woche. Um acht Uhr gibt es ein Kriminalstück und um neun einen bunten Abend.

HERBERT: Ein bunter Abend? Was ist das?

OTTO: Das sind Darbietungen verschiedener Art: Sänger, Tänzer, Komiker und so weiter.

HERBERT: Ah natürlich! — Aber sehen Sie mal! Das Kriminalstück ist ja amerikanisch.

OTTO: Oh, wir haben viele amerikanische Sendungen, besonders Filme aus dem wilden Westen. Die Deutschen lieben solche Sachen, wissen Sie.

HERBERT: Und die Indianer und die Cowboys sprechen alle Deutsch?

OTTO: Freilich. Das kommt Ihnen komisch vor, nicht wahr?

HERBERT: Ein bißchen schon.

HERR LENZ: So. Die Nachrichtensendung ist zu Ende. Ich habe das Radio abgestellt.

OTTO: Here. I've already tuned in your station. But what is the *matter?* We've never had such bad reception.

MR. LENZ: The storm! It's crackling like a machine gun. (*He turns the knob.*) There. Now it's a little better.

OTTO: (*speaks softly to Herbert.*) Here is the booklet with this week's TV programs. At eight o'clock there's a detective story and at nine a variety show.

HERBERT: A variety show? What's that?

OTTO: There are acts of different kinds: singers, dancers, comedians, and so on.

HERBERT: Of course. — But look here. The detective story is American.

OTTO: Oh, we have many American shows, especially movies about the Wild West. Germans love such things, you know.

HERBERT: And the Indians and the cowboys all speak German?

OTTO: That's right. That seems funny to you, doesn't it?

HERBERT: Yes, it does, a little.

MR. LENZ: Well, the news broadcast is over. I've turned the radio off.

OTTO: Es ist ein paar Minuten nach acht. Hoffentlich hat unser Kriminalstück noch nicht begonnen. (*Er dreht den Apparat an.*)

HERBERT: Das Bild flimmert ein wenig. Nun wird es deutlicher. — Aber, das ist ja eine Reklame! Ich dachte, es gäbe keine Reklamen im deutschen Fernsehen.

HERR LENZ: Im Radio gibt es keine. Aber im Fernsehen bekommen wir mehr als genug davon. Die Sendungen beginnen oft mit kleineren Verspätungen.

OTTO: Seid doch bitte still! Das Stück hat angefangen.

OTTO: It's a few minutes past eight. I hope our detective story hasn't begun yet. (*He turns the set on.*)

HERBERT: The picture is flickering a little. Now it's getting clearer. — Why, that's a commercial! I thought there weren't any commercials on German TV.

MR. LENZ: There aren't any on radio. But on TV we get more than enough of them. The programs are often slightly delayed at the beginning.

OTTO: Do be quiet, please. The play has begun.

Fragen

Antworten Sie auf deutsch!

1. Was hatte Herbert an diesem Abend vor?
2. Warum wollte er lieber zu Hause bleiben?
3. Was hat Herr Lenz vorgeschlagen?
4. Was für eine Sendung wollte Herr Lenz am Radio hören?
5. Warum war der Empfang im Rundfunk so schlecht?
6. Was für ein Heft hat Otto in die Hand genommen?
7. Woraus besteht ein bunter Abend?
8. Was für amerikanische Programme haben die Deutschen besonders gern?
9. Wann hat Herr Lenz das Radio abgestellt?
10. Was gibt es im deutschen Radio nicht?

Konversation

Fragen Sie Ihren Nachbar,

1. warum Herbert keine Lust hat auszugehen! [Ihr Nachbar muß selbstverständlich jede Frage beantworten.]
2. ob das amerikanische Fernsehen auch deutsche Filme bringt!
3. ob es im amerikanischen Radio viel Reklame gibt!
4. was für Sendungen er neulich im Fernsehen gesehen hat!
5. ob er gerne Nachrichtensendungen im Fernsehen sieht!
6. ob er oft Radio hört!
7. ob er mehr deutsche Filme im Fernsehen sehen möchte!
8. welche Sendungen er vorzieht, Kriminalstücke oder bunte Abende!

II. NÜTZLICHE AUSDRÜCKE

den Apparat ab-stellen	*to turn off the set*
den Apparat an-stellen	*to turn on the set*
einen Sender (eine Station) ein-stellen	*to tune in a station*
heute abend	*this evening*
keineswegs	*not at all, by no means*
am Knopf drehen	*to adjust a knob*

Was ist los?	*What's going on? What's the matter?*
vor-kommen	*to occur; to appear, seem*
Das kommt selten vor.	*That occurs seldom.*
Das kommt mir komisch vor.	*That seems funny to me.*
weiter- (*plus verb*)	*to keep on (doing something)*
weiter-regnen	*to keep on raining*
und so weiter, usw.	*and so forth, etc.*

III. GRAMMATIK

45. Predicate Adjectives

Marie ist **jung** und **hübsch.**
Mary is young and pretty.
Dieser Kaffee ist **gut.**
This coffee is good.

When used predicatively (that is, after the noun), descriptive adjectives never take endings.

46. Attributive Adjectives

Attributive adjectives (that is, adjectives that normally precede a noun) have certain endings.

(a) Adjectives Without **Der-** or **Ein-**Words

Kaltes Wasser ist erfrischend.
Cold water is refreshing.
Er schreibt mit **roter** Tinte.
He writes with red ink.

An adjective that is not preceded by a **der-** or an **ein-**word takes the endings of **der-**words, except that, in the genitive singular (masculine and neuter), the adjective ending is **-en** instead of **-es:**

		SINGULAR	
NOM.	gut**er** Kaffee	gut**e** Tinte	gut**es** Fleisch
GEN.	gut**en** Kaffees	gut**er** Tinte	gut**en** Fleisches
DAT.	gut**em** Kaffee	gut**er** Tinte	gut**em** Fleisch
ACC.	gut**en** Kaffee	gut**e** Tinte	gut**es** Fleisch

		PLURAL	
NOM.	gut**e** Männer	gut**e** Frauen	gut**e** Kinder
GEN.	gut**er** Männer	gut**er** Frauen	gut**er** Kinder
DAT.	gut**en** Männern	gut**en** Frauen	gut**en** Kindern
ACC.	gut**e** Männer	gut**e** Frauen	gut**e** Kinder

(b) Adjectives After **Der**-Words

Der **junge** Mann ist ihr Bruder.
The young man is her brother.
Ich kann den **jungen** Mann nicht mehr sehen.
I can't see the young man anymore.
Diese **hübsche** Dame ist seine Schwester.
This pretty lady is his sister.
Ich kenne diese **hübsche** Dame nicht.
I don't know this pretty lady.
Jedes **kleine** Kind liebt Süßigkeiten.
Every small child loves sweets.
Sie hat dieses **kleine** Kind nicht gehört.
She didn't hear this small child.
Die **bunten** Abende gefallen mir immer am besten.
I always like the variety shows best.
Der Name dieses **amerikanischen** Programmes ist mir unbekannt.
The name of this American program is unknown to me.
Sie haben lange mit der **jungen** Frau geredet.
They talked a long time with the young woman.

An adjective preceded by a **der**-word ends in **-en** except in the nominative singular (masculine, feminine, and neuter) and in the accusative singular (feminine and neuter), where it ends in **-e:**

		SINGULAR	
NOM.	der jung**e** Mann	die jung**e** Frau	das jung**e** Kind
GEN.	des jung**en** Mannes	der jung**en** Frau	des jung**en** Kindes
DAT.	dem jung**en** Manne	der jung**en** Frau	dem jung**en** Kinde
ACC.	den jung**en** Mann	die jung**e** Frau	das jung**e** Kind

		PLURAL	
NOM.	die jung**en** Männer	die jung**en** Frauen	die jung**en** Kinder
GEN.	der jung**en** Männer	der jung**en** Frauen	der jung**en** Kinder
DAT.	den jung**en** Männern	den jung**en** Frauen	den jung**en** Kindern
ACC.	die jung**en** Männer	die jung**en** Frauen	die jung**en** Kinder

(c) Adjectives After **Ein**-Words

Sie ist die Tochter eines **fremden** Diplomaten.
She's the daughter of a foreign diplomat.
Er ist mit seiner **kleinen** Schwester gekommen.
He came with his little sister.
Herr Klemper ist ein **guter** Freund meines Vaters.
Mr. Klemper is a good friend of my father's.
Herbert wollte eine **gute** Sendung finden.
Herbert wanted to find a good program.
Sie trug ein **schönes** Kleid.
She was wearing a pretty dress.

An adjective preceded by an **ein**-word ends in **-en,** except in the nominative singular masculine (ending **-er**), the nominative and accusative singular feminine (ending **-e**), and the nominative and accusative singular neuter (ending **-es**):[1]

SINGULAR

NOM.	mein gut**er** Freund	eine gut**e** Sendung
GEN.	meines gut**en** Freundes	einer gut**en** Sendung
DAT.	meinem gut**en** Freund	einer gut**en** Sendung
ACC.	meinen gut**en** Freund	eine gut**e** Sendung

NOM.	ein gut**es** Kleid
GEN.	eines gut**en** Kleides
DAT.	einem gut**en** Kleid
ACC.	ein gut**es** Kleid

PLURAL

NOM.	meine gut**en** Freunde	keine gut**en** Sendungen
GEN.	meiner gut**en** Freunde	keiner gut**en** Sendungen
DAT.	meinen gut**en** Freunden	keinen gut**en** Sendungen
ACC.	meine gut**en** Freunde	keine gut**en** Sendungen

NOM.	keine gut**en** Kleider
GEN.	keiner gut**en** Kleider
DAT.	keinen gut**en** Kleidern
ACC.	keine gut**en** Kleider

[1] Note that the *exceptional* adjective endings after **ein**-words correspond to the endings of **der**-words.

(d) Adjectives in a Series

Ein **anderes gutes** Fotogeschäft liegt in der nächsten Straße.
Another good camera shop is on the next street.
Otto hat seinen **jungen amerikanischen** Freund am Flughafen empfangen.
Otto met his young American friend at the airport.

All adjectives in a series have the same ending.

47. Numerical Adjectives

The following common numerical adjectives always have plural meaning:

alle	*all*
andere	*other*
beide	*both*
einige	*several, a few*
mehrere	*several*
viele	*many*
wenige	*few*

(a) Numerical adjectives, except **alle** and **beide,** function like unpreceded adjectives. They have the endings of **der**-words, as do descriptive adjectives following them:[1]

Einige gute Fotogeschäfte sind in der nächsten Straße.
Several good camera shops are on the next street.
Er hat **wenige gute** Freunde.
He has few good friends.

(b) **Alle** and **beide** function like **der**-words and are followed by descriptive adjectives with the ending **-en:**

Er hat **alle roten** Karten weggeworfen.
He threw away all the red cards.
Beide jungen Männer sprechen Deutsch.
Both young men speak German.

---

[1] Note that **andere, beide, viele, wenige** may also follow a **der**-word and function like descriptive adjectives preceded by a **der**-word:

diese anderen bekannten Programme	*these other well-known programs*
die wenigen guten Freunde	*the few good friends*

48. Adverbs

Otto fährt immer **langsam.**
Otto always drives slowly.
Ich höre ihn **gut.**
I hear him well.

Adverbs never have endings in German. Thus, an adverb is identical with its corresponding uninflected adjective.

49. Comparison of Adjectives and Adverbs: Forms

POSITIVE		COMPARATIVE	SUPERLATIVE	
lang	*long*	**länger**	**der längste**	**am längsten**
kurz	*short*	**kürzer**	**der kürzeste**	**am kürzesten**
langsam	*slow*	**langsamer**	**der langsamste**	**am langsamsten**

An adjective has three degrees of comparison: positive, comparative, and superlative. The comparative is formed with the suffix **-er,** the superlative with the suffix **-(e)st.** (Note that the superlative has two forms.) Most monosyllabic adjectives add umlaut in the comparative and superlative.

50. Comparison of Adjectives and Adverbs: Uses

(a) Comparison in the Positive Degree

Marie ist **so alt wie** Gertrud.
Mary is as old as Gertrude.
Sie singt **nicht so schön wie** Gertrud.
She doesn't sing as beautifully as Gertrude.

Comparison in the positive degree (affirmative or negative) is expressed by **so . . . wie** (*as . . . as*).

(b) Comparison in the Comparative Degree

Gertrud ist nicht **älter als** Marie.
Gertrude is not older than Mary.
Sie singt **schöner als** Marie.
She sings more beautifully than Mary.
Sie hat die **schönere** Stimme.
She has the more beautiful voice.

In the comparative degree, **als** is equivalent to English *than*. Note that, in attributive position, comparatives have regular adjective endings (die **schönere** Stimme).

(c) Superlative Degree

1. Der Frühling ist die **schönste** Jahreszeit.
Spring is the most beautiful season.
Er hat die Reise mit seinem **ältesten** Freund gemacht.
He took the trip with his oldest friend.

The superlative of an attributive adjective has regular adjective endings.

2. Die Suppe ist **am besten,** wenn sie heiß ist.
Soup is best when it's hot.
Gertrud singt **am schönsten.**
Gertrude sings the most beautifully.

The superlative of a predicate adjective and of an adverb is expressed by the **am . . . sten** form.

(d) Absolute Comparative

Ein **älterer** Mann stand an der Tür.
An elderly man was standing at the door.
Wir haben einen **längeren** Spaziergang durch die Stadt gemacht.
We took a rather long walk through the city.

The comparative may be used in an absolute sense, with no real comparison being made. It often has the meaning of *rather* or *somewhat*.

(e) Absolute Superlative

Es war eine **höchst interessante** Geschichte.
It was an extremely interesting story.
Er hat **äußerst leise** gesungen.
He sang very, very softly.

Höchst and **äußerst** are used with the positive degree of an adjective or adverb to express an idea in an absolute superlative sense.[1]

---

[1] The absolute superlative also occurs in set phrases, such as **in tiefster Trauer** (*in deepest mourning*); **Liebste Mutter!** (*Dearest Mother!*).

51. Irregular Comparisons

The following common adjectives and the two adverbs **bald** and **gern** have irregular comparative and superlative forms:

POSITIVE		COMPARATIVE	SUPERLATIVE	
groß	*big*	**größer**	**der größte**	**am größten**
gut	*good*	**besser**	**der beste**	**am besten**
hoch	*high*	**höher**	**der höchste**	**am höchsten**
nah	*near*	**näher**	**der nächste**	**am nächsten**
viel	*much*	**mehr**	**der meiste**	**am meisten**
bald	*soon*	**eher**		**am ehesten**
gern	*gladly*	**lieber**		**am liebsten**

Note the English equivalents for the forms of **gern:**

Ich trinke Milch **gern.** *I like to drink milk.*
Ich trinke Tee **lieber.** *I prefer to drink tea.*
Ich trinke Kaffee **am liebsten.** *I like most of all to drink coffee.*

52. Noun-Adjectives

Bekannte haben es mir gesagt.
Acquaintances told it to me.
Er ist **ein Bekannter** von mir.
He is an acquaintance of mine.
Das ist **die Deutsche,** von der ich gesprochen habe.
That's the German woman about whom I spoke.
Das Neue ist nicht immer besser als **das Alte.**
The new is not always better than the old.

Adjectives used as nouns have regular adjective endings, depending upon whether they are unpreceded or preceded by a **der-** or an **ein**-word. Such nouns are capitalized.

In the masculine singular, a noun-adjective refers to a male being; in the feminine singular, to a female being; in the neuter singular, to an abstraction.

53. Etwas, nichts, viel, wenig, alles

Er hat **etwas Gutes** gefunden.
He found something good.
Er hat **viel Schönes** gesagt.
He said many nice things.

Alles Neue ist nicht immer gut.
Everything that's new is not always good.

A neuter singular noun-adjective (capitalized) ending in **-es** follows **etwas** (*something*), **nichts** (*nothing*), **viel** (*much*), and **wenig** (*little, not much*).

A neuter singular noun-adjective ending in **-e** follows **alles** (*everything*).

IV. ÜBUNGEN

A. *Setzen Sie das Adjektiv in der korrekten Form vor das Substantiv!*

BEISPIEL: Ein Kind lief über die Straße. (klein)
Ein kleines Kind lief über die Straße.

1. Nachrichten sind immer willkommen. (gut)
2. Ein Mann wollte es ihr verkaufen. (fremd)
3. Er hat nichts als Wasser getrunken. (kalt)
4. Sein Vater hat ihn getadelt. (eigen)
5. Ein Gewitter kommt im Sommer oft vor. (klein)
6. Er ist mit Verspätung angekommen. (groß)
7. Unser Radio geht nicht. (neu)
8. Später sehen wir ein Kriminalstück. (amerikanisch)
9. Dies ist mein Wort. (letzt)
10. Männer hören nicht immer gut. (alt)

B. *Setzen Sie das Adjektiv in der korrekten Form vor das Substantiv!*

1. Ich habe seinen Freund nie gesehen. (amerikanisch)
2. Dieses Gewitter kann nichts schaden. (klein)
3. Alle Bücher sind ausverkauft. (deutsch)
4. Ich kann diesen Radioapparat nicht leiden. (neu)
5. Haben Sie das im Radio gehört? (deutsch)
6. Mancher Student sagt das Gleiche. (jung)
7. Wir haben keine Kartoffeln gefunden. (gut)
8. Ihre Kleider sehen altmodisch aus. (neu)
9. Die Reklamen langweilen mich. (viel)
10. Meine Schwestern sind musikalisch. (beide)

C. *Setzen Sie das Adjektiv in der korrekten Form vor das erste Substantiv!*

1. Kinder gehen früh zu Bett. (klein)
2. Er spielt gerne mit den Kindern. (klein)
3. Der Onkel hatte drei Fernsehapparate. (reich)
4. Er hat mit Tinte geschrieben. (rot)
5. Wir wollen ein Programm im Radio hören. (amerikanisch)
6. Wenige Leute glauben das. (vernünftig)
7. Mein Freund besucht mich nächstes Jahr. (deutsch)
8. Er kommt mit einem Freund nach Amerika. (holländisch)
9. Die Leute waren im Garten. (jung)
10. Das Radio ist kaputt. (alt)
11. Im Fernsehen gibt es oft Reklamen. (deutsch)
12. Das Radio bringt keine Reklamen. (deutsch)
13. Ein Fernsehapparat kostet ziemlich viel. (gut)
14. Er verkauft nur Zeitschriften. (amerikanisch)
15. Dieser Fernsehapparat ist billig. (neu)

D. *Beantworten Sie die folgenden Fragen mit „ja" und gebrauchen Sie dabei das angegebene Adjektiv!*

BEISPIEL: Stehen hohe Bäume im Park? (einige)
Ja, einige hohe Bäume stehen im Park.

1. Gibt es ausländische Studenten in Heidelberg? (viele)
2. Liest er deutsche Zeitschriften gerne? (alle)
3. Haben Sie alte Freunde getroffen? (einige)
4. Hat er Ihnen noch deutsche Zeitschriften gezeigt? (andere)
5. Haben Sie bunte Abende im Fernsehen gesehen? (mehrere)
6. Kommen kleine Verspätungen vor? (viele)
7. Kennen Sie die jungen Herren? (beide)
8. Hat er schöne Gemälde in seinem Hause? (einige)

E. *Beantworten Sie die folgenden Fragen mit „nein" und gebrauchen Sie dabei den Komparativ!*

BEISPIEL: Ist Ihr Bruder so alt wie Robert?
Nein, Robert ist älter als mein Bruder.

1. Ist ein Radioapparat so groß wie ein Fernsehapparat?
2. Gibt es im Fernsehen so viele Reklamen wie im Radio?

3. Ist die zweite Sendung so interessant wie die erste?
4. Sprechen Sie Deutsch so gern wie Englisch?
5. Finden Sie das alte Buch so schwierig wie das neue?
6. Schreibt dieser Dichter so gut wie der andere?
7. Finden Sie Ihren Deutschlehrer so streng wie Ihren Englischlehrer?
8. Ist Ihr Vater so reich wie Ihr Onkel?
9. Ist ein Volkswagen so teuer wie ein Mercedes-Benz?
10. Ist dieser Berg so hoch wie das Matterhorn?

F. *Ergänzen Sie die folgenden Sätze mit einem Superlativ!*

BEISPIELE: Wir alle haben schöne Häuser, aber er hat . . .
Wir alle haben schöne Häuser, aber er hat das schönste.

Der Baß singt besser als der Tenor, aber der Bariton singt . . .
Der Baß singt besser als der Tenor, aber der Bariton singt am besten.

1. In den Kleinstädten ist das Leben billiger als in Berlin, aber auf dem Lande ist das Leben . . .
2. Alfred singt besser als ich, aber Josef singt . . .
3. Ich habe gute Beziehungen, aber Werner hat . . .
4. Von meinen jüngeren Schwestern ist Eva . . .
5. Ich esse lieber Kuchen als Käse, aber Früchte esse ich . . .
6. Von allen berühmten Gemälden in diesem Museum ist die Mona Lisa . . .
7. Im November ist das Wetter kälter als im September, aber im Januar ist es . . .
8. Mit einem großen Dampfer fährt man schneller als mit einem kleinen Dampfer, aber mit dem Flugzeug fährt man . . .
9. Von allen hohen Gebirgen ist das Himalayagebirge . . .
10. Mein Onkel ist immer lustig, aber in Gesellschaft ist er . . .

G. *Ändern Sie die Sätze dem Beispiel entsprechend!*

BEISPIEL: Er hat nichts gelernt, was gut ist.
Er hat nichts Gutes gelernt.

1. Er wünschte uns alles, was gut ist.

2. Warum sagte er nie etwas, was neu ist?
3. In diesem Buche gibt es nichts, was interessant ist.
4. Er hat auf seiner Reise viel gesehen, was schön ist.
5. Sie hatte über die Sendung wenig zu sagen, was gut ist.
6. Ich weiß nichts über ihn, was schlecht ist.
7. Er hat mir in seinen Briefen alles mitgeteilt, was wichtig ist.
8. Er spricht immer gerne über etwas, was ungewöhnlich ist.

H. *Gebrauchen Sie sechs der Nützlichen Ausdrücke in ganzen Sätzen!*

I. *Sagen Sie zuerst und schreiben Sie danach auf deutsch!*

1. Before Otto und Herbert could watch TV, they had to listen to a short news broadcast on the radio.
2. A big thunderstorm caused very poor reception.
3. They looked for something good on TV but found only long commercials that were more boring than the American ones.
4. That seemed funny to Herbert.
5. What they finally found was a new detective story.
6. A wicked German and a more wicked Frenchwoman were going to rob an old Italian.
7. But the police were cleverer than the criminals, and the old man was the cleverest of all.
8. He had sold everything valuable or given it to his young nephews.
9. His money was in a very safe bank.
10. The police arrested the wicked couple at the end of this extremely exciting show.

Aufsatz

Sie sitzen nach dem Abendessen mit Ihrem Freund im Wohnzimmer. Da es draußen regnet, beschließen Sie, den Abend zu Hause am Radio und am Fernsehen zu verbringen. Schreiben Sie das Gespräch, das Sie mit Ihrem Freund führen, nieder! Schreiben Sie zum Beispiel:

(1) warum Sie beide nicht ausgehen;
(2) welche Sendungen im Radio Ihnen und Ihrem Freund am besten gefallen;
(3) warum man an gewissen Tagen schlechten Empfang hat;
(4) welche Sendungen im Fernsehen Ihnen am besten gefallen;
(5) warum Sie, wenn es möglich ist, doch lieber ins Kino gehen!

Pronouns: Personal, Demonstrative, Possessive, Interrogative.

Lektion 10

I. GESPRÄCH: Ausflug mit dem Fahrrad

OTTO: Ist es nicht herrlich, so in die frische Luft zu fahren?

HERBERT: Leider fühle ich mich noch etwas unsicher auf diesem Fahrrad.

OTTO: Das kann ich begreifen. Es ist das alte Rad meines Vaters. Wollen Sie tauschen? Sie können meines haben, und ich nehme Ihres.

HERBERT: So habe ich es nicht gemeint. Ich wollte sagen, daß ich schon seit Jahren nicht mehr radgefahren bin. In Amerika tut man so etwas nur als Junge, bevor man Auto fahren lernt.

OTTO: Hier fahren auch die meisten Leute lieber Auto. Aber ab und zu ist so ein Ausflug mit dem Rad sehr erfrischend, nicht wahr?

Bicycle Excursion

OTTO: Isn't it wonderful to ride like this in the fresh air?

HERBERT: Unfortunately I still feel a little insecure on this bicycle.

OTTO: I can understand that. It's my father's old bike. You want to switch? You may have mine and I'll take yours.

HERBERT: I didn't mean it that way. I meant that I haven't ridden a bicycle for years. In America we do that only as boys, before we learn to drive a car.

OTTO: Here, too, most people prefer to go by car. But every once in a while a bicycle outing like this is very refreshing, don't you think?

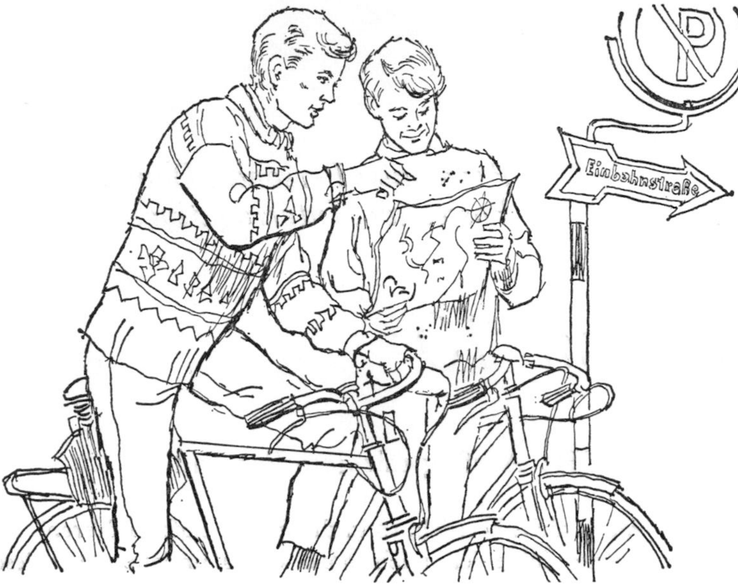

HERBERT: Ich finde diese Straße ganz ideal. Seit wir aus der Stadt heraus sind, sind wir kaum einem Wagen begegnet. Und das Land ist ganz eben.

OTTO: Verkehr gibt es hier kaum, denn dies ist keine Hauptstraße. Aber so mühelos geht es nicht lange weiter. Warten Sie nur, bis wir an die Hügel kommen. Dort müssen Sie kräftig in die Pedale treten.

HERBERT: Wo fahren wir eigentlich hin?

OTTO: Nach Bad Homburg. Das sind vielleicht zwanzig Kilometer, ich weiß es nicht genau. Wenn wir gemütlich fahren, so wie jetzt, dauert es etwa zwei Stunden.

HERBERT: Was geschieht, wenn wir eine Panne haben? Geht man dann zu Fuß weiter?

HERBERT: I think this road is just ideal. Since we've been out of the city, we've scarcely met a car. And the country is quite level.

OTTO: There's hardly any traffic here, because this isn't a main road. But it won't go on so easily for long. Just wait until we come to the hills. There you have to pedal hard.

HERBERT: Just where are we going?

OTTO: To Bad Homburg. That's about twenty kilometers. I don't know exactly. If we ride along at a leisurely pace, as we are doing now, it will take about two hours.

HERBERT: What happens if we have a breakdown? Will we continue on foot?

OTTO: Damit rechne ich natürlich nicht. Was für eine Panne meinen Sie denn?

HERBERT: Irgend etwas. Es fällt mir eben ein, daß man beim Autofahren immer mit einem Reserverad versehen ist. Beim Radfahren dagegen hat man keines.

OTTO: Dafür weiß jeder gute Radfahrer, wie man einen Reifen flickt. Schauen Sie hinter sich! Dort über Ihrem Hinterrad hängt eine schwarze Ledertasche.

HERBERT: Da ist wohl alles nötige Flickzeug drin? Gut.

OTTO: Ein Reifen läßt sich in zehn bis fünfzehn Minuten flicken.

HERBERT: Aber was tut man, wenn man keine Pumpe hat?

OTTO: Eine Pumpe hat man immer bei sich.

HERBERT: Es tut mir leid, aber ich sehe weder an Ihrem noch an meinem Fahrrad eine.

OTTO: Oh! Daran habe ich vor der Abfahrt gar nicht gedacht. — Na, wenn wir wirklich Pech haben, finden wir schon jemand, der uns hilft.

HERBERT: Gewiß. Ich habe keine Angst. Dagegen habe ich etwas Durst.

OTTO: Ich auch. Da vorne steht ein Wirtshaus. Steigen wir ab und nehmen wir eine Erfrischung!

OTTO: I don't expect that, of course. What kind of a breakdown do you mean?

HERBERT: Any kind. It just occurs to me that when you're going by car you always have a spare tire. By bicycle, on the other hand, you don't have any.

OTTO: In that case, every good cyclist knows how to repair a tire. Look behind you. There's a black leather bag over your rear wheel.

HERBERT: I suppose all necessary repair equipment is in there? Good.

OTTO: A tire can be repaired in ten to fifteen minutes.

HERBERT: But what do you do if you don't have a pump?

OTTO: You always have a pump with you.

HERBERT: I'm sorry, but I don't see one either on your bike or on mine.

OTTO: Oh! I didn't think about that at all before leaving. Well, if we really do have trouble, we'll find somebody who'll help us.

HERBERT: Certainly. I'm not worried. But I am a little thirsty.

OTTO: So am I. Up ahead there's an inn. Let's get off and get some refreshment.

Fragen

Antworten Sie auf deutsch!

1. Wem gehört das Fahrrad, auf dem Herbert fährt?
2. Warum fühlt sich Herbert ein bißchen unsicher auf dem Fahrrad?
3. Wie findet Herbert die Straße von Frankfurt nach Bad Homburg?
4. Warum ist nicht viel Verkehr auf dieser Straße?
5. Wie lange braucht man mit dem Fahrrad von Frankfurt nach Bad Homburg?
6. Was fällt Herbert während der Fahrt ein?
7. Was hat jeder gute Radfahrer immer bei sich, wenn er einen Ausflug macht?
8. Wie lange braucht man gewöhnlich, um einen Reifen zu flicken?
9. Was haben Otto und Herbert vergessen mitzunehmen?
10. Warum steigen Otto und Herbert ab?

Konversation

Fragen Sie Ihren Nachbar,

1. ob er radfahren kann! [Ihr Nachbar muß selbstverständlich jede Frage beantworten!]
2. warum Amerikaner so wenig radfahren!
3. warum die meisten amerikanischen Straßen für das Radfahren nicht sehr geeignet sind!
4. ob er mit dem Rad lieber bergab oder bergauf fährt!
5. wie viele Pannen er schon gehabt hat!
6. ob man in einem Auto gewöhnlich Flickzeug für Reifenpannen findet!
7. was man in einem Auto fast immer als Reserve findet!
8. was er am liebsten trinkt, wenn er Durst hat!

II. NÜTZLICHE AUSDRÜCKE

ab und zu	*now and then*
Angst haben	*to be afraid*
mit jemand aus-kommen	*to get along with somebody*
da vorne	*ahead, in front*

zu Fuß gehen	*to go on foot*
leiden	*to suffer*
jemand gut leiden können	*to like somebody*
Pech haben	*to have bad luck*
rechnen mit	*to count on, expect*
mit etwas versehen sein	*to be supplied with something; to have something*
einen Reifen wechseln	*to change a tire*
weder . . . noch	*neither . . . nor*

III. GRAMMATIK

54. Personal Pronouns

(a) Forms

SINGULAR

	I	*you*		*he*	*she*	*it*
NOM.	**ich**	**du**	**Sie**	**er**	**sie**	**es**
GEN.	**(meiner)**[1]	**(deiner)**[1]	**(Ihrer)**[1]	**(seiner)**[1]	**(ihrer)**[1]	**(seiner)**[1]
DAT.	**mir**	**dir**	**Ihnen**	**ihm**	**ihr**	**ihm**
ACC.	**mich**	**dich**	**Sie**	**ihn**	**sie**	**es**

PLURAL

NOM.	**wir**	**ihr**	**Sie**	**sie**
GEN.	**(unser)**[1]	**(euer)**[1]	**(Ihrer)**[1]	**(ihrer)**[1]
DAT.	**uns**	**euch**	**Ihnen**	**ihnen**
ACC.	**uns**	**euch**	**Sie**	**sie**

(b) Agreement of Personal Pronoun with Noun

Ist **der Reifen** kaputt? — Nein, **er** ist in gutem Zustand.
Is the tire ruined? — No, it's in good shape.

---

[1] Genitive forms, which are rare, occur as the objects of a few verbs and adjectives:

Erbarme dich **meiner!** *Have mercy on me!*
Sie war **seiner** nicht sicher. *She wasn't sure of him.*

Genitive forms are combined with the preposition **wegen;** final **r** changes to **t** except in **unser** and **euer,** which *add* **t: meinetwegen, unsertwegen** usw. *as far as I'm concerned, as far as we're concerned, etc.*

Ist **die Luft** kühl? — Ja, **sie** ist kühl.
Is the air cool? — Yes, it's cool.
Wo ist **Ihr Fahrrad?** — **Es** ist in der Garage.
Where's your bike? — It's in the garage.
Wo ist **das Mädchen?** — **Es** ist schon fortgegangen.
Where's the girl? — She has already left.

A personal pronoun agrees in gender and number with the noun for which it stands. Thus the English equivalent of **er** may be *he* or *it*, of **sie** *she* or *it*, and of **es** *he*, *she*, or *it*.

(c) **Da**-Compounds

Hatte er an diese Möglichkeit gedacht? — Nein, **daran** hatte **er** nicht gedacht.
Had he thought of this possibility? — No, he hadn't thought of it.
Hat er von seinem Ausflug gesprochen? — Ja, er hat **davon** gesprochen.
Did he talk about his outing? — Yes, he talked about it.

When used with a preposition, a personal pronoun referring to an object is normally replaced by **da-,** which is joined to the preposition (**dabei, damit, dazu**). **Dar-** is used if the preposition begins with a vowel (**daran, darüber**). Compare:

Er hat **an ihn** gedacht.	but	Er hat **daran** gedacht.
He thought of him.		*He thought of it.*

55. Selbst (selber)

Er hat es **selbst** (**selber**) getan.
Er **selbst** (**selber**) hat es getan.
He did it himself.
Die Leute sind **selbst** (**selber**) daran schuld.
It's the people's own fault.

The emphatic pronoun **selbst** (**selber**) is invariable. Note that when **selbst** precedes a noun or pronoun it means *even:*

Selbst der König hat ihn gelobt.
Even the king praised him.
Selbst ohne Hilfe vermochte er, das schwere Problem zu lösen.
Even without help he managed to solve the difficult problem.

56. Demonstrative Pronouns

(a) **Der**-Words

Mancher glaubt das nicht.
Many a person doesn't believe that.
Dieser Wagen gehört mir, **jener** gehört meinem Vater.
This car belongs to me, that one belongs to my father.
Gefallen Ihnen beide Bücher? — Nein, **dieses** gefällt mir besser als **jenes.**
Do you like both books? — No, I like this one better than that one.

Der-words may be used as demonstrative pronouns. In colloquial German, **jener** is often replaced by a form of **dieser da, der da, der dort, dieser dort:**

Der da gehört meinem Vater.
Dieses gefällt mir besser als **das da.**

(b) **Der, die, das** as Demonstrative Pronouns

Ist Gertrud hier? — Nein, **die** ist schon fortgegangen.
Is Gertrude here? — No, she has already left.
Wo sind die Jungen? — **Die** machen heute einen Ausflug.
Where are the boys? — They're having an outing today.
Was halten Sie von Herrn Schwarz? — Mit **dem** komme ich nicht aus.
What do you think of Mr. Schwarz? — I don't get along with him.

Forms of **der, die, das** may be used as demonstrative pronouns or as stressed personal pronouns. These forms are identical with those of the relative pronoun (See Lektion 6, paragraph 28).

(c) **Das, dies** as Subject

Wer ist die blonde Dame dort? — **Das** ist meine Schwester.
Who's the blond lady over there? — That's my sister.
Das (**dies**) sind meine Ansichten darüber.
Those (these) are my opinions about that.

Das or **dies,** both invariable in this usage, may function as subject of the verb **sein** followed by a noun. The verb agrees with the predicate. The English equivalent may be *this, that, these, those.*

57. Ein-Words as Pronouns; Possessive Pronouns

Hier steht mein Fahrrad, und dort steht **Ihres.**
Here's my bicycle and there's yours.
Da liegt Ihr Reifen. Wo ist **meiner?**
There's your tire. Where's mine?
Haben Sie Ihr Flickzeug bei sich? Ich habe **keines.**
Do you have your repair equipment with you? I don't have any.

Ein-words (possessive adjectives, **ein,** and **kein**) used as pronouns have **der**-word endings in all cases.

58. Interrogative Pronouns

(a) Wer, was

	MASCULINE AND FEMININE	NEUTER
NOM.	**wer**	**was**
GEN.	**wessen**	—
DAT.	**wem**	—
ACC.	**wen**	**was**

Wer hat Ihnen das gesagt?
Who told you that?
Wessen Fahrrad haben Sie?
Whose bicycle do you have?
Wem sind Sie begegnet?
Whom did you meet?
Was ist der Zweck dieser Übung?
What's the purpose of this exercise?
Wer sind diese beiden Herren?
Who are these two gentlemen?

(b) **Wo**-Compounds

Woran hat Otto nicht gedacht?
What did Otto not think of?
Worüber hat er geredet?
What did he talk about?

When used with a preposition, **was** is normally replaced by **wo-,** which is joined to the preposition (**womit, wozu**). **Wor-** is used if the preposition begins with a vowel (**woraus, worin, worüber**). (See Lektion 6, paragraph 29b, footnote, for **wo**-compounds in relative clauses.)

IV. ÜBUNGEN

A. *Ersetzen Sie die Substantive durch Personalpronomen!*

BEISPIEL: Ich schreibe meinen Eltern.
Ich schreibe ihnen.

1. Es gehörte meinem Onkel.
2. Hat mein Vater das gesagt?
3. Ich habe den Verkehr nie so stark gesehen.
4. Die Hauptstraße war fast leer.
5. Ich werde mit Anna kommen.
6. Ich finde die Straße ganz ideal.
7. Das Kind heißt Gerda.
8. Ich habe dem Mädchen gedankt.
9. Hast du das Flickzeug vergessen?
10. Die Erfrischungen waren nicht besonders teuer.
11. Was hast du bei deinen Freunden getan?
12. Ich habe die Mädchen gar nicht bemerkt.
13. Was hast du für deinen Vater gekauft?
14. Er spricht selten von seiner Freundin.
15. Ich warte auf meine Frau.

B. *Beantworten Sie die folgenden Fragen mit „ja“ und gebrauchen Sie dabei Personalpronomen anstelle der Substantive!*

BEISPIEL: Haben Sie die Zeitung gelesen?
Ja, ich habe sie gelesen.

1. Hat er seine Freundin eingeladen?
2. Ist er mit seiner Freundin ausgegangen?
3. Wollte er den neuen Film sehen?
4. War der Film sehr lang?
5. Hat sie den Film interessant gefunden?
6. Kennen Sie meinen Bruder?
7. Kennen Sie auch seine Frau?
8. Sie kommen oft mit meinem Bruder zusammen, nicht wahr?
9. Haben Sie seine Kinder schon gesehen?
10. Seine Wohnung ist sehr hübsch, nicht wahr?

C. *Ersetzen Sie das Präpositionalobjekt durch eine Zusammensetzung mit* **da-!**

BEISPIEL: Er hat über sein Pech gelacht.
Er hat darüber gelacht.

1. Ich habe viele Freude an dem Ausflug gehabt.
2. Er hat viel Pech mit diesem Schlauch gehabt.
3. Wir mußten nach dem Gewitter schnell weiterfahren.
4. Er hat mich um das Flickzeug gebeten.
5. Viele Fahrräder standen vor dem Brunnen.
6. Ich rechnete nicht mit einer Panne.
7. Was wissen Sie von der Geschichte?
8. Er hat lange über die Geschichte gelacht.
9. Eine Ledertasche hängt hinter dem Sitz.
10. Wir saßen auf einer niedrigen Bank.
11. Ich bin gegen diesen Vorschlag.
12. Wer ist für diesen Vorschlag?
13. Eine Panne gehört zu einem Ausflug.
14. Sie macht oft Fehler bei ihrer Arbeit.
15. Er ist durch diese Tat sehr berühmt geworden.

D. *Ersetzen Sie das erste Personalpronomen durch ein Demonstrativpronomen!*

BEISPIEL: Ihn sieht man selten hier.
Den sieht man selten hier.

1. Er ist nicht mein Freund.
2. Sie kenne ich nicht.
3. Mit ihr kann man nichts machen.
4. Ihn kann ich gut leiden.
5. Von ihm habe ich nichts gehört.
6. Bei ihr ißt man gut.
7. Sie weiß immer etwas Amüsantes zu erzählen.
8. Mit ihnen muß man sehr langsam fahren.
9. Sie waren sicher nicht dabei.
10. Ihn wollte ich besonders gerne singen hören.

E. *Ersetzen Sie das Substantiv im zweiten Satz durch ein* **Ein-***Wort:*

BEISPIEL: Er besitzt ein Auto. Ich habe kein Auto.
Er besitzt ein Auto. Ich habe keines.

1. Ihr Fahrrad gefällt mir. Wie gefällt Ihnen mein Fahrrad?
2. Ich sehe meine Pumpe. Ihre Pumpe sehe ich nicht.
3. Unser Ausflug war schön. Wie war Ihr Ausflug?
4. Ich habe meinen Reifen geflickt. Haben Sie Ihren Reifen auch geflickt?
5. Hier ist ein Hotel. Da drüben ist auch ein Hotel.
6. Ich finde mein Zimmer sehr hübsch. Wie finden Sie Ihr Zimmer?
7. Meine Landkarte habe ich verloren. Haben Sie Ihre Landkarte?
8. Meine Eltern sind sehr streng. Sind Ihre Eltern auch so streng?
9. Wir sangen zuerst ein Lied. Dann sangen wir noch ein Lied.
10. Hat er mit Ihrer Schwester gesprochen? Oder hat er mit meiner Schwester gesprochen?

F. *Bilden Sie Fragen dem Beispiel entsprechend!*

BEISPIEL: Mein Bruder hat es gesagt. (Who)
Wer hat es gesagt?

1. Dieser Mann ist mein Bruder. (Who)
2. Ich habe es Ihnen erklärt. (To whom)
3. Mein Buch liegt hier. (Whose)
4. Er hat mit meiner Schwester getanzt. (With whom)
5. Hans und Fritz sind die besten Studenten. (Who)
6. Wir haben einen schwarzen Pudel gefunden. (What)
7. Er hat meine Schwester getroffen. (Whom)
8. Meine Eltern sind eben angekommen. (Whose)
9. Er hat es für mich getan. (For whom)
10. Der Schlauch liegt auf dem Boden. (What)

G. *Fragen Sie nach dem Präpositionalobjekt, indem Sie eine Zusammensetzung mit* **wo-** *gebrauchen!*

BEISPIEL: Das Programm besteht aus mehreren kleinen Darbietungen.
Woraus besteht das Programm?

1. Sie schreibt mit einem Kugelschreiber.

2. Er hat auf dem Tisch gestanden.
3. Die Rede war von Freiheit und Treue.
4. Ich warte auf den Zug.
5. Er lebt vom Geld seiner Mutter.
6. Wir lernen aus unseren Büchern.
7. Er legte das Buch auf den Schreibtisch.
8. Er hat über den zweiten Weltkrieg geschrieben.
9. Wir sind mit der Eisenbahn gekommen.
10. Er hat es aus Holz gemacht.

H. *Gebrauchen Sie sechs der Nützlichen Ausdrücke in ganzen Sätzen!*

I. *Sagen Sie zuerst und schreiben Sie danach auf deutsch!*

1. Herbert, shall we go on a bicycle trip to the mountains?
2. I have two friends who want to go with us. They're very nice.
3. About whom are you talking? Are those the boys I met yesterday afternoon?
4. Unfortunately we have only three bicycles. We need one for you.
5. I'll use my father's bike, and you can use mine.
6. What will I fix this tire with? I see no repair materials.
7. Whose pump can I borrow? I must blow up this tire with it.
8. What are those things in the box behind the seat?
9. Oh. Those are the refreshments. Mother prepared them for us.
10. We'll make good use of them.

Aufsatz

Sie schreiben einen Brief nach Hause und erzählen darin von einem Ausflug, den Sie mit Ihrem Freund gemacht haben. Schreiben Sie zum Beispiel:

(1) über das Ausflugsziel, die Länge und die Dauer der Fahrt;
(2) über das Wetter, das Sie hatten;
(3) über die Vorteile, auf einer Nebenstraße zu fahren;
(4) weshalb und wie oft Sie angehalten haben;
(5) weshalb Ihr Freund der bessere Fahrer war;
(6) wie Sie sich bei Ihrer Rückkehr fühlten!

Indefinite Pronouns;
Numerals;
Expressions of Time.

Lektion 11

I. GESPRÄCH: Im Theater

HERBERT: Wie ist es bei den Prüfungen gegangen? Darf ich Ihnen gratulieren?

ILSE: Danke schön. Ich glaube, ich bin durchgekommen. Alles ist wie am Schnürchen gegangen.

HERBERT: Was haben Sie nun vor?

ILSE: Vorerst will ich mich ein wenig entspannen. Heute abend zum Beispiel möchte ich ins Theater.

HERBERT: Was wird gespielt?

ILSE: „Romulus der Große". Das ist ein Stück von Friedrich Dürrenmatt.

In the Theater

HERBERT: How did the exams go? May I congratulate you?

ILSE: Thank you. I think I passed. Everything went just like clockwork.

HERBERT: What do you plan to do now?

ILSE: For the time being I want to relax a little. This evening, for example, I'd like to go to the theater.

HERBERT: What's being given?

ILSE: *Romulus.* That's a play by Friedrich Dürrenmatt.

HERBERT: Das möchte ich auch gerne sehen. Ich habe schon lange mal in ein deutsches Theater gewollt. Darf ich Ihnen Gesellschaft leisten?

ILSE: Wenn Sie wollen. Ich bin eben auf dem Wege zur Theaterkasse. Hoffentlich müssen wir nicht zu lange Schlange stehen.

HERBERT: Um wieviel Uhr fängt die Vorstellung an?

ILSE: Der Vorhang geht um acht Uhr auf.

(*An der Theaterkasse.*)

ILSE: Wir haben es gut getroffen. Wir sind gleich an der Reihe.

HERBERT: Lassen Sie mich die Karten besorgen! (*Zum Fräulein an der Kasse.*) Haben Sie noch ein paar Plätze im Parkett für heute abend?

FRÄULEIN: Das ganze Parkett ist leider ausverkauft. Wir haben nur noch Balkonplätze, dritte Reihe links oder vierte Reihe rechts.

ILSE: Nehmen Sie links! Die sind gar nicht schlecht.

FRÄULEIN: Platz 112 und Platz 113. Vierundzwanzig Mark, bitte.

HERBERT: Können Sie mir auch zwei Programme geben?

FRÄULEIN: Die bekommen Sie von der Platzanweiserin im Theater.

HERBERT: I'd like to see that, too. I've wanted to go to a German theater for a long time. May I accompany you?

ILSE: If you want to. I'm just now on my way to the box office. I hope we don't have to stand in line too long.

HERBERT: What time does the performance begin?

ILSE: The curtain goes up at eight o'clock.

(*At the box office.*)

ILSE: We hit it right. It'll be our turn right away.

HERBERT: Let me get the tickets. (*To the girl at the box office.*) Do you still have a couple of orchestra seats for tonight?

CLERK: Unfortunately, the whole orchestra is sold out. We have only balcony seats, third row left or fourth row right.

ILSE: Take the left. They're not bad at all.

CLERK: Seat 112 and seat 113. Twenty-four marks, please.

HERBERT: Can you also give me two programs?

CLERK: You'll get them from the usher in the theater.

HERBERT: Danke.

ILSE: Sehen Sie, da drüben hängt ein Plakat mit den Namen der Darsteller! Wie ich gehört habe, sind alle sehr gut.

HERBERT: Ich kenne niemand außer dem Autor. Das ist doch der, der das Drama „Der Besuch der alten Dame“ geschrieben hat, nicht wahr?

ILSE: Ja, Dürrenmatt ist zweifellos einer der besten modernen Dramatiker. Die Komödie „Romulus der Große“ soll auch ein großer Erfolg sein.

HERBERT: Thank you.

ILSE: Look, over there is a poster with the names of the actors. From what I've heard, they're all very good.

HERBERT: I don't know anybody except the author. He's the one who wrote the play *The Visit*, isn't he?

ILSE: Yes. Dürrenmatt is undoubtedly one of the best modern dramatists. The comedy *Romulus* is supposed to be a great success, too.

Fragen

Antworten Sie auf deutsch!

1. Wie ist es Ilse bei den Prüfungen gegangen?
2. Was hat sie jetzt vor?
3. Von wem ist das Theaterstück „Romulus der Große"?
4. Was hat Herbert schon lange gewollt?
5. Wo besorgt man Plätze fürs Theater?
6. Wie lange mußten Herbert und Ilse an der Theaterkasse warten?
7. Wo mußte Herbert seine zwei Plätze nehmen?
8. Von wem kann man Programme bekommen?
9. Um wieviel Uhr fängt die Vorstellung an?
10. Worauf stehen die Namen der Darsteller?
11. Wer ist Dürrenmatt?

Konversation

Fragen Sie Ihren Nachbar,

1. was er für die Sommerferien vorhat! [Ihr Nachbar muß selbstverständlich jede Frage beantworten.]
2. ob er lieber ins Theater oder ins Kino geht!
3. was er lieber sieht, eine Komödie oder eine Tragödie!
4. wann er das letzte Mal ins Theater gegangen ist!
5. um wieviel Uhr der Vorhang im amerikanischen Theater meistens aufgeht!
6. ob er lieber im Parkett oder im Balkon sitzt!
7. was man im Programm findet!
8. wer Amerikas bester moderner Dramatiker ist!

II. NÜTZLICHE AUSDRÜCKE

das Beispiel	*example*
zum Beispiel, (*abbreviation*) **z.B.**	*for example*
bestehen auf (*plus acc.*)	*to insist on*
bestehen aus (*plus dat.*)	*to consist of*
jemand Gesellschaft leisten	*to keep somebody company*
die Meinung, -en	*opinion*
der Meinung sein	*to be of the opinion*
meiner Meinung nach	*in my opinion*

die Reihe	*row*
an der Reihe sein	*to be up*
Ich bin an der Reihe.	*It's my turn.*
die Schlange	*snake, line*
Schlange stehen	*to stand in line*
wie am Schnürchen gehen	*to go like clockwork*
treffen	*to meet*
es gut treffen	*to be lucky*
Du hast es gut getroffen.	*You've hit it right.*

III. GRAMMATIK

59. Indefinite Pronouns

(a) Man

Man kann nicht immer tun, was **man** will.
One can't always do what one wants to.
You can't always do what you want to.
Man sagt es überall.
They (people) are saying it everywhere.
Es macht **einem** Angst, solche Geschichten zu hören.
It frightens one to hear such stories.
Es wundert **einen,** daß sie nie fallen.
It surprises you that they never fall.

The indefinite pronoun **man** (dative **einem,** accusative **einen**) refers to an indefinite person or persons and is equivalent to English *one, you, they, people.* Note also the colloquial use of **man** in place of a personal pronoun:

Man kommt morgen an.
They are arriving tomorrow.
Man kann's kaum glauben.
I can scarcely believe it.

(b) Jemand, niemand

War **jemand** zu Hause? — Nein, **niemand.**
Was somebody at home? — No, nobody.
Sie ist mit **jemand** gekommen, den ich nicht kenne.
She came with somebody I don't know.

Haben Sie sonst **jemand** gesehen? — Nein, **niemand** anders.
Did you see anybody else? — No, nobody else.

Jemand and **niemand** are used chiefly in the uninflected nominative, dative, and accusative forms. The genitive (**jemandes**) is rarely used.

Von wem haben Sie das gehört? Oh, von **irgend jemand.**
From whom did you hear that? Oh, from someone (emphatic).

The word **irgend,** which emphasizes indefiniteness, occurs in combinations only, such as: **irgend jemand** (*anybody, somebody or other*), **irgendeiner** (*anyone, someone or other*), **irgend etwas** (*something or other*).

60. Anticipatory da

Ich erinnere Sie **daran,** daß Sie hier nicht rauchen dürfen.
I remind you that you're not allowed to smoke here.
Sie dankte mir **dafür,** daß ich die Karten besorgt hatte.
She thanked me for having got the tickets.
Ich mache Sie **darauf** aufmerksam, daß die Vorstellung Punkt acht anfängt.
I call it to your attention that the performance begins at eight sharp.
Er machte sich ein Vergnügen **daraus,** uns zu belästigen.
He took pleasure in bothering us.

After a verb, noun, or adjective requiring a preposition (**sich erinnern an** *to remember*, **danken für** *to thank for*, **aufmerksam machen auf** *to call attention to*, **sich ein Vergnügen machen aus** *to take pleasure in*), the preposition is joined with **da-** (**dar-**) in anticipation of a following clause.

61. Numerals

(a) Forms (Irregular forms are underscored)

	CARDINALS	ORDINALS
0	**null**	
1	**eins**	der, die, das **erste**
2	**zwei**	**zweite**
3	**drei**	**dritte**
4	**vier**	**vierte**
5	**fünf**	**fünfte**
6	**sechs**	**sechste**

7	**sieben**	**sieb(en)te**
8	**acht**	**achte**
9	**neun**	**neunte**
10	**zehn**	**zehnte**
11	**elf**	**elfte**
12	**zwölf**	**zwölfte**
13	**dreizehn**	**dreizehnte**
14	**vierzehn**	**vierzehnte**
15	**fünfzehn**	**fünfzehnte**
16	**sechzehn**	**sechzehnte**
17	**siebzehn**	**siebzehnte**
18	**achtzehn**	**achtzehnte**
19	**neunzehn**	**neunzehnte**
20	**zwanzig**	**zwanzigste**
21	**einundzwanzig**	**einundzwanzigste**
30	**dreißig**	**dreißigste**
31	**einunddreißig**	**einunddreißigste**
40	**vierzig**	**vierzigste**
50	**fünfzig**	**fünfzigste**
60	**sechzig**	**sechzigste**
70	**siebzig**	**siebzigste**
80	**achtzig**	**achtzigste**
90	**neunzig**	**neunzigste**
100	**hundert**	**hundertste**
101	**hunderteins**	**hunderterste**
200	**zweihundert**	**zweihundertste**
1,000	**tausend**	**tausendste**
1,000,000	**eine Million**	**millionste**
2,000,000	**zwei Millionen**	
1 billion	**eine Milliarde**	
1,000 billions	**eine Billion**	

FRACTIONS

1/2	**die Hälfte**[1]	1/8	**ein Achtel**
1/3	**ein Drittel**[2]	1/9	**ein Neuntel**
1/4	**ein Viertel**	1/10	**ein Zehntel**
1/5	**ein Fünftel**	1/20	**ein Zwanzigstel**
1/6	**ein Sechstel**	1/30	**ein Dreißigstel**
1/7	**ein Siebtel**	1/100	**ein Hundertstel**

[1] The adjective form for *one half* is **halb**: ein **halber** Apfel (*half an apple*).
[2] Except for **die Hälfte,** fractions are neuter.

(b) Cardinal Numbers

1. **Ein**undzwanzig und **eins** ist zweiundzwanzig.
Twenty-one and one is twenty-two.
Man braucht mehr als **einen** Tag, um Museen zu besichtigen.
You need more than one day to visit museums.

The form **eins** is used in counting (**eins, zwei, drei** usw.) but not before **und.** The form **ein** has normal **ein**-word endings before a noun. Other cardinal numbers have no endings.

2. Dieses Buch hat genau **hundert** Seiten.
This book has exactly one hundred pages.

The number **hundert** (*one hundred*) is generally not preceded by **ein.**

3. Das Jahr hat **dreihundertfünfundsechzig** Tage.
A year has three hundred and sixty-five days.

Numbers are written together as one word.

4. **Hunderte von Leuten** waren dort.
Hundreds of people were there.
Es gab **Tausende von Zuschauern.**
There were thousands of spectators.

Hundert (*hundred*) and **Tausend** (*thousand*) may function as neuter nouns. In the plural they are followed by the preposition **von.**

5. Berlin hat über **vier Millionen** Einwohner.
Berlin has over four million inhabitants.

Million—also **Milliarde** and **Billion**—are feminine nouns.

(c) Ordinal Numbers

Ich habe es jetzt zum **fünfzehnten** Mal versucht.
I have tried it for the fifteenth time.
Heute abend sehen wir die **hundertste** Vorstellung des Stückes.
This evening we'll be seeing the hundredth performance of the play.

Ordinal numbers from **zwei** to **neunzehn** add **-t,** from **zwanzig** on **-st,** to the cardinal form. Ordinal numbers have normal adjective endings.

(d) Fractions

In acht Tagen[1] können wir **ein Fünftel der Arbeit** tun.
In a week we can complete a fifth of the work.
Die Hälfte der Darsteller stammt aus Österreich.
Half (of) the actors come from Austria.

Fractions are neuter nouns formed by adding **-el** to the ordinal numbers, with the exception of **die Hälfte.** They are followed by nouns in the genitive.

62. Expressions of Time

(a) Clock Time

Wieviel Uhr ist es? (**Wie spät ist es?**) — **Es ist . . .**
What time is it? — It is . . .

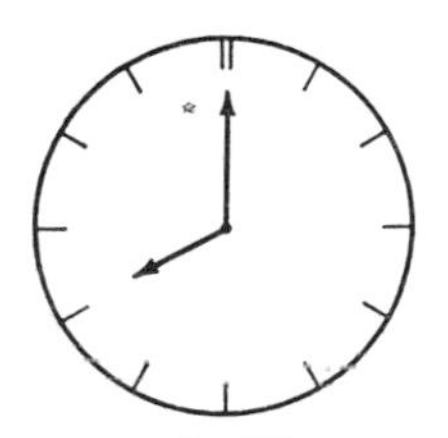

acht Uhr

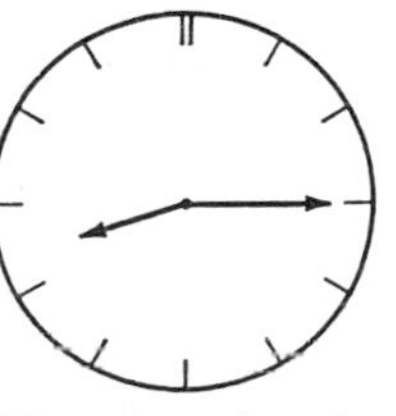

Viertel nach acht; Viertel (auf) neun; acht Uhr fünfzehn

halb neun; acht Uhr dreißig

Viertel vor neun; dreiviertel neun; acht Uhr fünfundvierzig

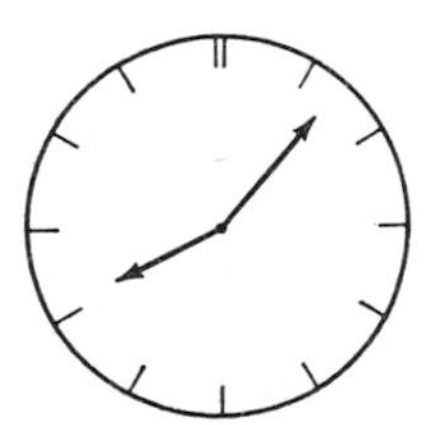

sieben (Minuten) nach acht; acht Uhr sieben

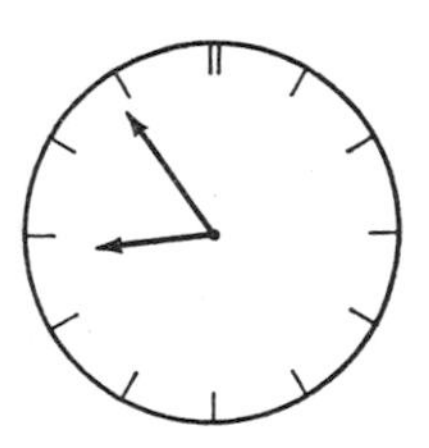

sechs (Minuten) vor neun; acht Uhr vierundfünfzig

[1] Germans usually say **acht Tage** for *a week* and **vierzehn Tage** for *two weeks*, although **eine Woche** and **zwei Wochen** are not uncommon.

1. **Uhr** is normally used only with an even hour (**acht Uhr**) or when stating the hour first, followed by the number of minutes (**acht Uhr sieben**).

2. The half hour is expressed in relation to the next hour (**halb neun** *half past eight*).

(b) Adverbial Time Expressions

1. **Um wieviel Uhr** kommt er an? — **Um acht Uhr.**
At what time is he arriving? — At eight o'clock.

   Um is the German equivalent for *at* in time expressions.[1]

2. Ich stehe **morgens** um sieben Uhr auf.
I get up at seven o'clock in the morning.
Meinen Sie **acht Uhr morgens oder abends?**
Do you mean eight A.M. *or* P.M.?

   The adverbs **morgens, vormittags, nachmittags, abends, nachts,** in addition to their basic meaning (*in the morning*, etc.), are used to distinguish A.M. and P.M.

   Similar adverbs and adverbial forms for the days of the week (**sonntags, montags, dienstags, mittwochs, donnerstags, freitags, samstags, sonnabends**) express customary time:

   Er geht **sonntags** immer in die Kirche.[2]
He always goes to church on Sundays.

3. Die Vorstellung fängt **um zwanzig Uhr** (20^{00}) an.
The performance begins at 8 P.M.
Der Zug fährt (**um**) **siebzehn Uhr fünfzehn** (**17^{15}**) von Köln ab.
The train leaves Cologne at 5:15 P.M.

   Germans use the twenty-four hour system for official documents, public announcements, theater performances, transportation schedules, and telegrams.

---

[1] When **Punkt** (*at exactly, on the dot of*) is used, **um** is omitted:

Er kommt **Punkt acht Uhr** abends.
He's coming at exactly eight P.M.

[2] Compare: Er geht **Sonntag** in die Kirche.
He's going to church (next) Sunday.

63. Dates

(a) Days of the Month

Heute ist **der 28. (achtundzwanzigste) Februar.**
Today is February 28th.
Das geschah **am 4. (vierten) Juli.**
That happened on July 4th.

In dates, ordinal numbers express the day of the month. In writing, these ordinals are normally expressed as figures followed by a period.

Note: On letter heads or in official documents, dates are expressed in the accusative: **den 23. (dreiundzwanzigsten) Januar** (*January 23rd*).

(b) Years

Im Jahre 1918 (neunzehnhundertachtzehn) wurde Deutschland eine Republik.
In 1918 Germany became a republic.
Ich war **1964 (neunzehnhundertvierundsechzig)** in München.
I was in Munich in 1964.

Years are expressed in cardinal numbers, either with or without the phrase **im Jahre; hundert** may not be omitted in German.[1]

IV. ÜBUNGEN

A. *Ersetzen Sie die angegebenen Wörter durch die korrekte Form von* **man!**

BEISPIEL: Es tut den Leuten leid, dies zu hören. (den Leuten)
Es tut einem leid, dies zu hören.

1. Wir müssen in der Schule viel arbeiten. (wir)
2. Das Volk möchte mehr Freiheit haben. (das Volk)
3. Der Lehrer gibt uns die Gelegenheit, viel zu lernen. (uns)
4. Waren die Zuhörer aufmerksam? (die Zuhörer)

---

[1] As in English, Germans may use abbreviated forms:

Ich war **64** in München. *I was in Munich in '64.*

5. Er bringt uns jeden Tag Blumen aus seinem Garten. (uns)
6. Er ladet uns oft ein, nicht wahr? (uns)
7. Wir sehen ihn immer gerne. (wir)
8. Bei schönem Wetter machen die Leute gern Ausflüge. (die Leute)

B. *Verbinden Sie die beiden Sätze dem Beispiel entsprechend!*

BEISPIEL: Er war traurig. Er erhielt keine Briefe.
Er war traurig darüber, daß er keine Briefe erhielt.

1. Ich warte. Die Platzanweiserin bringt mir ein Programm.
2. Wir erkannten ihn. Er war so klein.
3. Er war stolz. Seine Schwester war eine bekannte Schauspielerin.
4. Ich erinnere mich jetzt. Der Zug kommt um zehn Uhr fünfzehn an.
5. Sie machte uns aufmerksam. Der Präsident spricht heute im Rundfunk.
6. Ich habe ihr gedankt. Sie hat meinen Freund auch eingeladen.
7. Ich dachte gar nicht. Ich hatte eine andere Verabredung.
8. Wir sind froh. Wir konnten dir ein wenig helfen.

C. *Antworten Sie auf deutsch!*

1. Wieviel ist 17 und 3?
2. Wieviel ist 12 und 9?
3. Wieviel ist 85 und 10?
4. Wieviel ist 150 und 75?
5. Wieviel ist 780 und 91?
6. Wieviel ist ein Viertel von 60?
7. Wieviel ist ein Drittel von 900?
8. Wieviel ist ein Achtel von 32?
9. Wieviel ist die Hälfte von 24?
10. Wieviel ist ein Fünftel von 75?

D. *Ergänzen Sie das angegebene Zahlwort auf deutsch!*

1. (eleventh) Dies ist die ______ Lektion.

2. (fifth)	Ich kann das ______ Kapitel nicht verstehen.
3. (35th)	Kennedy war der ______ Präsident der Vereinigten Staaten.
4. (16th)	Lincoln war unser ______ Präsident.
5. (twelfth)	Der Dezember ist der ______ Monat des Jahres.
6. (third)	Kennen Sie den Film „Der ______ Mann"?
7. (20th)	Wir leben im ______ Jahrhundert.
8. (43rd)	Meine Mutter hatte gestern ihren ______ Geburtstag.
9. (72nd)	Heute ist der ______ Geburtstag meines Großvaters.
10. (100th)	Morgen ist die ______ Vorstellung dieses Stückes.

E. *Antworten Sie mit „nein" und erhöhen Sie die Zeitangaben in den Antworten um zehn Minuten!*

BEISPIEL: Ist Herbert um sieben Uhr angekommen?
Nein, Herbert ist um zehn nach sieben angekommen.

1. Hören Sie Ihren Wecker morgens um 7^{15}?
2. Gehen Sie um 7^{35} zum Frühstück?
3. Verlassen Sie das Haus um 8^{05}?
4. Kommen Sie um 8^{40} im Büro an?
5. Fängt der Arbeitstag nicht um 8^{45} an?
6. Trinken Sie um 10^{25} eine Tasse Kaffee?
7. Gehen Sie um 11^{50} zum Mittagessen?
8. Beginnt die Arbeit um 12^{30} wieder?
9. Hören Sie um 5^{15} auf zu arbeiten?
10. Fahren Sie um 5^{20} wieder nach Hause?

F. *Beantworten Sie die folgenden Fragen!*

1. Wann ist Weihnachten?
2. Wann ist Neujahr?
3. Wann ist Washingtons Geburtstag?
4. Wann ist Lincolns Geburtstag?
5. Welchen Tag im Juli feiert man überall in Amerika?
6. Nennen Sie das Datum des letzten Tages des Jahres!
7. In welchem Jahr ist der zweite Weltkrieg ausgebrochen?

8. In welchem Jahrhundert lebte Lincoln?
9. Welcher Tag kommt nur einmal alle vier Jahre?
10. Welches ist der letzte Tag im September?

G. *Gebrauchen Sie sechs der Nützlichen Ausdrücke in ganzen Sätzen!*

H. *Sagen Sie zuerst und schreiben Sie danach auf deutsch!*

1. My friends called to my attention that it is very difficult to get seats for this play.
2. I remind you that the performance begins at eight sharp.
3. In all, the theater has only 933 seats.
4. About one half of these are in the orchestra.
5. A third are in the first balcony, that is, about 311; the others are in the second balcony.
6. Although the curtain in German theaters usually goes up at eight sharp, this performance will begin at 7:45.
7. One of the leading actors is sick this evening.
8. He was supposed to play the role of the third brother.
9. Too bad he's ill; they like him very much here in Frankfurt.
10. But after a hundred performances he has a right to be ill.

Aufsatz

Sie gehen mit einer Freundin ins Theater. Während Sie an der Theaterkasse Schlange stehen, unterhalten Sie sich mit Ihrer Freundin. Schreiben Sie das Gespräch, das Sie mit der Freundin und anschließend mit dem Fräulein an der Theaterkasse führen, nieder! Sie sprechen zum Beispiel über:

(1) das Stück, das gespielt wird;
(2) den Autor und andere Stücke dieses Autors;
(3) die Darsteller, die Sie kennen;
(4) die vermutliche Länge des Stückes;
(5) ein anderes Stück, das Sie kürzlich gesehen haben;
(6) den Preis der Plätze, die Sie nehmen möchten.

Future and Future Perfect;
als, wenn, wann.

Lektion 12

I. GESPRÄCH: Ferienpläne

HERBERT: Nehmen wir eine Taxe! Es ist schon halb zwölf und ich bin etwas müde.

ILSE: Wo denken Sie hin! Eine Taxe ist viel zu teuer. Wir nehmen die Straßenbahn!

HERBERT: Die ist eben abgefahren.

ILSE: Die nächste wird in zehn Minuten hier sein — solange werden wir wohl warten können. Hier ist die Haltestelle.

HERBERT: Sagen Sie, steht da nicht die junge Dame, die im Theater in der Reihe vor uns saß?

Vacation Plans

HERBERT: Let's take a taxi. It's already half past eleven, and I'm a little tired.

ILSE: Whatever are you thinking of! A taxi is much too expensive. We'll take the streetcar.

HERBERT: It just left.

ILSE: The next one will be here in ten minutes. Surely we can wait that long. Here is the stop.

HERBERT: Say, isn't that the young lady who sat in the row in front of us in the theater?

ILSE: Tatsächlich, Erika Waiblinger, eine Studienkollegin von mir. Sie fährt in der gleichen Richtung. Ich habe Sie bereits vorgestellt, nicht wahr?

HERBERT: Gewiß. — Guten Abend, Fräulein Waiblinger.

ERIKA: Guten Abend, Herr Becker. Guten Abend, Ilse. Angenehm kühl, die Nacht, finden Sie nicht?

ILSE: Ja. Dafür wird's morgen wieder recht heiß werden.

HERBERT: Nach dem Wetterbericht müssen wir uns auf eine ganze Woche heißes Wetter gefaßt machen. Zum Glück verreise ich übermorgen auf einige Tage.

ILSE: Stimmt. Herr Lenz hat mir gesagt, daß Sie eine Ferienfahrt mit ihm vorhaben.

HERBERT: Frau Lenz und Otto fahren auch mit. Ich freue mich sehr darauf.

ERIKA: Wo geht die Reise hin?

HERBERT: Nach München, wo wir drei Tage bleiben werden.

ERIKA: Das wird Ihnen bestimmt gefallen. Ich finde München die schönste Stadt . . .

ILSE: Natürlich! Erika ist Münchnerin!

ILSE: You're right, Erika Waiblinger, a fellow student of mine. She's going in the same direction. I've already introduced you, haven't I?

HERBERT: Yes. — Good evening, Miss Waiblinger.

ERIKA: Good evening, Mr. Becker. Good evening, Ilse. Pleasantly cool tonight, don't you think?

ILSE: Yes. But tomorrow it's going to be quite hot again.

HERBERT: According to the weather report we have to prepare ourselves for a whole week of hot weather. Fortunately I'm going out of town for a few days the day after tomorrow.

ILSE: That's right. Mr. Lenz told me you were going to take a vacation trip with him.

HERBERT: Mrs. Lenz and Otto are going along, too. I'm looking forward to it very much.

ERIKA: Where are you going?

HERBERT: To Munich, where we'll stay for three days.

ERIKA: You'll certainly like that. I think Munich is the most beautiful city . . .

ILSE: Naturally! Erika is from Munich.

ERIKA: Nun, Spaß beiseite, München ist eine alte Residenzstadt, wo es sehr viel zu sehen gibt. Sie müssen aber auch nach Füssen zu den Königsschlössern fahren. Von denen werden Sie wohl schon gehört haben.

HERBERT: Neuschwanstein, zum Beispiel, nicht wahr?

ERIKA: Ein richtiges Märchenschloß. Von dort ist es auch nicht weit nach Oberammergau. Ein entzückender Ort.

HERBERT: Ja, aber Herr Lenz sagt, daß diesen Sommer dort nichts los ist.

ERIKA: Passionsspiele gibt es dieses Jahr keine, aber in Oberammergau werden Sie auch sonst viel Betrieb finden.

HERBERT: Ich werde es Herrn Lenz sagen.

ERIKA: Rufen Sie mich an, wenn Sie in München sind!

HERBERT: Sehr liebenswürdig von Ihnen.

ILSE: Hier kommt unsere Straßenbahn!

ERIKA: Well, all joking aside, Munich is an old royal residence, where there's a lot to be seen. But you must also go to the royal castles at Füssen. You have probably heard about them already.

HERBERT: Neuschwanstein, for example, right?

ERIKA: A real fairy castle. From there it's not far to Oberammergau. A delightful place.

HERBERT: Yes, but Mr. Lenz says there's nothing going on there this summer.

ERIKA: There isn't any Passion Play this year, but in Oberammergau you'll find a lot of other activity.

HERBERT: I'll tell Mr. Lenz.

ERIKA: Call me up when you're in Munich.

HERBERT: That's very nice of you.

ILSE: Here comes our streetcar.

Fragen

Antworten Sie auf deutsch!

1. Um wieviel Uhr kommen Herbert und Ilse aus dem Theater?
2. Warum nehmen Sie keine Taxe?
3. Wann kommt die nächste Straßenbahn?
4. Wen sehen Herbert und Ilse bei der Haltestelle?
5. In welcher Richtung fährt Fräulein Waiblinger?
6. Mit wem wird Herbert eine Ferienfahrt machen?
7. Wohin geht die Reise?
8. Wie lange wird er in München bleiben?
9. Wie findet Fräulein Waiblinger München?
10. Warum findet Fräulein Waiblinger München so schön?
11. Was soll Herbert tun, wenn er in München ist?

Konversation

Fragen Sie Ihren Nachbar,

1. ob er lieber mit einer Taxe oder mit der Straßenbahn fährt! [Ihr Nachbar muß selbstverständlich jede Frage beantworten.]
2. ob es überhaupt Straßenbahnen in seiner Stadt gibt!
3. wie er das Wetter heute findet!
4. ob er heißes oder kaltes Wetter vorzieht!
5. wohin er eine Ferienfahrt machen möchte!
6. was er zu einem Freund sagt, wenn er ihm morgens begegnet!
7. was er zu einem Freund sagt, wenn er ihn abends trifft!
8. was eine „Residenzstadt" ist!
9. ob er schon einmal die Passionsspiele in Oberammergau gesehen hat!
10. wie viele Reisen er schon nach Europa gemacht hat!

II. NÜTZLICHE AUSDRÜCKE

auf einige Tage	*for a few days (in the future)*
der Betrieb	*workshop, factory; activity*
Dort ist Betrieb.	*There's something going on there.*
Wo denken Sie hin!	*What are you thinking of? That's impossible.*

sich freuen auf (*plus acc.*)	*to look forward to, anticipate*
sich gefaßt machen auf (*plus acc.*)	*to prepare oneself for, expect*
zum Glück	*fortunately, luckily*
Wo geht die Reise hin?	*Where are you going (on your trip)?*
nach	*after; according to*
nach dem Wetterbericht	*according to the weather report*
der Spaß	*joke*
Spaß beiseite.	*All joking aside.*

III. GRAMMATIK

64. Future Tense

(a) Forms

ich **werde singen**	*I shall (will) sing*
du **wirst singen**	*you will sing*
er **wird singen**	*he will sing*
wir **werden singen**	*we shall (will) sing*
ihr **werdet singen**	*you will sing*
sie **werden singen**	*they will sing*

The future tense consists of the present tense of the auxiliary verb **werden** plus the infinitive of the main verb.

(b) Uses of the Future

1. Future Time

Sie **werden** morgen **kommen.**
They will (are going to) come tomorrow.
Wir **werden** nächste Woche nach München **fahren.**
We shall (will) drive to Munich next week.

In general, the future tense is used in German as in English, that is, to express an idea in future time.[1]

---

[1] An infinitive (including a double infinitive) stands at the end of a main clause:

Ich werde morgen **abfahren.** *I'll leave tomorrow.*
Wir werden es morgen **tun können.** *We'll be able to do it tomorrow.*

Note: As in English, the present tense in German is frequently preferred for expressing future action, especially when the context clearly indicates future time:

Sie **kommen** morgen.
They're coming tomorrow.
Wir **fahren** nächste Woche nach München.
We're driving to Munich next week.

2. Probability

Sie **werden** das (wohl) **wissen.**
You probably know that. You must know that.
Das **wird** (schon) richtig **sein.**
That's probably right. That must be right.

The future tense is used to express present probability. Either **wohl** or **schon** is often added to reinforce the idea of probability.

65. Future Perfect Tense

(a) Forms

ich **werde getan haben**	*I shall (will) have done*
du **wirst getan haben**	*you will have done*
er **wird getan haben**	*he will have done*
wir **werden getan haben**	*we shall (will) have done*
ihr **werdet getan haben**	*you will have done*
sie **werden getan haben**	*they will have done*

The future perfect tense consists of the present tense of the auxiliary verb **werden** plus the perfect infinitive of the main verb. The perfect infinitive stands at the end of a main clause.

(b) Uses of the Future Perfect

1. Sie **werden** die Nachricht schon **bekommen haben,** bevor er anruft.
They will already have got the news before he telephones.

In general, the future perfect tense is used in German, as in English, to express an action that will be completed before another action in future time. This use of the future perfect is as rare in German as in English, however. The above sentence would normally be expressed as follows:

Sie **werden** die Nachricht **bekommen,** bevor er anruft.
They will get the news before he telephones.

2. Past Probability

Er **wird** sie (wohl) **gesehen haben.**
He probably saw her. He must have seen her.
Die Straßenbahn **wird** schon **abgefahren sein.**
I guess the streetcar has already left.

The most common use of the future perfect is to express past probability. Either **wohl** or **schon** is often added to reinforce the idea of probability.

66. Als, wenn, wann

Als, wenn, and **wann** all mean *when*, but they are used in different ways.

(a) **Als**

Ich habe sie sofort erkannt, **als** ich sie sah.
I recognized her at once when I saw her.
Die Straßenbahn war eben abgefahren, **als** wir zur Haltestelle kamen.
The streetcar had just left when we arrived at the stop.

Als refers to a single past action.

(b) **Wenn**

Rufen Sie mich an, **wenn** Sie in München sind!
Call me up when (whenever) you're in Munich.
Er war nie zu Hause, **wenn** ich ihn besuchen wollte.
He was never at home when I wanted to visit him.

Wenn refers to repeated action in any tense or to a future action, often with the meaning of *whenever.*[1]

---

[1] **Wenn** may also mean *if:*

Wenn er Geld hat, kann er es bezahlen.
If he has money, he can pay for it.

(c) **Wann**

Wann ist er abgefahren?
When did he leave?
Wissen Sie, **wann** er abfahren will?
Do you know when he wants to leave?

Wann is used with any tense to introduce a direct or indirect question.

IV. ÜBUNGEN

A. *Setzen Sie die Verben in den folgenden Sätzen ins Futur!*

1. Sie gehen morgen abend ins Theater.
2. Ich komme nächste Woche zurück.
3. Sie schicken die Kinder zu den Großeltern.
4. Er nimmt das Geld nicht an.
5. Machst du das ohne Hilfe?
6. Warum muß er es ein zweites Mal machen?
7. Das Wetter ist morgen sicher wieder sehr heiß.
8. Bleibt er nur drei Tage bei dem Onkel?
9. Wir können ihn in Heidelberg treffen.
10. Er muß nach Füssen fahren.

B. *Beginnen Sie die folgenden Sätze mit* **Ich weiß nicht, ob** *und setzen Sie sie ins Futur!*

BEISPIEL: Das Stück gefällt Ihnen.
Ich weiß nicht, ob Ihnen das Stück gefallen wird.

1. Er nimmt eine Taxe.
2. Erika fährt in der gleichen Richtung.
3. Sie sitzen in der Reihe vor uns.
4. Wir verreisen morgen.
5. Du hilfst uns gerne.
6. Wir bleiben drei Tage.
7. Er vergißt die Sache.
8. Die Vorstellung fängt um drei Uhr an.
9. Du siehst viel.
10. Es dauert zwei Stunden.

C. *Ersetzen Sie das Futur durch das Präsens!*

1. Werden Sie ihn abholen müssen?
2. Ich werde sofort zurückkommen, wenn er nicht dort ist.
3. Werden Sie lange fortbleiben?
4. Er wird doch nicht mitfahren.
5. Das wirst du allein machen müssen.
6. Wird sie den Flug machen dürfen?
7. Der Bericht wird morgen in den Zeitungen erscheinen.
8. Wohin werdet ihr heute abend fahren?
9. Wann werden wir Sie wiedersehen?
10. Wann wird er mit dem Paket kommen?

D. *Ändern Sie die folgenden Sätze, indem Sie* **wohl** *oder* **schon** *gebrauchen und eine Möglichkeit oder Wahrscheinlichkeit ausdrücken!*

BEISPIEL: Das weiß er.
Das wird er wohl wissen.

1. Er ist im Kino.
2. Sie hat es gern.
3. Du verstehst das.
4. Sie kennt ihn.
5. Du bist sehr müde.
6. Sie will allein sein.
7. Es ist unmöglich.
8. Ihr dürft kommen.
9. Wir haben genug Geld.
10. Er hat recht.

E. *Ändern Sie die folgenden Sätze, indem Sie* **wohl** *oder* **schon** *gebrauchen und eine Möglichkeit oder Wahrscheinlichkeit ausdrücken!*

BEISPIEL: Er wußte es nicht.
Er wird es wohl nicht gewußt haben.

1. Er hat den Kuchen gegessen.
2. Sie hat ihn gesehen.
3. Wir haben es falsch gemacht.
4. Ich habe es zu billig verkauft.
5. Sie hat deine Geschichte vergessen.

6. Sie sind gestern abend gekommen.
7. Ich habe es zu teuer gekauft.
8. Er hat das Problem gelöst.
9. Er kannte ihn nicht.
10. Sie hat eine Ferienreise gemacht.
11. Sie ist ins Theater gegangen.

F. *Ergänzen Sie mit* **als, wenn** *oder* **wann!**

1. Wir trafen ihn, _____ wir auf die Straßenbahn warteten.
2. Wir treffen meistens einige Bekannte, _____ wir nach Hause fahren.
3. Er las gerade die Zeitung, _____ wir ihn begrüßten.
4. Er trägt immer seinen besten Anzug, _____ er ins Theater geht.
5. Ich möchte wissen, seit _____ er diesen Anzug hat.
6. Er verreist übermorgen, aber nur _____ das Wetter schön bleibt.
7. Er wird uns eine Postkarte schicken, _____ er in Berlin ist.
8. Hat er Ihnen gesagt, _____ er zurückkommt?
9. Das hat er noch nicht gewußt, _____ ich ihn fragte.
10. Er wird es uns bestimmt mitteilen, _____ er uns schreibt.

G. *Gebrauchen Sie sechs der Nützlichen Ausdrücke in ganzen Sätzen!*

H. *Sagen Sie zuerst und schreiben Sie danach auf deutsch!*

1. Mr. Becker, I hear you're going to take a vacation trip to Munich.
2. Will you go to Oberammergau when you're there?
3. That's probably one of the best-known little villages in Bavaria.
4. You must also have heard of Garmisch.
5. Next winter I'll go to Garmisch during my vacation.
6. Mr. Lenz says we will make several excursions, but I don't really know where we'll go.
7. He must know Bavaria very well, because he studied at the University of Munich.
8. I would like to go to the opera. But will there be performances in August?

9. Of course, I will also want to go to the great art museums.
10. I think Mr. and Mrs. Lenz will probably accompany me and explain everything to me.

Aufsatz

Sie machen Pläne für eine Ferienfahrt nach Bayern und unterhalten sich mit einem Freund, der aus München stammt und Ihnen Auskunft gibt. Schreiben Sie Ihre Fragen und die Auskünfte, die Sie erhalten, in der Form eines Gespräches nieder! Sie möchten zum Beispiel wissen:
(1) ob die Hotels in München teuer sind und ob Ihr Freund Ihnen eins besonders empfehlen kann;
(2) wie viele Tage man braucht, um München zu besichtigen;
(3) ob es in Bayern viele Schlösser gibt;
(4) wie man von München am besten nach Oberammergau fährt (mit dem Wagen oder mit dem Zug);
(5) was es in Oberammergau zu sehen gibt;
(6) ob das Wetter dort im Sommer auch heiß ist.

Subjunctive;
Contrary-to-Fact Clauses.

Lektion 13

I. GESPRÄCH: Ankunft im Hotel

HERR LENZ:	So, nun sind wir in München. Wir nähern uns bereits dem Stadtzentrum.
FRAU LENZ:	Jetzt müssen wir nur noch unser Hotel finden.
HERR LENZ:	Das liegt ganz nahe beim Bahnhofsplatz. „Eden" heißt es.
FRAU LENZ:	Hier ist furchtbar viel Verkehr. Wäre es nicht besser gewesen, wenn wir in einem Hotel in der Vorstadt abgestiegen wären? Wenn wir nur schon einen Parkplatz hätten!
HERR LENZ:	Laß das nur meine Sorge sein! Ich kenne eine Garage in der Nähe, wo ich den Wagen immer einstellen kann.

Arrival at the Hotel

MR. LENZ:	Well, now we're in Munich. We're already nearing the center of the city.
MRS. LENZ:	Now all we have to do is find our hotel.
MR. LENZ:	It's quite close to the Bahnhofsplatz. It's called the "Eden."
MRS. LENZ:	There's an awful lot of traffic here. Wouldn't it have been better if we had stopped at a hotel in the suburbs? If we only had a parking place already!
MR. LENZ:	Let me worry about that! I know a garage in the vicinity where I can always put the car up.

OTTO: Der Bahnhof liegt da drüben, Vater. Bei dieser Kreuzung mußt du nach links abbiegen.

HERR LENZ: Mein Junge, wenn ich das täte, würde ich eine Strafe bekommen. Hier ist jedes Abbiegen verboten. Wir müssen geradeaus fahren.

OTTO: Verzeihung! Ich habe das Verkehrszeichen gar nicht bemerkt. — Wir hätten eben schon früher nach links abbiegen sollen!

HERR LENZ: Das macht nichts aus. Wir kommen früh genug zum Hotel.

FRAU LENZ: Du hast doch die Zimmer vorausbestellt?

HERR LENZ: Bestimmt. Wenn wir sie nicht vorausbestellt hätten, könnten wir überhaupt nicht auf Unterkunft rechnen. Es findet hier gegenwärtig eine Tagung von Ärzten oder Zahnärzten statt, und alle Hotels sind voll besetzt.

OTTO: Da geht es zum Bahnhofsplatz. Wir brauchen nur diesen Straßenbahngeleisen zu folgen.

(*Im Hotel.*)

EMPFANGSCHEF: Guten Tag. Womit kann ich dienen?

OTTO: The railroad station is over there, father. You have to turn left at this intersection.

MR. LENZ: If I did that, my boy, I'd get a ticket. Turns are not permitted here. We have to go straight ahead.

OTTO: I'm sorry. I didn't notice the traffic sign at all. We should have turned left sooner.

MR. LENZ: It doesn't make any difference. We'll get to the hotel soon enough.

MRS. LENZ: You did reserve the rooms?

MR. LENZ: Certainly. If we hadn't reserved them, we couldn't count on accommodations at all. Right now there's a meeting here of doctors or dentists, and all the hotels are fully occupied.

OTTO: There's the way to the Bahnhofplatz. All we have to do is follow those streetcar tracks.

(*At the hotel.*)

HEAD CLERK: How do you do? May I help you?

HERR LENZ: Mein Name ist Lenz. Ich habe mir zwei Zimmer reservieren lassen. Hier ist die Bescheinigung.

EMPFANGSCHEF: Stimmt. Ihre Zimmer sind im dritten Stock, gleich nebeneinander.

HERR LENZ: Herbert, ich hoffe, es macht Ihnen nichts aus, ein Zimmer mit Otto teilen zu müssen.

HERBERT: Keineswegs. Aber ein Bad hätte ich gerne gehabt.

EMPFANGSCHEF: Alle Zimmer im Hotel haben Bad. — Dürfte ich Sie noch bitten, dieses Formular auszufüllen?

HERR LENZ: Gerne. — Wo sind die Schlüssel?

EMPFANGSCHEF: Hier, bitte. Ich lasse Ihr Gepäck gleich auf die Zimmer bringen. Der Fahrstuhl ist hier nebenan.

FRAU LENZ: Ein feines Hotel! Mir ist, als wäre ich schon einmal hier gewesen.

HERR LENZ: Das kommt dir nur so vor. Alle Hotels gleichen sich ein wenig.

MR. LENZ: My name is Lenz. I have reservations for two rooms. Here is the confirmation.

HEAD CLERK: That's correct. Your rooms are on the fourth floor, right next to each other.

MR. LENZ: Herbert, I hope you don't mind having to share a room with Otto.

HERBERT: Not at all. But I would have liked a bathroom.

HEAD CLERK: All rooms in the hotel have bathrooms. — May I ask you to fill out this form?

MR. LENZ: Gladly. — Where are the keys?

HEAD CLERK: Here you are, sir. I'll have your baggage taken up to your rooms immediately. The elevator is right over here.

MRS. LENZ: A fine hotel. It seems to me as though I've been here before.

MR. LENZ: It just seems that way to you. All hotels are a little bit alike.

Fragen

Antworten Sie auf deutsch!

1. Wie heißt das Hotel, das die Familie Lenz sucht?
2. Wo liegt das Hotel „Eden"?
3. Warum meint Frau Lenz, es wäre besser, in einem Hotel in der Vorstadt abzusteigen?
4. Warum hat Herr Lenz keine Schwierigkeiten, den Wagen zu parken?
5. In welcher Richtung sollte Herr Lenz abbiegen?
6. Warum fährt Herr Lenz jedoch geradeaus?
7. Was hat Herr Lenz vor der Abreise getan, um mit Sicherheit Unterkunft zu finden?
8. In welchem Stock sind die Zimmer?
9. Mit wem wird Herbert sein Zimmer teilen müssen?
10. Welche Tatsache zeigt, daß das „Eden" ein modernes Hotel ist?

Konversation

Fragen Sie Ihren Nachbar,

1. ob er im Stadtzentrum oder in der Vorstadt wohnt! [Ihr Nachbar muß selbstverständlich jede Frage beantworten.]
2. ob er jemand kennt, der immer in einem Hotel wohnt!
3. wie oft er beim Autofahren schon eine Strafe bekommen hat!
4. wann und wo er Schwierigkeiten beim Parken hat!
5. ob er lieber in einem Hotel oder in einem Motel übernachtet!
6. warum man Zimmer vorausbestellen muß!
7. wie viele Hausschlüssel er bei sich hat!
8. wer das Gepäck auf die Hotelzimmer bringt!

II. NÜTZLICHE AUSDRÜCKE

ein Formular aus-füllen	*to fill out a form*
einen Wagen ein-stellen	*to put away (park) a car*
etwas aus-machen	*to make a difference*
Das macht nichts aus.	*That doesn't matter.*

etwas voraus-bestellen	*to order something in advance*
gar nicht	*not at all*
geradeaus fahren	*to drive straight ahead*
in einem Hotel ab-steigen	*to stay at a hotel*
nach links ab-biegen	*to turn left*
nach rechts ab-biegen	*to turn right*

III. GRAMMATIK

The Subjunctive

The terms *indicative* and *subjunctive* describe two basic aspects of verbs in German. In previous lessons we have reviewed indicative forms, which express facts and certainty. The *subjunctive* expresses uncertainty, doubt, supposition, conjecture, wishful thinking, politeness, and conditions contrary to fact or reality.

67. Forms of the Subjunctive

The two tenses of the subjunctive most commonly used are the present and the past. Each has two forms, called Subjunctive I and Subjunctive II. Subjunctive endings are the same for all tenses of all verbs, except **sein** (*to be*).

(a) Subjunctive I

1. Present Subjunctive I

kaufen *to buy*	**fahren** *to drive, go*
ich kaufe[1]	fahre
du kauf**est**	fahr**est**
er kauf**e**	fahr**e**
wir kauf**en**	fahr**en**
ihr kauf**et**	fahr**et**
sie kauf**en**	fahr**en**

[1] The meanings of subjunctive forms vary widely with the context. Study these meanings carefully in the examples given in this and the following lessons.

haben *to have*	**sein** *to be*	**werden** *to become*
ich hab**e**	**sei**[1]	werd**e**
du hab**est**	**seiest**	werd**est**
er hab**e**	**sei**	werd**e**
wir hab**en**	**seien**	werd**en**
ihr hab**et**	**seiet**	werd**et**
sie hab**en**	**seien**	werd**en**

The present subjunctive I consists of the infinitive stem plus the subjunctive endings.

2. Past Subjunctive I

kaufen *to buy*	**fahren** *to drive, go*
ich **habe gekauft**	**sei gefahren**
du **habest gekauft**	**seiest gefahren**
er **habe gekauft**	**sei gefahren**
wir **haben gekauft**	**seien gefahren**
ihr **habet gekauft**	**seiet gefahren**
sie **haben gekauft**	**seien gefahren**

The past subjunctive I of all verbs consists of the present subjunctive I of **haben** or **sein** plus the past participle of the main verb.

(b) Subjunctive II

1. Present Subjunctive II

kaufen *to buy*	**fahren** *to drive, go*
ich kaufte[2]	führ**e**
du kauft**est**	führ**est**
er kauft**e**	führ**e**
wir kauft**en**	führ**en**
ihr kauft**et**	führ**et**
sie kauft**en**	führ**en**

[1] **Sein** is the only verb with irregular forms in the present subjunctive I.

[2] Note that present subjunctive II forms of regular (weak) verbs are identical with past-indicative forms.

	haben *to have*	**sein** *to be*	**werden** *to become*
ich	**hätte**	**wäre**	**würde**
du	**hättest**	**wärest**	**würdest**
er	**hätte**	**wäre**	**würde**
wir	**hätten**	**wären**	**würden**
ihr	**hättet**	**wäret**	**würdet**
sie	**hätten**	**wären**	**würden**

The present subjunctive II consists of the simple-past stem plus subjunctive endings. In strong verbs, the stem vowel is umlauted wherever possible.

Note: Some irregular weak verbs and modals umlaut the past-stem vowel in the present subjunctive II:

INFINITIVE		PAST INDICATIVE	PRESENT SUBJUNCTIVE II
bringen	*to bring*	brachte	**brächte**
denken	*to think*	dachte	**dächte**
dürfen	*to be allowed*	durfte	**dürfte**
können	*to be able*	konnte	**könnte**
mögen	*to like*	mochte	**möchte**
müssen	*to have to*	mußte	**müßte**
wissen	*to know*	wußte	**wüßte**

Four irregular weak verbs with stem vowel **a** in the past indicative have **e** in the present subjunctive II:

INFINITIVE		PAST INDICATIVE	PRESENT SUBJUNCTIVE II
kennen	*to know*	kannte	**kennte**
nennen	*to name*	nannte	**nennte**
rennen	*to run*	rannte	**rennte**
brennen	*to burn*	brannte	**brennte**

2. Past Subjunctive II

	kaufen *to buy*	**fahren** *to drive, go*
ich	**hätte gekauft**	**wäre gefahren**
du	**hättest gekauft**	**wärest gefahren**
er	**hätte gekauft**	**wäre gefahren**
wir	**hätten gekauft**	**wären gefahren**
ihr	**hättet gekauft**	**wäret gefahren**
sie	**hätten gekauft**	**wären gefahren**

The past subjunctive II of all verbs consists of the present subjunctive II of **haben** or **sein** plus the past participle of the main verb.

68. Contrary-to-Fact Conditions

There are two major uses of the subjunctive in German: in *contrary-to-fact conditions* and in *indirect discourse.* In contrary-to-fact conditions, subjunctive II forms are used. In indirect discourse, which will be reviewed in Lektion 14, both subjunctive I and II forms are used.

(a) Contrary-to-Fact Conditions in Present Time

Wenn ich Zeit **hätte, ginge** ich ins Kino.
Wenn ich Zeit **hätte, würde** ich ins Kino **gehen.**
If I had time, I'd go to the movies.
Wenn er hier **wäre, wüßten** wir es.
Wenn er hier **wäre, würden** wir es **wissen.**[1]
If he were here, we would know it.

The present subjunctive II is used to express contrary-to-fact conditions in present time. In the result clause, either the present subjunctive II or **würde** (*would*) plus infinitive is used.[2]

Note:

(1) In informal usage, **würde**-forms are usually preferred to the present subjunctive II in the result clause.[3] For auxiliaries and modals, however, the present subjunctive II is generally preferred:

---

[1] As in English, the result clause may precede the conditional clause:

Ich **würde** ins Kino **gehen,** wenn ich Zeit **hätte.**
I'd go to the movies, if I had time.
Wir **würden** es **wissen,** wenn er hier **wäre.**
We would know it, if he were here.

[2] The form **würde** plus infinitive is also called "present conditional."

[3] There are also regional differences: In southern Germany **würde**-forms are more common. In northern Germany, present subjunctive II is favored.

Wenn wir Hilfe bekämen, **müßten** wir nicht so lange arbeiten.
If we were to get help, we wouldn't have to work so long.
Wenn ich einen Wagen hätte, **könnte** ich hinfahren.
If I had a car, I could drive there.

(2) In contrary-to-fact conditions, **wenn** may be omitted, but the finite verb must then be first in the clause, and the result clause is commonly introduced by **so** or **dann:**

Hätte ich Zeit, **so würde ich** ins Kino **gehen.**
If I had time, I'd go to the movies.
Wäre er hier, **dann würden wir** es **wissen.**
If he were here, we would know it.

(b) Contrary-to-Fact Conditions in Past Time

Wenn ich Zeit **gehabt hätte, wäre** ich ins Kino **gegangen.**
Hätte ich Zeit **gehabt,** so **wäre** ich ins Kino **gegangen.**
If I had had time, I'd have gone to the movies.
Wenn er hier **gewesen wäre, hätten** wir es **gewußt.**
Wäre er hier **gewesen,** dann **hätten** wir es **gewußt.**
If he had been here, we'd have known it.

The past subjunctive II is used to express a contrary-to-fact condition in past time. In the result clause, the past subjunctive II is generally preferred to the more cumbersome **würde** plus perfect infinitive.[1]

69. Other Uses of Subjunctive II

(a) Unfulfilled Wishes

Wenn ich nur reich wäre!
Wäre ich nur reich!
If only I were rich!
Wenn ich es (nur) gewußt hätte!
Hätte ich es (nur) gewußt!
If (only) I had known it!

An unfulfilled wish is expressed by a **wenn**-clause with subjunctive II. Present time is expressed by the present subjunctive II; past time, by the past subjunctive II.

[1] The form **würde** plus perfect infinitive (**ich würde gegangen sein**) is also called "perfect conditional."

Likewise, subjunctive II is used in a separate result clause (with a **wenn**-clause merely implied) to express a contrary-to-fact situation or unrealized wish:

Aber ein Bad **hätte** ich gerne.
But I would like a bathroom [if I could get one].
Aber ein Bad **hätte** ich gerne **gehabt.**
But I would have liked a bathroom [if I could have got one].

(b) **Als ob**

Sie tat, **als ob sie krank wäre.**
She acted as though (if) she were ill.
Es war uns, **als ob er uns gesehen hätte.**
It seemed to us as though (if) he had seen us.

Clauses introduced by **als ob** (*as though*, *as if*) require subjunctive II. Present time is expressed by the present subjunctive II; past time, by the past subjunctive II. Note that **ob** may be omitted, with the finite verb directly following **als:**

Sie tat, **als wäre sie krank.**
Es war uns, **als hätte er uns gesehen.**

(c) Could have, should have

Er **hätte** es allein **machen können**!
He could have done it alone.
Sie **hätten** früher **aufhören sollen**!
You should have stopped earlier.

Could have and *should have* are expressed by the past subjunctive II of **können** and **sollen.** Note the double infinitive.

IV. ÜBUNGEN

A. *Verbinden Sie die Satzpaare den Beispielen entsprechend!*

BEISPIELE: Es ist möglich. Ich tue es.
Wenn es möglich wäre, würde ich es tun.
Wenn es möglich wäre, täte ich es.

1. Er ist hier. Ich gebe es ihm.
2. Es ist möglich. Wir verkaufen das alte Haus.

3. Sie hat Fieber. Wir rufen den Arzt.
4. Er reist hier früher ab. Er kommt dort früher an.
5. Er hat einen Wagen. Er fährt nach Oberammergau.
6. Wir haben ein freies Zimmer. Wir geben es ihm.
7. Sie fahren zu schnell. Sie bekommen eine Strafe.
8. Ich weiß es. Ich sage es Ihnen.
9. Das Zimmer hat kein Bad. Ich nehme es nicht.
10. Ich darf reden. Ich schweige trotzdem.

B. *Wiederholen Sie Übung A den Beispielen entsprechend!*

BEISPIELE: Es ist möglich. Ich tue es.
Wäre es möglich, so würde ich es tun.
Wäre es möglich, so täte ich es.

C. *Verbinden Sie die Satzpaare dem Beispiel entsprechend!*

BEISPIEL: Das Wetter ist schöner. Wir machen einen Ausflug.
Wenn das Wetter schöner gewesen wäre, hätten wir einen Ausflug gemacht.

1. Er kommt zeitig. Wir fahren nicht ohne ihn ab.
2. Wir nehmen den längeren Weg. Wir vermeiden den großen Verkehr.
3. Sie nimmt den späteren Zug. Sie kommt erst um Mitternacht an.
4. Er bestellt sein Zimmer voraus. Er hat keine Schwierigkeiten.
5. Sie rufen vorher an. Sie erledigen alles schneller.
6. Wir fahren nicht so schnell. Wir haben keinen Unfall.
7. Sie weiß das. Sie fragt uns nicht.
8. Der Film dauert nicht so lange. Wir kommen früher nach Hause.
9. Er winkt uns nicht. Wir erkennen ihn nicht.
10. Sie helfen uns. Wir werden schneller fertig.

D. *Verbinden Sie die Satzpaare in Übung C dem Beispiel entsprechend!*

BEISPIEL: Das Wetter ist schöner. Wir machen einen Ausflug.
Wäre das Wetter schöner gewesen, so hätten wir einen Ausflug gemacht.

E. *Verbinden Sie die Satzpaare den Beispielen entsprechend!*

BEISPIELE: Ich kaufe das Gemälde. Ich habe Geld.
Ich würde das Gemälde kaufen, wenn ich Geld hätte.

Er kann uns alles erklären. Er ist hier.
Er könnte uns alles erklären, wenn er hier wäre.

1. Er besucht uns öfter. Er hat mehr Zeit.
2. Er lacht. Er hört diese Geschichte.
3. Wir nehmen sie alle mit. Unser Volkswagen ist nicht so klein.
4. Ich fahre schneller. Es ist nicht verboten.
5. Er tut es nicht. Es ist nicht nötig.
6. Ich kann ihn besser verstehen. Er spricht nicht so leise.
7. Er sagt es uns bestimmt. Er weiß es.
8. Du kannst es tun. Du willst.
9. Er ist nicht immer so müde. Er geht früher zu Bett.
10. Ich esse weniger. Ich bin nicht so hungrig.

F. *Verbinden Sie die Satzpaare dem Beispiel entsprechend!*

BEISPIEL: Ich schreibe dir. Ich kenne deine Adresse.
Ich hätte dir geschrieben, wenn ich deine Adresse gekannt hätte.

1. Ich glaube es nicht. Ich sehe es nicht selbst.
2. Wir verstehen das Stück besser. Die Schauspieler sprechen nicht so schnell.
3. Wir haben Zimmer. Er bestellt sie voraus.
4. Sie schreibt uns. Sie vergißt die Adresse nicht.
5. Er bekommt keine Strafe. Er fährt nicht so schnell.
6. Wir kommen früher an. Wir haben keine Panne.
7. Er nimmt den kürzeren Weg. Er kennt ihn.
8. Die Fahrt dauert weniger lange. Wir nehmen die Autobahn.
9. Er spricht nicht solchen Unsinn. Er versteht die Sache.
10. Sie kommt mit. Ich lade sie ein.

G. *Ändern Sie die Sätze den Beispielen entsprechend!*

BEISPIELE: Er ist hier.
Wenn er nur hier wäre!
Wäre er nur hier!

1. Ich bin reich.

2. Sie ist gesund.
3. Sie sind hier.
4. Sie hat viel Geld.
5. Ich habe einen Wagen.
6. Ich kann schwimmen.
7. Ich darf gehen.
8. Wir haben mehr Zeit.
9. Er hat Geduld.
10. Er kommt bald.

H. *Ändern Sie die Sätze den Beispielen entsprechend!*

BEISPIELE: Er ist hier gewesen.
Wenn er nur hier gewesen wäre!
Wäre er nur hier gewesen!

1. Ich habe daran gedacht.
2. Sie hat es mir gesagt.
3. Sie sind etwas länger geblieben.
4. Sie hat mehr Geld gehabt.
5. Ich habe einen Wagen gehabt.
6. Er ist früher gekommen.
7. Es hat nicht geregnet.
8. Wir haben mehr Zeit gehabt.
9. Er hat Geduld gehabt.
10. Ich habe das gewußt.

I. *Verbinden Sie die folgenden Sätze mit* **als ob!**

BEISPIEL: Er tut. Er weiß es nicht.
Er tut, als ob er es nicht wüßte.

1. Wir taten. Er war nicht hier.
2. Es kommt ihm vor. Er hat es schon einmal gesehen.
3. Sie kleidet sich. Sie ist eine Königin.
4. Er sah uns an. Er hatte uns nicht verstanden.
5. Sie tat. Sie hatte es nicht gehört.
6. Er ging an uns vorbei. Er hatte uns nicht gesehen.
7. Es war mir. Ich habe den Film schon einmal gesehen.
8. Trotz der Nachricht lächelte sie. Nichts war geschehen.
9. Es gab einen Lärm. Das ganze Haus stürzte zusammen.

10. Sie war vor ihrer Abreise so aufgeregt. Sie hatte noch nie eine Reise gemacht.

J. *Verbinden Sie die Sätze in Übung I mit* **als!**

BEISPIEL: Er tut. Er weiß es nicht.
Er tut, als wüßte er es nicht.

K. *Gebrauchen Sie sechs der Nützlichen Ausdrücke in ganzen Sätzen!*

L. *Sagen Sie zuerst und schreiben Sie danach auf deutsch!*

1. If I had the time, I'd like very much to go to Darmstadt with you this afternoon.
2. But if I did that, I couldn't finish my work; and that wouldn't be very smart.
3. I know that my friend Rainer wants to go with you.
4. He acts as if he had more time to travel than I.
5. If only I had done my work last night!
6. It would have been easy, but I was lazy and wanted to watch a TV program.
7. If the program had been good, I wouldn't be unhappy.
8. It always seemed as though something interesting were going to happen, but nothing happened.
9. If you could wait until next week, perhaps I could find a car, and we could go to Darmstadt and Heidelberg together.
10. Perhaps it would be better if you went to Darmstadt today; we'll spend a whole day in Heidelberg next week.

Aufsatz

Sie befinden sich mit Ihren Eltern auf einer Ferienreise. Sie kommen gegen Abend in einer Stadt an, in der Sie ein Hotel suchen. Erzählen Sie in einem Aufsatz, in dem Sie auch Konjunktivformen (*subjunctive forms*) gebrauchen:

(1) Ihre Fahrt zum Stadtzentrum;
(2) Ihre Ankunft im Hotel;
(3) Ihr Gespräch mit dem Empfangschef (z.B. über die Lage der Zimmer, ob die Zimmer mit oder ohne Bad sind, über den Preis der Mahlzeiten usw.);
(4) Ihre ersten Eindrücke im Hotel!

Subjunctive in Indirect Discourse.

Lektion 14

I. GESPRÄCH: Besorgungen

FRAU LENZ: Sie scheinen Einkäufe gemacht zu haben. Sie kommen ja mit einem ganzen Haufen Schachteln und Papiertüten daher.

HERBERT: Ich habe heute Gelegenheit gehabt, alle meine Besorgungen zu machen.

FRAU LENZ: Herbert, ich glaubte immer, Sie seien sparsam.

HERBERT: Das bin ich auch. Alles war sehr billig.

FRAU LENZ: Wie können Sie das wissen? Sie haben mir selbst einmal gesagt, Sie hätten keine Ahnung von Preisen.

HERBERT: Es hat mir jemand geholfen. Erika Waiblinger, eine Studienkollegin von Ilse. Ich habe sie angerufen, und sie sagte mir, sie wolle mir München zeigen.

Shopping

MRS. LENZ: You seem to have done some shopping. Here you are with a whole heap of packages and paper bags.

HERBERT: I had the opportunity today to do all my shopping.

MRS. LENZ: Herbert, I always thought you were thrifty.

HERBERT: I am. Everything was very inexpensive.

MRS. LENZ: How can you know that? You told me yourself once that you had no idea about prices.

HERBERT: Somebody helped me. Erika Waiblinger, a fellow student of Ilse's. I telephoned her and she told me she wanted to show me Munich.

FRAU LENZ: Dann hat sie Ihnen die Läden gezeigt! Schön. Was haben Sie denn gekauft?

HERBERT: Ein Paar Lederhosen, sehen Sie!

FRAU LENZ: Für wen sind die? Ich glaubte, in Amerika würde man keine Lederhosen tragen.

HERBERT: Ich schon. Die haben übrigens nur 35 Mark gekostet.

FRAU LENZ: 35 Mark? Das finde ich gar nicht besonders billig.

HERBERT: Aber dieser farbige Pullover, ist der nicht schneidig?

FRAU LENZ: Ja, der ist sehr hübsch. Nach dem Preis will ich nicht fragen.

HERBERT: Der Pullover ist natürlich für den Winter. Aber Erika sagte, man müßte so einen Artikel im Sommer kaufen, denn später würde er viel mehr kosten.

FRAU LENZ: Im Herbst wäre er etwas teuerer, das stimmt. Aber dann hätte man auch eine größere Auswahl in den Läden.

HERR LENZ: Ich weiß nicht, warum du so kritisch bist. Herbert muß ja denken, er hätte alles falsch gemacht.

FRAU LENZ: Er sollte sich nicht von einer Person beraten lassen, die er kaum kennt.

HERBERT: Ich habe mir auch einige Sachen zu meiner Skiausrüstung angeschafft.

MRS. LENZ: And so she showed you the stores! Fine. What did you buy?

HERBERT: A pair of leather shorts, see?

MRS. LENZ: For whom? I thought nobody wore leather shorts in America.

HERBERT: I do. Incidentally, they cost only 35 marks.

MRS. LENZ: 35 marks? I don't think that's especially cheap.

HERBERT: But this colorful sweater, isn't it smart?

MRS. LENZ: Yes, it's very attractive. I won't ask about the price.

HERBERT: Naturally the sweater is for the winter. But Erika said one ought to buy such an article in the summer, because it would cost much more later.

MRS. LENZ: In the fall it would be somewhat more expensive, that's true. But then you'd have a bigger selection in the stores.

MR. LENZ: I don't know why you are so critical. Herbert must think he did everything wrong.

MRS. LENZ: He shouldn't take advice from somebody he scarcely knows.

HERBERT: I also got a few things for my skiing equipment.

HERR LENZ: Und diese Bierkrüge. Die werden wohl Geschenke für Ihre Freunde sein?

HERBERT: Ja. Sie sind etwas groß und wiegen ziemlich viel. Ich will alles zusammen verpacken und mit der Post nach Hause schicken.

HERR LENZ: Das ist gewiß am besten. Gehen Sie ins Büro und sagen Sie, man solle Ihnen eine starke Schachtel und braunes Packpapier geben! Nein, warten Sie, ich komme mit und helfe Ihnen!

MR. LENZ: And these beer mugs. I suppose they are presents for your friends?

HERBERT: Yes. They are a little big and weigh quite a bit. I want to pack everything together and mail it home.

MR. LENZ: That's certainly best. Go to the office and tell them to give you a strong carton and brown wrapping paper. No, wait, I'll come with you and help you.

Fragen

Antworten Sie auf deutsch!

1. Womit ist Herbert nach Hause gekommen?
2. Was hat Frau Lenz von Herbert immer geglaubt?
3. Wer hat Herbert bei seinen Einkäufen geholfen?
4. Was hat sich Herbert in München gekauft?
5. Trägt man Lederhosen in Amerika?
6. Wieviel hat Herbert für seine Lederhosen ausgegeben?
7. Wie findet Herbert seinen Pullover?
8. Warum hat Herbert seinen Pullover im Sommer gekauft?
9. Was für Geschenke hat Herbert für seine Freunde gekauft?
10. Was wird Herbert mit den schweren Sachen tun?
11. Wer wird Herbert beim Verpacken helfen?

Konversation

Fragen Sie Ihren Nachbar,

1. ob er Einkäufe lieber allein oder mit einem Freunde macht! [Ihr Nachbar muß jede Frage beantworten.]
2. in welchem Monat er die meisten Einkäufe macht!
3. was er neulich gekauft hat!
4. ob 35 Mark für ein Paar Lederhosen teuer oder billig ist!
5. wann man gewöhnlich Winterartikel kauft!
6. warum man manchmal Winterartikel im Sommer kauft!
7. für wen er Bierkrüge kaufen würde!
8. was man braucht, um ein Paket zu packen!
9. wann und an wen er das letzte Mal ein Paket mit der Post geschickt hat!

II. NÜTZLICHE AUSDRÜCKE

keine Ahnung von etwas haben	*to have no idea about something*
die Gelegenheit haben	*to have the opportunity*
etwas falsch machen	*to do something the wrong way*
mit der Post schicken	*to send by mail*
nach etwas fragen	*to ask, inquire, about something*
sich beraten lassen	*to take advice*

so ein	*such a*
für so einen Artikel	*for such an article*

III. GRAMMATIK

70. Indirect Discourse

Direct discourse *quotes* the words of a speaker directly. Indirect discourse merely *reports* the same words, with appropriate changes of subject, verb, and pronoun objects.

DIRECT: He said, "We are not ready for you."
INDIRECT: He said (that) they were not ready for us.

German uses the *subjunctive* in indirect discourse to indicate that what is reported or expressed is not necessarily true. Indirect discourse occurs in dependent clauses, usually after verbs like **sagen** (*to say, tell*), **fragen** (*to ask*), **behaupten** (*to claim*), **meinen** (*to have or to express an opinion*), **denken** (*to think, believe*), **glauben** (*to believe*), **hoffen** (*to hope*), **zweifeln** (*to doubt*).

(a) DIRECT: Sie hat gesagt: „Ich gehe gerne ins Theater."
She said, "I like to go to the theater."
INDIRECT: Sie hat gesagt, sie **ginge** (**gehe**) gerne ins Theater.
She said she liked to go to the theater.
DIRECT: Er behauptet: „Ich weiß nichts von der Sache."
He claims, "I don't know anything about it."
INDIRECT: Er behauptet, er **wüßte** (**wisse**) nichts von der Sache.[1]
He claims he doesn't know anything about it.

The present subjunctive is used in indirect discourse if the direct statement was or would have been in the present tense. Either the present subjunctive I or II may be used in indirect discourse, although subjunctive II is generally preferred in conversation and informal writing, except when it is identical with the past indicative, in which case subjunctive I is often favored.

---

[1] Indirect discourse may also be expressed as a **daß**-clause:

Sie sagte, daß sie gerne ins Theater **ginge** (**gehe**).
Er behauptet, daß er nichts von der Sache **wüßte** (**wisse**).

Note that, unlike in English, the tense of the introductory verb has no bearing on the tense of the verb in the dependent clause:

Er sagt, er **wüßte** (**wisse**) nichts von der Sache.
He says he knows nothing about the matter.
Er hat gesagt, er **wüßte** (**wisse**) nichts von der Sache.
He said he knew nothing about the matter.
Er wird gewiß sagen, er **wüßte** (**wisse**) nichts von der Sache.
He will surely say he knows nothing about the matter.

(b) DIRECT: Er sagte: „Ich habe ihn öfter gesehen."
He said, "I have often seen him."
INDIRECT: Er sagte, er **hätte** (**habe**) ihn öfter **gesehen.**
He said he had often seen him.
DIRECT: Sie sagten: „Wir fuhren ziemlich langsam."
They said, "We were driving quite slowly."
INDIRECT: Sie sagten, sie **wären** (**seien**) ziemlich langsam **gefahren.**
They said they were driving quite slowly.

The past subjunctive is used in indirect discourse if the direct statement was or would have been in a past tense.

(c) DIRECT: Sie sagt: „Ich werde morgen kommen."
She says, "I'll come tomorrow."
INDIRECT: Sie sagt, sie **würde** (**werde**) morgen **kommen.**
She says she'll come tomorrow.
DIRECT: Er hat gesagt: „Wir werden gerne mit Ihnen gehen."
He said, "We'll be glad to go with you."
INDIRECT: Er hat gesagt, sie **würden** (**werden**) gerne mit uns **gehen.**
He said they'd be glad to go with us.

To express indirect discourse in the future, use a subjunctive form of **werden.**[1]

---

[1] To express a command in indirect discourse, use **sollte** or **solle** plus infinitive:

Sie schrieb uns, wir **sollten** (**sollen**) ihr sofort **antworten.**
She wrote us to answer her right away.
Er sagte mir, ich **sollte** (**solle**) ihm eine Schachtel **geben.**
He told me to give him a box.

Note that, contrary to English, German uses a full clause to express an indirect command.

Note: Some speakers prefer a present subjunctive to express future time in indirect discourse:

Sie sagt, sie **käme** (**komme**) morgen.
She says she'll come tomorrow.
Er hat gesagt, sie **gingen** (**gehen**) gerne mit uns.
He said they'd be glad to go with us.

71. Indirect Discourse in the Indicative

The indicative is normally used in indirect discourse

(a) when the main clause is in the first person:

Ich habe ihm gesagt, daß ich ihm gerne helfen **will.**
I told him that I'll be glad to help him.
Wir haben ihr geschrieben, daß du krank **bist.**
We wrote to her that you are sick.

(b) when reporting facts:

Er sagt, daß der Bierkrug zwölf Mark **gekostet hat.**
He says the beer mug cost twelve marks.
Sie hat mir gesagt, daß ihre Mutter **gestorben ist.**
She told me that her mother died.

In indirect discourse expressed in the indicative, **daß**-clauses are generally preferred.

Note: The indicative is often favored when the speaker reports a question in indirect discourse:

Sie wollte wissen, was er hier **tut.**
She wanted to know what he's doing here.
Er hat mich gefragt, warum ich nicht kommen **kann.**
He asked me why I can't come.

72. Other Uses of the Subjunctive

(a) In Expressions of Possibility (Subjunctive II)

Der andere Weg **wäre** besser **gewesen.**
The other road would have been better.
Das **würde** ich nicht **tun.**
I wouldn't do that.
Das **könnte** möglich **sein.**
That might be possible.

Subjunctive II forms are used to express possibility. Note that these statements imply an introductory phrase like **Ich glaube** or **Es scheint mir.**

(b) In Expressions of Politeness (Subjunctive II)

Dürfte ich noch eine Tasse Kaffee haben?
May I have another cup of coffee?
Ich **möchte** diese Sachen mit der Post schicken.
I'd like to mail these things.
Sie **sollten** doch nicht so viel arbeiten!
You really shouldn't work so much!
Hätten Sie zufällig jetzt Zeit?
Would you by any chance have time now?

Subjunctive II forms, especially of modals and auxiliaries, are frequently used in set expressions of politeness.[1]

(c) In Wishes (Subjunctive I)

Es **lebe** der König!
Long live the king!
Gott **sei** Dank!
Thank goodness!

(d) In Third-Person Singular and First-Person Plural Commands (Subjunctive I)

Man **beachte** die Regeln!
Observe the rules!
Gehen wir!
Let's go!
Seien wir ehrlich!
Let's be honest!

Note that only the verb **sein** has a plural command form that is distinctively subjunctive.

IV. ÜBUNGEN

A. *Ersetzen Sie die direkte Rede durch die indirekte Rede!*

---

[1] See Lektion 6, Section 32, for other examples of the subjunctive in idiomatic phrases of politeness.

BEISPIELE: Er sagte: „Ich habe kein Geld."
Er sagte, er hätte kein Geld.
Er sagte, er habe kein Geld.

1. Er sagte: „Ich bin krank."
2. Er hat gesagt: „Ich muß nach Stuttgart."
3. Sie haben geantwortet: „Wir können nicht kommen."
4. Er behauptet: „Ich kenne ihn nicht."
5. Er hat gesagt: „Sie hat ein Geschenk mitgebracht."
6. Sie sagt: „Ich kann es nicht verstehen."
7. Er meinte: „Es gibt zwei Möglichkeiten."
8. Er erklärte: „Mein Freund erwartet mich."
9. Sie hat geschrieben: „Es ist sehr heiß in München."
10. Er hat gesagt: „Ich bleibe nur zwei Tage."

B. *Wiederholen Sie die Sätze in Übung A, wobei Sie die Nebensätze mit* **daß** *beginnen!*

BEISPIELE: Er sagte: „Ich habe kein Geld."
Er sagte, daß er kein Geld hätte.
Er sagte, daß er kein Geld habe.

C. *Ersetzen Sie die direkte Rede durch die indirekte Rede!*

BEISPIELE: Sie sagte: „Ich bin ganz langsam gefahren."
Sie sagte, sie wäre ganz langsam gefahren.
Sie sagte, sie sei ganz langsam gefahren.

1. Er sagte: „Ich habe Einkäufe gemacht."
2. Er sagte: „Ich habe viele Geschenke gekauft."
3. Er erzählte: „Erika hat eine große Schachtel getragen."
4. Er erklärte: „Erika ist nicht allein gewesen."
5. Er sagte: „Erika hat es gewollt."
6. Sie sagte: „Er hat es mit der Post geschickt."
7. Sie sagten: „Wir haben keine Zeit dazu gehabt."
8. Sie sagte: „Ich habe ihn im Büro gesehen."
9. Sie sagte: „Er hat immer gerne gesungen."
10. Sie sagten: „Wir haben das Stück schon einmal gesehen."
11. Er sagte: „Ich habe das Hotel nicht gefunden."
12. Sie sagten: „Wir sind ins Theater gegangen."

13. Sie sagten: „Wir haben die Straßenbahn genommen."
14. Er sagte: „Ich habe nur wenig Geld ausgegeben."

D. *Wiederholen Sie die Sätze in Übung C, wobei Sie die Nebensätze mit* **daß** *beginnen!*

BEISPIELE: Sie sagte: „Ich bin ganz langsam gefahren."
Sie sagte, daß sie ganz langsam gefahren wäre.
Sie sagte, daß sie ganz langsam gefahren sei.

E. *Ersetzen Sie die direkte Rede durch die indirekte Rede!*

BEISPIEL: Er sagte: „Ich werde es morgen tun."
Er sagte, er würde es morgen tun.

1. Er versprach mir: „Ich werde es Ihnen schicken."
2. Er sagte: „Das Paket wird bald ankommen."
3. Er meinte: „München wird Ihnen gefallen."
4. Sie versprachen uns: „Wir werden Sie heute nachmittag besuchen."
5. Er schrieb: „Mein Brief wird alles erklären."
6. Sie meinte: „Sie werden es bald genug erfahren."
7. Er hat gesagt: „Ich werde meine Besorgungen machen müssen."
8. Sie sagten: „Er wird viel Freude daran haben."
9. Er erklärte: „Niemand wird es hören."
10. Sie hat geschrieben: „Ich werde Deutsch lernen."

F. *Wiederholen Sie die Sätze in Übung E, wobei Sie die Nebensätze mit* **daß** *beginnen!*

BEISPIEL: Er sagte: „Ich werde es morgen tun."
Er sagte, daß er es morgen tun würde.

G. *Verbinden Sie die Satzpaare und gebrauchen Sie je nach dem Fall den Indikativ oder den Konjunktiv!*

BEISPIELE: Ich wollte wissen. Wie heißt seine Schwester?
Ich wollte wissen, wie seine Schwester heißt.

Sie hatte gehofft. Man wird ihr Bescheid geben.
Sie hatte gehofft, man würde ihr Bescheid geben.

1. Er wünschte. Wir werden mit ihm gehen.
2. Wir haben ihm gesagt. Sie bleibt zu Hause.
3. Sie dachte. Wir haben es schon getan.
4. Er hoffte. Sie wird den Brief rechtzeitig erhalten.
5. Ich habe sie gefragt. Wann ist sie angekommen?
6. Er hat sich vorgestellt. Die Arbeit wird leichter sein.
7. Sie befürchtete. Es wird den ganzen Tag regnen.
8. Wir haben ihnen geschrieben. Wir schicken die Geschenke mit der Post.
9. Man könnte glauben. Er ist Deutscher.
10. Sie hatte gedacht. Du weißt es schon.

H. *Ersetzen Sie die direkten Befehle (commands) durch indirekte!*

BEISPIEL: Ich sagte ihm: „Geben Sie nicht soviel Geld aus!"
Ich sagte ihm, er sollte nicht soviel Geld ausgeben.

1. Ich sagte ihm: „Zeigen Sie mir den anderen Fotoapparat!"
2. Ich sagte ihr: „Hören Sie sofort auf!"
3. Er sagte mir: „Nehmen Sie Platz!"
4. Ich sagte ihm: „Geben Sie mir Kleingeld dafür!"
5. Sie sagte mir: „Schicken Sie das Paket nach Amerika!"
6. Sie sagte uns: „Gehen wir zuerst in das Geschäft an der Ecke!"
7. Wir haben ihm geschrieben: „Senden Sie uns keine Zigaretten mehr!"
8. Er sagte uns: „Sprechen Sie nicht so laut!"
9. Ich sagte ihnen: „Machen Sie Ihre Einkäufe morgen!"
10. Er sagte dir: „Fahre langsamer!"

I. *Gebrauchen Sie sechs der Nützlichen Ausdrücke in ganzen Sätzen!*

J. *Sagen Sie zuerst und schreiben Sie danach auf deutsch!*

1. Mrs. Lenz told me that my purchases were too expensive.
2. But I answered that Erika Waiblinger had told me where to buy them.
3. Erika claimed that sweaters were cheaper in the summer.
4. She said I should buy them in Munich because the selection was better there.

5. When the salesgirl asked me how much I wanted to pay for leather shorts, I answered that I didn't know.
6. Erika thought that I didn't have much money.
7. I said I could pay about 35 marks, and the salesgirl replied that she had a good pair for that price.
8. She explained that Americans had made many purchases in her shop.
9. They said that they found her prices lower than elsewhere.
10. She would have my leather shorts wrapped and mailed to my address in New York.

Aufsatz

Sie tragen ein Paket, das Sie von Deutschland nach Amerika schicken wollen, zur Post. Sie erkundigen sich am Postschalter, und der Beamte gibt Ihnen Auskunft. Schreiben Sie Ihr Gespräch mit dem Beamten nieder! Sie sprechen zum Beispiel über:

(1) das Gewicht des Paketes (etwa 2,5 Kilogramm);
(2) das Porto (mit Luftpost sehr hoch, mit gewöhnlicher Post etwa 15 Mark);
(3) den Inhalt des Paketes und das Formular, das Sie für die Zollkontrolle ausfüllen müssen;
(4) die Dauer der Sendung (etwa 3 bis 4 Wochen).

Cases and Their Functions.

Lektion 15

I. GESPRÄCH: Ein Fußballspiel

HERBERT: Stimmt es wirklich, daß die Deutschen kein Interesse für Fußball haben?

OTTO: Mensch, wer hat Ihnen das gesagt? Fußball[1] ist doch der beliebteste Sport in Deutschland. Wissen Sie nicht, daß Deutschland vor einigen Jahren Weltmeister war?

HERBERT: Verzeihung, aber ich meine Fußball, wie wir ihn in Amerika kennen und spielen.

OTTO: Ach so, Sie meinen Rugby? Nein, das ist bei uns kaum bekannt.

HERBERT: Rugby ist ein englisches Spiel. Aber Sie haben recht, es ist dem amerikanischen Fußball ähnlich.

A Football Game

HERBERT: Is it really true that Germans aren't interested in football?

OTTO: Say, who told you that? Why, football[1] is the most popular sport in Germany. Don't you know that a few years ago Germany was world champion.

HERBERT: Excuse me, but I mean football as we know and play it in America.

OTTO: Oh, you mean rugby? No, that's almost unknown here.

HERBERT: Rugby is an English game. But you're right, it's similar to American football.

[1] German has no special word for American football; hence Herbert's and Otto's confusion over the word **Fußball.**

OTTO: Ich habe mir so ein Spiel einmal im Fernsehen angeschaut. Verstanden habe ich es nicht. Beim Fußball darf niemand den Ball mit den Händen berühren, das heißt niemand außer dem Torwart.

HERBERT: Das weiß ich. Ich habe es auch schon im Fernsehen gesehen.

OTTO: Sie sollten mal zwei wirklich gute Mannschaften spielen sehen! Warten Sie, übermorgen gibt es hier in Frankfurt einen spannenden Kampf. Wollen Sie mitkommen?

HERBERT: Gerne. Vielleicht sollte ich auch Ilse einladen.

OTTO: Das würde ich nicht tun. Frauen interessieren sich kaum für Fußball.

(*Im Stadion.*)

OTTO: Die blauweißen Spieler sind Hertha Berlin, die gelben sind Borussia Dortmund.

HERBERT: Und der schwarzgekleidete Mann ist wohl der Schiedsrichter?

OTTO: Ja, das ist der Mann mit der Pfeife. Wie Sie sehen, unterbricht er das Spiel nur selten.

HERBERT: Wer wird Ihrer Meinung nach gewinnen?

OTTO: I watched one of those games on TV once. I didn't understand it. In soccer nobody is allowed to touch the ball with his hands, that is, except the goalie.

HERBERT: I know that. I, too, have already seen that on TV.

OTTO: You ought to see two really good teams play some time. Wait, day after tomorrow there's an exciting game here in Frankfurt. Do you want to come along?

HERBERT: I'd like to. Perhaps I should also invite Ilse.

OTTO: I wouldn't do that. Women aren't interested in soccer.

(*At the stadium.*)

OTTO: The blue and white players are Hertha Berlin; the yellows are Borussia Dortmund.

HERBERT: And the man in black is presumably the referee?

OTTO: Yes, that's the man with the whistle. As you see, he seldom interrupts the game.

HERBERT: In your opinion, who's going to win?

OTTO: Dortmund, ohne Zweifel. Man sieht doch auf den ersten Blick, daß die Dortmunder den Berlinern weit überlegen sind.

HERBERT: Die Berliner verteidigen sich aber ausgezeichnet. Sehen Sie, jetzt kommt ein Blauweißer mit dem Ball nach vorne, er läuft die Seitenlinie entlang, jetzt stößt er den Ball zur Mitte, und . . .

OTTO: Tor! Ein Tor für die Berliner! Der Spieler in der Mitte hat den Ball mit dem Kopf ins Tor gestoßen. Das hatte ich nicht erwartet.

HERBERT: Alles klatscht. Aber wo bleibt die Musik?

OTTO: Die kommt erst in der Halbzeit.

HERBERT: Das ist aber schade. In Amerika würde jetzt bestimmt die Kapelle spielen.

OTTO: Dortmund, without a doubt. You can see at first glance that the Dortmund players are far superior to the Berliners.

HERBERT: But the Berliners are defending very well. Look, a Blue-White is now running the ball forward, he's running along the sideline, now he kicks the ball to the middle, and . . .

OTTO: Goal! A goal for the Berliners! The player in the middle headed the ball into the net. I hadn't expected that.

HERBERT: Everybody is applauding. But where's the music?

OTTO: We won't have any until half-time.

HERBERT: That's really too bad. In America the band would certainly be playing now.

Fragen

Antworten Sie auf deutsch!

1. Was für eine Art Fußball meint Herbert, wenn er von Fußball spricht?
2. Was versteht Otto unter dem Wort Fußball?
3. Was sagt Otto über die Beliebtheit des Fußballs in Deutschland?
4. Welchem englischen Spiel ist der amerikanische Fußball ähnlich?
5. Welcher Spieler im deutschen Fußball darf den Ball in die Hände nehmen?
6. Warum meint Otto, daß Herbert Ilse nicht einladen sollte?
7. Woran erkennt man den Schiedsrichter sofort?
8. Wer wird Ottos Meinung nach das Fußballspiel gewinnen?
9. Wie hat ein blauweißer Spieler ein Tor erzielt?
10. Wann spielt die Musik bei einem deutschen Fußballspiel?

Konversation

Fragen Sie Ihren Nachbar,

1. welches Wort Otto mißversteht! [Ihr Nachbar muß jede Frage beantworten.]
2. ob der amerikanische Fußball in Deutschland gut bekannt ist!
3. welche Mannschaften Otto und Herbert spielen sehen!
4. welche Mannschaft der anderen überlegen ist!
5. wo Otto einmal ein Rugbyspiel gesehen hat!
6. ob er auch schon ein Fußballspiel in Europa gesehen hat!
7. wie der Schiedsrichter gekleidet ist!
8. an welchen Tagen man in Amerika sportliche Veranstaltungen hat!
9. in welcher Jahreszeit man in Amerika Fußball spielt!
10. was er bei sportlichen Veranstaltungen während der Pause macht!

II. NÜTZLICHE AUSDRÜCKE

Ach so!	*Oh! Oh, I see.*
auf den ersten Blick	*at first sight*
bleiben	*to remain*
Wo bleibt er denn?	*Why isn't he here yet?*

d. h. (**das heißt**) *that is to say, that is*
Interesse haben für (*plus acc.*) *to be interested in*
nach vorne *forward*
recht haben *to be right*
unrecht haben *to be wrong*
schade *too bad; it's a pity*
  Wie schade! *What a pity!*

III. GRAMMATIK

Cases and Their Functions

73. Nominative

Der schwarzgekleidete Mann ist **der Schiedsrichter.**
The man dressed in black is the referee.
Sportliche Veranstaltungen sind hier immer am Sonntag.
Sports events are always on Sundays here.

The nominative is the case of the subject and predicate noun.

74. Genitive

(a) Die Kostüme **der Berliner** sind blauweiß.
The uniforms of the Berliners are blue and white.
Die Freunde **des Spielers** waren alle dort.
The player's friends (*The friends of the player*) *were all there.*

The genitive is the case primarily of possession.

Note: Genitive nouns normally follow the nouns they modify. Genitives of proper names and of nouns denoting family membership precede, as in English, but do not have an apostrophe: **Ottos Fahrrad** (*Otto's bicycle*), **Mutters Geburtstag** (*mother's birthday*).

(b) Ist das Stadion **diesseits** oder **jenseits des Flusses?**
Is the stadium on this side or on that side of the river?
Während der Pause spielt die Kapelle.
During the intermission the band plays.

The genitive is used with the following prepositions:[1]

anstatt	*instead of*
diesseits	*on this side of*
jenseits	*on that side of*
oberhalb	*above*
trotz	*in spite of*
um . . . willen	*for the sake of*
unterhalb	*below*
während	*during*
wegen	*because of*

75. Dative

(a) Er hat es **dem Schiedsrichter** gesagt.
He said it to the referee.
Ich möchte es **meinem Bruder** geben.
I'd like to give it to my brother.

The dative is the case primarily of the indirect object.[2]

Note: The dative also indicates *to whom* or *for whom* something is done:

Er schaute **dem Mädchen** ins Gesicht.
He looked into the girl's face.
Sie hat **ihrem Mann** die Schuhe geputzt.
She cleaned her husband's shoes.
Der Dieb hat **der Frau** alles gestohlen.
The thief stole everything from the woman.
Man hat es **ihm** genommen.
They took it away from him.

---

[1] Genitive phrases before certain adjectives (**fähig** *capable*, **schuldig** *guilty*, etc.) and after certain verbs (**sich erinnern** *to remember*, **sich schämen** *to be ashamed of*, etc.) occur in formal German only. In conversation, prepositional dative and accusative phrases are preferred:

Er ist **an dem Mord schuldig.** (instead of **des Mordes schuldig**)
He is guilty of the murder.
Ich erinnere mich **an seinen Besuch.** (instead of **seines Besuches**)
I remember his visit.

[2] For word-order patterns affecting objects, see the Appendix.

(b) Die Spieler müssen **dem Schiedsrichter gehorchen.**
The players must obey the referee.
Man kann **ihm** nicht **glauben.**
You can't believe him.

The dative is used for the object of the following verbs:

antworten	*to answer*	**gehören**	*to belong*
befehlen	*to command*	**gelingen**	*to succeed*
begegnen	*to meet (by chance)*	**glauben**[1]	*to believe*
danken	*to thank*	**helfen**	*to help*
dienen	*to serve*	**passen**	*to fit, be suitable*
drohen	*to threaten*	**schaden**	*to damage, hurt*
folgen	*to follow*	**scheinen**	*to seem*
gefallen	*to please*	**trauen**	*to trust*
gehorchen	*to obey*		

(c) **Beim Fußball** darf niemand den Ball **mit der Hand** berühren.
In football, nobody is allowed to touch the ball with his hands.
Er stammt **aus einem kleinen Dorf** bei Wien.
He's from a small village near Vienna.

The dative is used with the following prepositions:

aus	*out of, from*
außer	*except*
bei	*at*
entgegen	*toward*
gegenüber	*opposite*
mit	*with*
nach	*after; to, toward; according to*
seit	*since*
von	*from, of*
zu	*to*

Note:

(1) **Nach** in the sense of *according to* frequently follows the noun:

[1] **Glauben** is followed by a dative personal object and an accusative nonpersonal object:

Ich glaube **ihm** nicht.
I don't believe him.
Ich glaube **die Geschichte** nicht.
I don't believe the story.

Meiner Meinung nach hat er unrecht.
In my opinion he's wrong.

(2) **Entgegen** and **gegenüber** usually follow the noun:

Er ging **den Kindern entgegen.**
He went toward the children.
Der Park liegt **dem Hause gegenüber.**
The park is located opposite the house.

(3) **Von** may be used in combination with an adverb, most commonly **an** or **aus:**

Vom ersten Tag an hat er gut gearbeitet.
From the first day on his work has been good.
Vom Fenster aus sieht man den See.
From the window you see the lake.

In constructions like **von . . . an, von . . . aus,** the adverb often merely indicates direction without affecting the meaning of the preposition (compare English *from here on*).

(d) Berlin ist **der anderen Mannschaft überlegen.**
Berlin is superior to the other team.
Das war **dem armen Mann** sehr **angenehm.**
That was very pleasant for the poor man.

The dative is used with certain adjectives, which always follow the noun (or pronoun):

ähnlich	*similar*
angenehm	*pleasant, agreeable*
begreiflich	*comprehensible*
bekannt	*known*
gleich	*like, equal*
möglich	*possible*
nützlich	*useful*
treu	*faithful*
überlegen	*superior*
verwandt	*related*
verständlich	*comprehensible*

76. Accusative

(a) Berlin hat **den Kampf** gewonnen.
Berlin has won the game.

Er stößt **den Ball** zur Mitte.
He kicks the ball to the middle.

The accusative is the case primarily of the direct object.

Note: Two accusative objects may be used after the following verbs:

fragen	*to ask*
heißen	*to call*
kosten	*to cost*
lehren	*to teach*
nennen	*to name*

Die Kinder nennen **ihn ihren Onkel.**
The children call him their uncle.
Seine Mutter hat **ihn das** gelehrt.
His mother taught him that.

(b) **Ohne gute Spieler** kann keine Mannschaft gewinnen.
Without good players no team can win.
Man muß **durch die ganze Stadt** fahren.
You have to drive through the whole city.

The accusative is used with the following prepositions:

bis	*until, up to*
durch	*through*
entlang	*along*
für	*for*
gegen	*against*
ohne	*without*
um	*around*
wider	*against*

Note:

(1) The preposition **bis** is often used adverbially with another preposition (**an, auf, nach, zu,** etc.), which determines the case of the noun:

Er hat **bis zum letzten Tag** gearbeitet.
He worked up to the last day.
Er ist **bis an die Grenze** gefahren.
He drove all the way to the border.
But:
Er ist **bis Weihnachten** geblieben.
He stayed until Christmas.

(2) **Ohne** is frequently used without an article:

Ohne Ball kann man nicht spielen.
You can't play without a ball.

(3) **Entlang** follows the noun:

Er läuft **die Seitenlinie entlang.**
He's running along the sideline.

77. Dative or Accusative

The following prepositions are used with both the dative and the accusative:

an	*at, on*
auf	*on*
hinter	*behind*
in	*in, into*
neben	*near, next to*
über	*over, above, via*
unter	*below, beneath*
vor	*in front of*
zwischen	*between*

The dative expresses location:

Er steht **an der Tür.**
He's standing at the door.
Sie sind **im Zimmer** herumgelaufen.
They ran around in the room.

The accusative expresses motion or direction:

Er ging **an die Tür.**
He went to the door.
Er legt das Buch **auf den Tisch.**
He's laying the book on the table.
Sie kamen **ins Zimmer** hereingelaufen.
They came running into the room.

Note: **Auf** with the accusative is sometimes used with **zu: auf . . . zu** (*to, up to*):

Er ging mit drohender Miene **auf den Schiedsrichter zu.**
He walked up to the referee with a threatening look on his face.

78. Cases in Time Expressions

(a) **Eines Nachmittags** habe ich im Fernsehen ein Rugbyspiel gesehen.
One afternoon I watched a rugby game on TV.
Er ist **eines Abends** plötzlich gekommen.
He suddenly arrived one evening.

The genitive expresses indefinite time.

(b) **Den ganzen Abend** saßen wir vor dem Fernsehapparat.
We sat in front of the TV set the whole evening.
Er mußte **eine Stunde** zu Fuß gehen.
He had to walk for an hour.
Vorigen Monat haben wir ihn in München gesehen.
Last month we saw him in Munich.
Nächsten Sonntag gibt es einen spannenden Fußballkampf.
Next Sunday there'll be an exciting football game.

The accusative expresses definite time and duration.

(c) **Im August** mache ich eine Reise nach Europa.
In August I'm taking a trip to Europe.
Am Sonntag haben wir oft sportliche Veranstaltungen.
On Sundays we often have sports events.
Vor vielen Jahren habe ich selbst Fußball gespielt.
Many years ago I played football myself.

The dative is used with **in, an, vor** to express a point in time.

IV. ÜBUNGEN

A. *Bilden Sie Sätze den Beispielen entsprechend!*

BEISPIELE: Junge, Schüler
Der Junge ist ein Schüler.

Damen, Tanten
Die Damen sind seine Tanten.

1. Mann, Onkel
2. Mädchen, Freundinnen
3. Frauen, Lehrerinnen
4. Arzt, Vater
5. Krankenhaus, großes Gebäude

6. Berliner Mannschaft, gute Mannschaft
7. Bücher, Stolz
8. Löwe, Tier
9. Student, Bruder
10. Musiker, Künstler

B. *Ergänzen Sie die Sätze mit den korrekten Formen der angegebenen Wörter!*

BEISPIEL: Hans ist der Sohn. (mein Freund)
Hans ist der Sohn meines Freundes.

1. Das Vorwort ist der beste Teil. (dieses Buch)
2. Rolf ist der älteste Spieler. (diese Mannschaft)
3. Was ist der Zweck? (seine Rede)
4. Die Augen sind ein Teil. (der Kopf)
5. Die Finger sind Teile. (die Hand)
6. Dieses Gemälde zeigt die Hand. (ein Meister)
7. Wie groß ist die Zahl? (die Einwohner)
8. Wie heißt die Frau? (Ihr Bruder)
9. Jetzt ißt er den Rest. (der Kuchen)
10. Hier ist das Resultat. (meine Versuche)

C. *Ergänzen Sie die Sätze mit den korrekten Formen der angegebenen Wörter!*

BEISPIEL: Er hat die Zeitung verkauft. (der Mann)
Er hat dem Mann die Zeitung verkauft.

1. Der Lehrer erklärt die Lektion. (seine Schüler)
2. Er hat es gesagt. (der Professor)
3. Ich habe einen langen Brief geschrieben. (mein Freund)
4. Wir haben ein kleines Geschenk geschickt. (unser Chef)
5. Sie hat ein Lied gesungen. (ihr Kind)
6. Er hat einen Gefallen getan. (sein Nachbar)
7. Das Spiel hat nicht gefallen. (die Zuschauer)
8. Er hat Blumen geschickt. (seine Mutter)
9. Wir werden eine Uhr kaufen. (unser Vater)
10. Du hast nichts davon gesagt. (deine Freunde)

D. *Ergänzen Sie die Sätze mit den korrekten Formen der angegebenen Wörter!*

BEISPIEL: Er ist sehr dankbar. (sein Helfer)
Er ist seinem Helfer sehr dankbar.

1. Es war nicht möglich. (meine Schwester)
2. Dieses Buch ist ähnlich. (das andere Buch)
3. Die blauen Spieler waren überlegen. (die gelben Spieler)
4. Das war sehr angenehm. (ihr Mann)
5. Er bleibt treu. (seine Freunde)
6. Das Werkzeug war sehr nützlich. (der Arbeiter)
7. Der Entschluß des Sohnes war unbegreiflich. (die Eltern)
8. Das Problem ist wohl bekannt. (der Forscher)
9. Sein neues Buch ist unverständlich. (alle Leser)
10. Diese Prüfung war sehr unangenehm. (alle Studenten)

E. *Bilden Sie neue Sätze dem Beispiel entsprechend!*

BEISPIEL: Er hat gearbeitet. (the whole afternoon)
Er hat den ganzen Nachmittag gearbeitet.

1. Die Zusammenkunft findet statt. (in September)
2. Er hat uns ins Theater eingeladen. (one evening)
3. Ich habe sie angerufen. (half an hour ago)
4. Er ist plötzlich abgereist. (one day)
5. Es gibt ein spannendes Fußballspiel. (next Sunday)
6. Wir haben immer schönes Wetter. (in spring)
7. Wir haben auf ihn gewartet. (one hour)
8. Die Kapelle spielt. (during the intermission)
9. Wir waren in Europa. (last year)
10. Er kommt gewöhnlich. (on Mondays)

F. *Ergänzen Sie die Sätze mit den angegebenen Wörtern!*

BEISPIEL: Er hat angerufen. (während, meine Abwesenheit)
Er hat während meiner Abwesenheit angerufen.

1. Er hat geraucht. (trotz, das Verbot)
2. Haben Sie ihn gesehen? (während, die Pause)
3. Er hat nicht spielen können. (wegen, seine Verletzungen)
4. Im Theater ist ein Lustspiel gegeben worden. (anstatt, das Trauerspiel)
5. Er hat sich ein neues Haus gekauft. (jenseits, der Fluß)
6. Wir sind wach geblieben. (trotz, unsere Müdigkeit)
7. Sie hat geschlafen. (während, die Vorstellung)

8. Er hat Lob dafür bekommen. (anstatt, eine Strafe)
9. Ich habe nicht schlafen können. (wegen, der Lärm)
10. Italien liegt im Süden. (jenseits, die Alpen)

G. *Ergänzen Sie die Sätze mit den angegebenen Wörtern!*

BEISPIEL: Er raucht nicht mehr. (seit, ein halbes Jahr)
Er raucht seit einem halben Jahr nicht mehr.

1. Samstags sind wir nicht gegangen. (zu, die Schule)
2. Sie wohnte in Hamburg. (bei, ihr Onkel)
3. Er wollte es besprechen. (mit, der Schiedsrichter)
4. Gehen Sie jeden Tag? (zu, die Arbeit)
5. Sie sind nicht mehr hier. (seit, zwei Tage)
6. Wir haben die Lieder gelernt. (von, unsere Mutter)
7. Sie hat sich ein Kleid gekauft. (aus, reine Seide)
8. Haben Sie nichts gelesen? (außer, die Dramen von Schiller)
9. Er wohnt in einem neuen Hause. (der Park, gegenüber)
10. Sie ist sofort heimgekehrt. (nach, die Vorstellung)

H. *Ergänzen Sie die Sätze mit den angegebenen Wörtern!*

BEISPIEL: Sie hat ein Geschenk gekauft. (für, ihr Vater)
Sie hat für ihren Vater ein Geschenk gekauft.

1. Man kann nicht spielen. (ohne, ein Ball)
2. Der Spieler ist gelaufen. (auf . . . zu, das Tor)
3. Er hat gearbeitet. (bis auf, der letzte Tag)
4. Sie hat es getan. (gegen, mein Wille)
5. Sie ist hereingekommen. (durch, diese Tür)
6. Er beschloß zu gehen. (ohne, wir)
7. Er hat immer geredet. (gegen, ich)
8. Sie hat nie etwas getan. (für, er)
9. Er ging herum. (um, der ganze Sportplatz)
10. Wir sind gefahren. (der See, entlang)

I. *Ersetzen Sie die Verben in den folgenden Sätzen!*

BEISPIELE: Er ist in der Schule geblieben. (gehen)
Er ist in die Schule gegangen.

Ich habe es auf den Zettel geschrieben. (lesen)
Ich habe es auf dem Zettel gelesen.

1. Sie legte das Buch auf den Stuhl. (bemerken)
2. Sie saß oft in diesem Park. (gehen)
3. Sie kam ans Fenster. (stehen)
4. Der Hund schlief unter dem Tisch. (laufen)
5. Er legte die Decke über das schlafende Kind. (betrachten)
6. Er hat den Wagen hinter das Haus gefahren. (stehenlassen)
7. Mein Onkel wohnt in der Schweiz. (reisen)
8. Er stellte das Radio auf den Tisch. (anstellen)
9. Er klopfte an die Tür. (stehenbleiben)
10. Sie fand den Brief unter ihren Büchern. (schieben)

J. *Ergänzen Sie die Sätze mit den korrekten Formen der angegebenen Pronomen!*

BEISPIEL: Er hat nicht geantwortet. (ich)
Er hat mir nicht geantwortet.

1. Man wird kaum glauben. (sie)
2. Wer kann helfen? (wir)
3. Das schadet nichts. (du)
4. Sie haben gedroht. (er)
5. Hat das gepaßt? (Sie)
6. Das gefällt nicht immer. (wir)
7. Das Experiment ist gelungen. (ich)
8. Was hat er befohlen? (er)
9. Ihr Hund gehorcht immer. (sie)
10. Hat er sofort geantwortet? (du)

K. *Gebrauchen Sie sechs der Nützlichen Ausdrücke in ganzen Sätzen!*

L. *Sagen Sie zuerst und schreiben Sie danach auf deutsch!*

1. Sunday I saw a German soccer game with Otto and another friend.
2. The stadium is on the far side of the river.
3. Otto drove along the river and left the car in a parking lot.
4. At the stadium we ran into other friends.

5. Otto knew they were there, because he had seen them drive into the parking lot.
6. We had followed them through the parking lot and into the stadium.
7. Otto's friend thought the yellow team was far superior to the other team, but what happened? They lost!
8. After the half-time it seemed as if their players couldn't see the ball.
9. Two years ago this team won every game except the last one.
10. The band played only during the intermission and after the end of the game.

Aufsatz

Sie schreiben einen Brief an einen Freund und erzählen darin von einem Fußballspiel, das Sie kürzlich gesehen haben. Sie schreiben zum Beispiel über:

(1) die Beliebtheit dieses Sports in Deutschland;
(2) die Zahl der Spieler in jeder Mannschaft (elf), und wie die Spieler und der Schiedsrichter gekleidet sind;
(3) die Unterschiede zwischen dem amerikanischen und dem deutschen Fußball;
(4) die Zahl der Tore, die jede Mannschaft erzielt hat;
(5) die Stimmung der Zuschauer, und wie Ihnen das Spiel gefallen hat.

Reflexive Verbs;
Impersonal Constructions.

Lektion 16

I. GESPRÄCH: Rheinfahrt

HERR LENZ: Morgen machen wir unsere Rheinfahrt, Herbert. Darauf haben Sie sich doch schon lange gefreut.

HERBERT: Sehr. Hartungs fahren auch mit, nicht wahr?

HERR LENZ: Ja. Wir treffen uns in Mainz, wo wir das Schiff nehmen.

HERBERT: Könnten wir nicht zusammen nach Mainz fahren?

HERR LENZ: Sechs Personen? Mit unserem Opel läßt sich das nicht machen, und Herrn Hartungs Wagen ist ebenfalls zu klein dazu.

HERBERT: Klar. Das hätte ich mir denken sollen!

Trip on the Rhine

MR. LENZ: Tomorrow we'll take our trip on the Rhine, Herbert. You've been looking forward to it for a long time.

HERBERT: Yes indeed. The Hartungs are going along too, aren't they?

MR. LENZ: Yes, we're meeting in Mainz, where we get the boat.

HERBERT: Couldn't we drive to Mainz together?

MR. LENZ: Six people? Can't be done in our Opel, and Mr. Hartung's car is also too small.

HERBERT: Of course. I should have realized it.

HERR LENZ:	Das Schiff fährt um elf Uhr dreißig. Wir werden uns gleich zum Mittagessen in den Speisesaal setzen. Später ist dort kaum mehr Platz zu finden.
HERBERT:	Wo steigen wir aus?
HERR LENZ:	In Bonn. Von dort kommen wir mit der Bahn zurück. (*Auf dem Rheindampfer.*)
HERBERT:	Herrlich, diese Weinberge zu beiden Seiten des Rheins. Und alle paar Minuten zeigt sich auf der Höhe eine Burg oder eine Ruine.

MR. LENZ:	The boat leaves at eleven-thirty. We'll have lunch in the dining room right away. Later there's scarcely a place to be found there.
HERBERT:	Where are we getting off?
MR. LENZ:	In Bonn. From there we'll come back by train. (*On the boat.*)
HERBERT:	Magnificent, these vineyards on both sides of the Rhine. And every few minutes you see a fortress or a ruin on the heights.

ILSE:	Ja, aber bitte fragen Sie mich nicht nach den Namen! Es sind so viele, daß selbst unser Schiffskapitän nicht alle nennen könnte.
HERBERT:	Ihre Mutter hat mir gesagt, sie kenne die Gegend ziemlich gut.
ILSE:	Meine Mutter interessiert sich für Burgen und Schlösser. Glücklicherweise ist sie noch im Speisesaal beim Kaffee, sonst müßten Sie sich die längsten Vorträge über alte Sagen anhören.
HERBERT:	Sagen Sie, sind wir schon an der Loreley vorbei?
ILSE:	Nein. Der Loreleyfelsen kommt erst in fünfzehn oder zwanzig Minuten. Bewahren Sie sich bis dahin noch etwas Film auf! Sie machen ja in einem fort Aufnahmen.

ILSE:	Yes, but please don't ask me for the names. There are so many that even the captain of our ship couldn't name them all.
HERBERT:	Your mother told me she knows the area quite well.
ILSE:	My mother is interested in fortresses and castles. Fortunately she's still having her coffee in the dining room; otherwise you'd have to listen to long lectures about old legends.
HERBERT:	Say, have we already passed the Loreley?
ILSE:	No. We won't reach the Loreley Rock for another fifteen or twenty minutes. Save a little film for then. You're continuously taking pictures.

HERBERT: Ich hatte mir nie vorgestellt, daß auf einem Fluß so viel Verkehr sein könnte. Der Rhein ist ja ganz international. Man sieht Schiffe mit französischen, holländischen und sogar schweizerischen Flaggen. — Übrigens habe ich noch bei weitem genug Film.

ILSE: Lassen Sie mich einmal eine Aufnahme von Ihnen machen, damit Sie später beweisen können, daß Sie auf dem Rhein gefahren sind!

HERBERT: Gerne. Hier ist die Kamera. — Vielen Dank! — Es weht ein kalter Wind hier auf dem oberen Deck. Ich hätte Lust nach einem heißen Getränk.

ILSE: Bedienung gibt es hier oben keine. Wenn Sie eine Tasse Kaffee wollen, müssen Sie sich selbst eine besorgen.

HERBERT: Gehen wir doch hinunter aufs untere Deck!

ILSE: Ja, mich friert jetzt auch ein wenig. — Dort kommt Herr Lenz.

HERR LENZ: Kinder, ich glaube, es wird heute noch regnen. Paßt auf, daß ihr euch nicht erkältet!

HERBERT: I had never imagined there could be so much activity on a river. Why, the Rhine is quite international. You see ships with French, Dutch, and even Swiss flags. — By the way, I still have plenty of film.

ILSE: Let me take a picture of you, so that you can prove later you took a trip on the Rhine.

HERBERT: Gladly. Here's the camera. — Thank you very much! — There's a cold wind blowing here on the upper deck. I feel like having a hot drink.

ILSE: There's no service up here. If you want a cup of coffee, you must get one yourself.

HERBERT: Let's go down to the lower deck.

ILSE: Yes. Now I'm a little cold, too. — There comes Mr. Lenz.

MR. LENZ: Children, I think it will rain before the day is over. Be careful you don't catch cold!

Fragen

Antworten Sie auf deutsch!

1. Mit wem macht Herbert eine Rheinreise?
2. Hat er sich darauf gefreut?
3. Wo werden sich die Familien Hartung und Lenz treffen?
4. Um wieviel Uhr fährt der Rheindampfer?
5. Wie werden die Leute von Bonn zurückkommen?
6. Was sieht man zu beiden Seiten des Rheins?
7. Wer interessiert sich besonders für Burgen und Schlösser?
8. Warum sagt Herbert, der Rhein sei international?
9. Von wem will Ilse eine Aufnahme machen?
10. Was wird Herbert mit dieser Aufnahme beweisen können?

Konversation

Fragen Sie Ihren Nachbar,

1. worauf sich Herbert schon lange gefreut hat! [Ihr Nachbar muß jede Frage beantworten.]
2. wo die Familien Lenz und Hartung das Schiff nehmen!
3. ob das Schiff morgens oder nachmittags abfährt!
4. was Herbert zu beiden Seiten des Rheins sieht!
5. was für Flaggen man auf den Schiffen sieht!
6. warum Bonn eine bekannte Stadt ist!
7. wie lange die Fahrt von Mainz nach Bonn dauert!
8. was er schon von der Loreley gehört hat!
9. ob er auch eine Kamera besitzt — und was für eine!
10. warum Herbert und Ilse das obere Deck verlassen!

II. NÜTZLICHE AUSDRÜCKE

alle — *all*
  alle paar Minuten — *every few minutes*
  alle zwei Wochen — *every two weeks*
beim Kaffee, Essen usw.:
  Sie sagte mir das beim Kaffee. — *She told me that while having coffee.*

bei weitem	*by far*
bei weitem genug	*plenty of*
bei weitem nicht so gut	*not nearly so good*
bis dahin	*until then*
eine Aufnahme machen	*to take a picture*
Lust haben nach etwas	*to want (to have) something*
schon lange	*for a long time (looking backward)*
sich freuen über (*plus acc.*)	*to be pleased with, be happy about*
sich interessieren für	*to be interested in*
zu beiden Seiten	*on both sides*

III. GRAMMATIK

79. Reflexive Verbs

A reflexive verb consists of a basic verb and a pronoun object (reflexive pronoun), which refers back to the subject of the verb. Some verbs, like **sich fürchten** (*to be afraid*), have an accusative reflexive pronoun; others, like **sich denken** (*to imagine*), have a dative reflexive pronoun.

Some reflexive verbs are logical extensions of simple verbs: **waschen** (*to wash*), **sich waschen** (*to wash oneself*); **bedienen** (*to serve*), **sich bedienen** (*to serve oneself*). Others are never used *without* reflexive pronoun: **sich schämen** (*to be ashamed*), **sich befinden** (*to be, feel*). Many German reflexive verbs have non-reflexive English equivalents.

(a) Reflexive Pronouns

ACCUSATIVE		DATIVE	
ich fürchte mich	*I am afraid*	**ich denke mir**	*I imagine*
du fürchtest dich		**du denkst dir**	
er fürchtet sich		**er denkt sich**	
sie fürchtet sich		**sie denkt sich**	
es fürchtet sich		**es denkt sich**	
wir fürchten uns		**wir denken uns**	
ihr fürchtet euch		**ihr denkt euch**	
sie fürchten sich		**sie denken sich**	
Sie fürchten sich		**Sie denken sich**	

Reflexive pronouns are identical with accusative and dative personal pronouns, except for the form **sich** used with the third person singular and plural and the **Sie**-form.

(b) Reflexive Verbs with Accusative Pronoun

Ich habe mich gestern **erkältet.**[1]
I caught cold yesterday.
Er freut sich auf die Rheinfahrt.
He's looking forward to the Rhine trip.

Common reflexive verbs with an accusative (direct) pronoun object are:

sich amüsieren	*to have a good time*
sich anziehen	*to get dressed*
sich ärgern über (*plus acc.*)	*to be angry about*
sich ausruhen	*to rest*
sich ausziehen	*to get undressed*
sich bedienen	*to serve oneself*
sich beeilen	*to hurry*
sich befinden	*to be, feel*
sich benehmen	*to act, behave*
sich bewegen	*to move*
sich entschuldigen	*to excuse oneself, beg pardon*
sich erinnern an (*plus acc.*)	*to remember*
sich erkälten	*to catch cold*
sich erkundigen nach	*to inquire about*
sich fragen	*to wonder*
sich freuen über (*plus acc.*)	*to be happy about*
sich freuen auf (*plus acc.*)	*to look forward to*
sich fürchten vor (*plus dat.*)	*to be afraid of*
sich interessieren für	*to be interested in*
sich irren	*to make a mistake*
sich legen	*to lie down*
sich nähern	*to approach*
sich setzen	*to sit down*
sich verabschieden	*to take leave*

[1] All reflexive verbs have the auxiliary **haben** in the compound past and past perfect:

Ich habe mich beeilt. *I hurried.*
Sie hatten sich genähert. *They had approached.*

sich verlassen auf (*plus acc.*)	*to rely on*
sich vorstellen	*to present oneself*
sich waschen	*to wash oneself, get washed*
sich wundern über (*plus acc.*)	*to be amazed at*

(c) Reflexive Verbs with Dative Pronoun

Ich muß mir etwas Zucker **besorgen.**
I have to get myself some sugar.
Hast du dir weh getan?
Did you hurt yourself?

Common reflexive verbs with dative (indirect) pronoun object are:

sich ansehen	*to look at*
sich aufbewahren	*to save for oneself*
sich besorgen	*to get for oneself*
sich bestellen	*to order*
sich denken	*to imagine*
sich einbilden	*to imagine*
sich helfen	*to help oneself*
sich leisten	*to afford*
sich Sorgen machen um	*to worry about*
sich vorstellen	*to imagine*
sich weh tun	*to hurt oneself*

(d) Emphatic Reflexive Pronouns

1. **Selbst**

Ich habe **mir selbst** weh getan, nicht ihm.
I hurt myself, not him.
Endlich hat die Gastgeberin **sich selbst** bedient.
Finally the hostess served herself.

Selbst (invariable) may follow a reflexive pronoun to intensify its meaning. (English depends upon special stress on the reflexive.)

2. **Einander**

The invariable pronoun **einander** (*one another*) may be substituted for **sich** in the sense of *each other, one another* to avoid ambiguity:

Sie kaufen **sich** Geschenke. (or:) Sie kaufen **einander** Geschenke.
They're buying presents for one another.
Die Kinder waschen **sich.** (but:) Die Kinder waschen **einander.**[1]
The children wash themselves. *The children wash one another.*

80. Impersonal Verbs

Impersonal Verbs have **es** as the grammatical subject and are used only in the third person singular.

(a) **Es blitzt.** *It's lightening.*
Es dämmert. *It's dawning. It's getting dark.*
Es donnert. *It's thundering.*
Es friert. *It's freezing.*
Es hagelt. *It's hailing.*
Es regnet. *It's raining.*
Es schneit. *It's snowing.*
Es ist kalt, heiß usw. *It's cold, hot, etc.*

Many phenomena of nature are expressed by impersonal verbs.

(b) **Es friert mich.**[2] **(Mich friert.)** *I'm cold.*
Es ist mir heiß. **(Mir ist heiß.)** *I'm hot.*
Es ist mir kalt. **(Mir ist kalt.)** *I'm cold.*
Es ist mir übel. **(Mir ist übel.)** *I'm sick.*
Es ist mir warm. **(Mir ist warm.)** *I'm warm.*
Es ist mir wohl. **(Mir ist wohl.)** *I'm well.*
Es hungert mich.[3] **(Mich hungert.)** *I'm hungry.*

Several impersonal verbs express emotions or physical conditions. Note that in many of these expressions **es** may be

---

[1] Note also these other emphatic reflexive expressions with reciprocal meaning:

Sie haben **sich gegenseitig** gelobt.
They praised one another.
Sie haben **einer dem andern** gratuliert.
They congratulated one another.

[2] In everyday German, the verb **frieren** is more commonly used as a personal verb: **Ich friere.** *I'm cold.*

[3] In everyday German, the following personal expressions are more common: **Ich habe Hunger. Ich bin hungrig.**

omitted (especially with first-person pronouns), but the pronoun is then placed before the verb.

(c) **Es gefällt mir nicht,** daß Sie immer Aufnahmen machen.
I don't like your taking pictures continually.
Es tat ihnen leid, daß sie ihm nicht helfen konnten.
They were sorry they couldn't help him.
Es ist mir recht, wenn Sie hier bleiben.
It's all right with me if you stay here.

In a number of phrases the grammatical subject **es** is used to anticipate a dependent clause.[1] The most common of these phrases are:

Es gefällt mir.	*I like.*
Es gelingt mir.	*I succeed.*
Es paßt mir.	*It suits me.*
Es stimmt.	*It's correct.*
Es tut mir leid.	*I'm sorry.*
Es tut mir weh.	*It hurts me.*
Es ist mir recht.	*It suits me.*
Es ist mir lieber (**am liebsten.**)	*I prefer.*

Note that these verbs are also used in personal constructions:

Diese Aufnahmen gefallen mir nicht.
I don't like these pictures.
Die Frau tat ihnen leid.
They felt sorry for the woman.
Das stimmt nicht.
That isn't right.

(d)	**es amüsiert mich**	**ich amüsiere mich**	*I'm amused*
	es ärgert mich	**ich ärgere mich**	*I'm angry, annoyed*
	es freut mich	**ich freue mich**	*I'm glad*
	es fürchtet mich	**ich fürchte mich**	*I'm afraid*

---

[1] Most of such phrases with anticipatory **es** are often followed by an infinitive construction with **zu** if there is no change of subject:

Es gefällt mir nicht, **immer Aufnahmen zu machen.**
I don't like to take pictures all the time.
Es tat ihnen leid, **nicht helfen zu können.**
They were sorry they couldn't help.

es interessiert mich	**ich interessiere mich**	*I'm interested*
es schämt mich	**ich schäme mich**	*I'm ashamed*
es wundert mich	**ich wundere mich**	*I'm amazed*

A number of impersonal verbs have equivalent reflexive constructions:

Es freut ihn, daß Sie gekommen sind.
Er freut sich, daß Sie gekommen sind.
He's happy that you have come.
Es wundert mich, daß er das getan hat.
Ich wundere mich, daß er das getan hat.
I'm amazed that he did that.

Note:

(1) The grammatical subject **es** may be omitted in some expressions (especially with first-person pronouns), but the pronoun then precedes the verb:

Mich ärgert, daß er nicht gekommen ist.
I'm angry that he didn't come.
Mich wundert, daß er das getan hat.
I'm amazed that he did that.

(2) The verbs **klopfen** (*to knock*), **klingeln** (*to ring*), and **läuten** (*to ring*) are used impersonally when no specific subject is expressed:

Es klopft.
Somebody is knocking (at the door).
Es klingelt.
The bell (doorbell) is ringing.
Es hat geläutet.
The bell rang.

(3) The verbs **sich verstehen** (*to be understood*) and **sich handeln um** (*to be a question of*) occur as impersonal reflexives:

Es versteht sich von selbst.
That's understood. (That goes without saying.)
Es handelt sich um seine Zukunft.
It's a question of his future.

81. Anticipatory es

Es weht ein kalter Wind hier oben.
There's a cold wind blowing up here.
Es sind heute abend Gäste gekommen.
Guests came this evening.

To make a statement emphatic, **es** is sometimes used to anticipate the real subject, which then follows the verb. The verb is singular or plural according to the real subject.

82. There is, there are

(a) Es gibt

Es gibt zwei Möglichkeiten.
There are two possibilities.
Es gibt keinen solchen Mann.
There isn't any such man.

Es gibt (*there is*, *there are*), which may be followed by a singular or plural accusative object, expresses mere existence.[1]

(b) Es ist, es sind

Es ist nur ein Junge hier.
There's only one boy here.
Es sind zwanzig Schüler in der deutschen Klasse.
There are twenty students in the German class.

Es ist (*there is*) is followed by a singular subject; **es sind** (*there are*), by a plural subject. Both phrases express specific facts or situations.[2]

---

[1] Note the special use of **es gibt** in phrases like the following:

Es gibt heute Schnee.
It will snow today. We'll have snow today.
Es gibt heute Bohnensuppe.
There's bean soup today. We're having bean soup today.

[2] **Es ist** (**sind**) phrases may also be expressed by a personal construction:

Nur ein Junge ist hier.
Zwanzig Schüler sind in der deutschen Klasse.

(c) Da ist, da sind (dort ist, dort sind)

Da ist unser Hotel!
There's our hotel!
Da sind unsere Freunde.
There are our friends.

Da ist (*there is*), followed by a singular subject, and **da sind** (*there are*), followed by a plural subject, are used to point to something.

IV. ÜBUNGEN

A. *Ändern Sie die Sätze, indem Sie das angegebene Pronomen als Subjekt gebrauchen!*

BEISPIELE: Er ärgert sich. (du)
Du ärgerst dich auch.

Er hat sich geirrt. (wir)
Wir haben uns auch geirrt.

1. Er freut sich. (ich)
2. Er hat sich gefürchtet. (wir)
3. Er hat sich erkältet. (du)
4. Er wird sich amüsieren. (Sie)
5. Er muß sich beeilen. (ihr)
6. Er hat sich vorgestellt. (wir)
7. Er sollte sich ausruhen. (du)
8. Er hat sich erkundigt. (ich)
9. Er erinnert sich nicht. (ihr)
10. Er möchte sich verabschieden. (sie)

B. *Antworten Sie mit „ja"!*

BEISPIEL: Haben Sie sich das Haus angesehen?
Ja, ich habe mir das Haus angesehen.

1. Machen Sie sich Sorgen um ihn?
2. Haben Sie sich das Bild angesehen?
3. Haben Sie sich die Sache anders vorgestellt?

4. Können wir uns einen neuen Wagen leisten?
5. Hat sie sich die Fahrkarte besorgt?
6. Haben Sie sich die ganze Rede angehört?
7. Hat er sich weh getan?
8. Müssen wir uns die Getränke selbst besorgen?
9. Haben Sie sich große Hoffnungen gemacht?
10. Hat er sich diesen Erfolg nur eingebildet?

C. *Ändern Sie die Sätze, indem Sie die angegebenen reflexiven Verben gebrauchen!*

BEISPIELE: Du hast einen Fehler gemacht. (sich irren)
Du hast dich geirrt.

Ich habe die Fahrkarte schon geholt. (sich besorgen)
Ich habe mir die Fahrkarte schon besorgt.

1. Ich habe Abschied genommen. (sich verabschieden)
2. Das Kind hat Angst vor der Nacht. (sich fürchten vor)
3. Du bist immer um ihn besorgt. (sich Sorgen machen um)
4. Wir haben Freude an ihrem Besuch gehabt. (sich freuen über)
5. Ich habe das Gemälde betrachtet. (sich ansehen)
6. Wir haben großes Interesse für Burgen und Schlösser. (sich interessieren für)
7. Sie haben keine Bewegung gemacht. (sich bewegen)
8. Es hat ihn gewundert, daß sie fortgegangen war. (sich wundern)
9. Ich bat um Entschuldigung. (sich entschuldigen)
10. Hast du Schmerzen gehabt? (sich weh tun)

D. *Setzen Sie die Verben ins Perfekt!*

BEISPIEL: Es war mir recht.
Es ist mir recht gewesen.

1. Es war schade.
2. Gefiel es Ihnen?
3. Es tat ihr weh.
4. Ging es ihr gut?

5. Es war mir nicht wohl.
6. Tat es ihm leid?
7. Es interessiert ihn nicht.
8. Es gelang ihnen.
9. Paßte es ihm?
10. Es stimmte nicht.

E. *Ergänzen Sie mit den passenden unpersönlichen oder reflexiven Ausdrücken!*

1. (She is afraid) __________, wenn sie nachts allein ist.
2. (He is glad) ______ immer, wenn man ihn besucht.
3. (I liked) __________, daß er immer pünktlich war.
4. (She was amazed) __________, daß wir es noch nicht wußten.
5. (I was glad) __________, Sie kennenzulernen.
6. (They were sorry) __________, nicht länger bleiben zu können.
7. (I was cold) __________, als ich abends auf ihn warten mußte.
8. (They were annoyed) __________, auf uns warten zu müssen.
9. (He succeeded) __________, alle zu überreden.
10. (It rains and snows) __________ hier oft im Dezember.

F. *Beginnen Sie die Sätze mit* **es**!

BEISPIEL: Ein kalter Wind hat geweht.
Es hat ein kalter Wind geweht.

1. Viele Gäste sind gekommen.
2. Ein großer Lärm entstand.
3. Viel Schnee war gefallen.
4. Ein Unglück ist geschehen.
5. Nur neue Bilder waren ausgestellt.
6. Nichts ist mir eingefallen.
7. Viel Unkraut ist im Garten gewachsen.
8. Niemand hat uns gesehen.

9. Etwas ist mir in den Sinn gekommen.
10. Jemand hat ihm geholfen.

G. *Ergänzen Sie mit den entsprechenden deutschen Formen von „there is, there are"!*

1. ______ mehr Mädchen als Jungen in dieser Klasse.
2. Heute ______ kein Fleisch zum Mittagessen.
3. ______ der Mann, den Sie suchen?
4. ______ in Amerika keine wild lebenden Löwen.
5. Die ganze Familie ist ausgegangen. ______ niemand zu Hause.
6. ______ nur eine einzige Lösung zu diesem Problem.
7. Sie müssen zum Stadtzentrum fahren. Dort ______ die besten Fotogeschäfte.
8. Ich glaube, ______ heute noch Regen.
9. In München ______ viel zu sehen.

H. *Gebrauchen Sie sechs der Nützlichen Ausdrücke in ganzen Sätzen!*

I. *Sagen Sie zuerst und schreiben Sie danach auf deutsch!*

1. Herbert was looking forward to the Rhine trip he was going to take with a few German friends.
2. He was glad that Ilse was with them, because they understood each other very well.
3. Naturally they looked at everything on both banks of the river.
4. Herbert was very interested in the vineyards, but his friend Ilse liked the old castles better.
5. When he inquired about one of the ruins, Ilse's mother gave (halten) a long lecture about the Rhine.
6. He thought to himself that she had read many books about it.
7. There was a very cool wind blowing, and he was cold on deck.
8. He didn't want to catch cold, and so he went to the dining room.
9. There were many Americans on the steamer.
10. They were sorry they couldn't speak German, but they were having a good time nevertheless.

Aufsatz

Sie treffen einen Bekannten, der noch nie mit einem Schiff gefahren ist, und erzählen ihm von einer Rheinfahrt, die Sie kürzlich mit einigen Freunden gemacht haben. — Schreiben Sie in der Form eines Gespräches, wie Sie Ihrem Bekannten Ihre Erlebnisse und Eindrücke vom Rhein schildern! Sie sprechen zum Beispiel über:

(1) die Personen, mit denen Sie die Fahrt gemacht haben;
(2) die Dauer der Fahrt, und wo Sie ein- und ausgestiegen sind;
(3) den Verkehr auf dem Fluß und die Dinge, die Sie zu beiden Seiten des Rheins gesehen haben;
(4) die Erfrischungen, die Sie auf dem Schiff eingenommen haben;
(5) das Wetter;
(6) und ob Ihnen die Fahrt gefallen hat.

The Passive.

Lektion 17

I. GESPRÄCH: Ein Krankenbesuch

FRAU LENZ:	Guten Tag, Ilse. Bitte kommen Sie herein!
ILSE:	Ich danke Ihnen für Ihren Anruf. Wir waren bestürzt zu hören, daß Herbert krank ist.
FRAU LENZ:	Herbert wird sich freuen, Sie zu sehen.
ILSE:	Er wird sich wohl vergangenen Sonntag bei der Rheinfahrt erkältet haben.
FRAU LENZ:	Sehr wahrscheinlich. Er hat gestern den ganzen Tag gehustet, und abends hat er etwas Fieber gehabt.
ILSE:	Haben Sie den Arzt kommen lassen?
FRAU LENZ:	Ich habe unseren Hausarzt, Doktor Roberts, angerufen. Leider ist er diese Woche nicht zu sprechen.

A Sick Call

MRS. LENZ:	Hello, Ilse. Please come in.
ILSE:	Thank you for your call. We were upset to hear that Herbert is ill.
MRS. LENZ:	Herbert will be glad to see you.
ILSE:	He must have caught cold last Sunday on our Rhine trip.
MRS. LENZ:	Very likely. He coughed all day yesterday, and in the evening he had a slight fever.
ILSE:	Have you sent for the doctor?
MRS. LENZ:	I telephoned our family doctor, Dr. Roberts. Unfortunately, he can't be reached this week.

ILSE: Doktor Roberts hat aber einen Stellvertreter, Doktor Jung, der sehr tüchtig sein soll. Ich bin schon von ihm behandelt worden.

FRAU LENZ: Ja, Doktor Jung ist auch gekommen. Er scheint sogar in Amerika studiert zu haben. Jedenfalls hat er mit Herbert nur Englisch gesprochen.

ILSE: Wann war er hier?

FRAU LENZ: Heute morgen. Aber kommen Sie! Hier ist Herberts Zimmer.

ILSE: Herbert! Wie befinden Sie sich?

HERBERT: Danke, es geht mir schon viel besser.

ILSE: Was fehlt Ihnen denn?

HERBERT: Der Arzt sagt, es handelt sich um eine Halsentzündung. Er hat mir eine Einspritzung gegeben — Penicillin oder etwas ähnliches.

ILSE: Müssen Sie auch Pillen schlucken?

HERBERT: Gewiß, gelbe und rote. Und Frau Lenz bringt mir in einem fort Tee.

FRAU LENZ: Mit einem Schluck Tee lassen sich Pillen viel leichter einnehmen.

ILSE: But Dr. Roberts has a substitute, Dr. Jung, who is supposed to be very capable. I've been treated by him already.

MRS. LENZ: Yes, Dr. Jung did come. Apparently he even studied in America. In any case, he spoke only English with Herbert.

ILSE: When was he here?

MRS. LENZ: This morning. But come along. Here is Herbert's room.

ILSE: Herbert! How do you feel?

HERBERT: Thank you. I feel much better already.

ILSE: What's wrong with you?

HERBERT: The doctor says it's a throat infection. He gave me an injection — penicillin or something like that.

ILSE: Do you have to swallow pills, too?

HERBERT: Yes indeed, yellow and red ones. And Mrs. Lenz is always bringing me tea.

MRS. LENZ: Pills can be taken a lot more easily with a sip of tea.

ILSE:	Ich sehe, Sie haben ein offenes Buch auf Ihrem Nachttisch. Was lesen Sie?
HERBERT:	„Die Blechtrommel“, von Günter Grass. Erinnern Sie sich? Der Roman ist mir kürzlich von Ihnen empfohlen worden.
ILSE:	Aber nicht als Lektüre für einen Fieberkranken! „Die Blechtrommel“ ist nicht leicht zu lesen. Sie sollten sich überhaupt nicht anstrengen.
HERBERT:	Ich fühle mich schon gar nicht mehr so krank. Ich glaube sogar, ich habe kein Fieber mehr.
FRAU LENZ:	Gut, aber heute und morgen bleiben Sie mir noch im Bett!
HERBERT:	Morgen? Morgen abend gehe ich mit Ilse ins Konzert.
FRAU LENZ:	Das bezweifle ich. Na, wir werden ja sehen.

ILSE:	I see you have an open book on your night table. What are you reading?
HERBERT:	*The Tin Drum*, by Günter Grass. You remember? You recommended the novel to me recently.
ILSE:	But not for reading by a man sick with a fever. *The Tin Drum* isn't easy to read. You shouldn't exert yourself in any way.
HERBERT:	I don't feel at all that ill anymore. I even believe I don't have a fever anymore.
MRS. LENZ:	Good. But today and tomorrow I do want you to stay in bed.
HERBERT:	Tomorrow? Tomorrow evening I'm going to a concert with Ilse.
MRS. LENZ:	I doubt that. Well, we'll see.

Fragen

Antworten Sie auf deutsch!

1. Von wem hat Ilse erfahren, daß Herbert krank ist?
2. An was für einer Krankheit leidet Herbert?
3. Welchen Arzt wollte Frau Lenz kommen lassen?
4. Warum ist Dr. Jung und nicht Dr. Roberts gekommen?
5. In welcher Sprache hat Dr. Jung mit Herbert geredet?
6. Was hat Herbert vom Arzt bekommen?
7. Welches Getränk nimmt Herbert beim Pillenschlucken?
8. Was für ein Buch sieht Ilse auf Herberts Nachttisch liegen?
9. Von wem ist ihm dieser Roman empfohlen worden?
10. Wie lange sollte Herbert noch im Bett liegen?

Konversation

Fragen Sie Ihren Nachbar,

1. ob er sich oft erkältet! [Ihr Nachbar muß jede Frage beantworten.]
2. wann er das letzte Mal beim Arzt war!
3. ob er immer zum selben Arzt geht!
4. ob er den Arzt gewöhnlich zu sich ins Haus kommen läßt!
5. wie er sich fühlt, wenn er Fieber hat!
6. mit welcher Flüssigkeit er gewöhnlich Pillen einnimmt!
7. was er liest, wenn er krank ist!
8. ob er ein Radio oder einen Fernsehapparat in seinem Zimmer hat!
9. wann er das letzte Mal einen Krankenbesuch gemacht hat!
10. wie der Verfasser des Romans „Die Blechtrommel" heißt!

II. NÜTZLICHE AUSDRÜCKE

es handelt sich um — *it's (a question of), it deals with, concerns*

der Fall — *case*
  jedenfalls — *in any case, anyway*

fehlen — *to be missing*
  Was fehlt Ihnen? — *What's wrong (with you)? What ails you?*

Fieber haben	*to have a temperature, fever*
in einem fort	*continually*
jemand kommen lassen	*to send for a person, have a person come*
nicht zu sprechen sein	*to be unavailable*
Der Arzt ist jetzt nicht zu sprechen.	*The doctor is busy now. (You can't talk with the doctor now.)*

III. GRAMMATIK

83. The Passive

In the active voice, the subject performs the action of the verb; in the passive voice, the subject receives the action of the verb.

gelobt werden (*to be praised*)[1]

PRESENT

ich **werde gelobt**	*I am (being) praised*
du **wirst gelobt**	*you are (being) praised*
er **wird gelobt**	*he is (being) praised*
wir **werden gelobt**	*we are (being) praised*
ihr **werdet gelobt**	*you are (being) praised*
sie **werden gelobt**	*they are (being) praised*

PAST

ich **wurde gelobt**[2] — *I was (being) praised*

FUTURE

ich **werde gelobt werden**[2] — *I will be praised*

COMPOUND PAST

ich **bin gelobt worden**[2] — *I have been praised, I was praised*

PAST PERFECT

ich **war gelobt worden**[2] — *I had been praised*

---

[1] The passive infinitive consists of the infinitive of the auxiliary **werden** and the past participle of the main verb: Sie will gern **gelobt werden.** *She likes to be praised.*

[2] For complete forms, see the Appendix.

The passive consists of a form of the auxiliary **werden** and the past participle of the main verb. Note that the normal past participle of **werden, geworden,** becomes **worden** in the passive compound tenses.[1]

Note:

(1) Das Paket wird **von dem Zollbeamten** aufgemacht.
The parcel is being opened by the customs official.
Das Buch ist mir **von einem Freund** empfohlen worden.
The book was recommended to me by a friend.

The agent of a passive construction (by whom something is done) is expressed by **von** plus dative.

(2) Die Scheune ist **durch Feuer** zerstört worden.
The barn was destroyed by fire.
Ich bin **durch seine letzte Rede** sehr beeinflußt worden.
I was greatly influenced by his last speech.

The instrument of a passive construction (by means of which something is done) is expressed by **durch** plus accusative.

(3) To express a state or condition (also called "apparent passive"), use a form of **sein** plus past participle. Compare:

TRUE PASSIVE	APPARENT PASSIVE
Das Haus **wird verkauft.**	Das Haus **ist verkauft.**
The house is being sold.	*The house is (already) sold.*
Die Türen **wurden geschlossen.**	Die Türen **waren geschlossen.**
The doors were (being) closed.	*The doors were (already) closed.*

---

[1] The verb **werden** has three uses:

(1) as an independent verb meaning *to become:*
Im Winter **wird** es sehr kalt.
In the winter it becomes very cold.

(2) as the auxiliary for the future:
Der Arzt **wird** bald hier **sein.**
The doctor will be here soon.

(3) as the auxiliary for the passive:
Er **wird** von Dr. Jung **behandelt.**
He's being treated by Dr. Jung.

A true passive describes an action in the process of taking place; an apparent passive describes a condition or state that is the result of an earlier passive action.

84. Passive of Verbs with Dative Object

Ihm wurde vom Arzt **geraten,** noch zwei Tage im Bett zu bleiben.
He was advised by the doctor to stay in bed another two days.
Mir ist von niemand **geholfen worden.**
I wasn't helped by anybody.

Verbs that require dative personal objects in active constructions (such as **antworten, glauben, helfen, raten**) do so also in the passive. The impersonal grammatical subject **es** is sometimes expressed:

Es wurde ihm vom Arzt **geraten,** noch zwei Tage im Bett zu bleiben.
Es ist mir von niemand **geholfen worden.**

Note: In conversational German, such passive constructions are often replaced by active constructions:

Der Arzt hat ihm geraten, noch zwei Tage im Bett zu bleiben.
Niemand hat mir geholfen.

85. Impersonal Use of the Passive without Subject

Die ganze Nacht **wurde getanzt und gesungen.**
There was dancing and singing the whole night long.
Hier **ist** von den guten alten Zeiten **gesprochen worden.**
Here there was talk about the good old times. (*Here they talked about the good old times.*)

A passive verb may be used without subject to indicate a general activity.[1] Equivalent active constructions with **man** are:

Man hat die ganze Nacht **getanzt und gesungen.**
Hier **hat man** von den guten alten Zeiten **gesprochen.**

---

[1] The impersonal grammatical subject **es** may introduce such sentences:

Es wurde die ganze Nacht **getanzt und gesungen.**
Es ist von den guten alten Zeiten **gesprochen worden.**

86. Word Order in the Passive

(a) Der Wagen wird morgen **repariert werden.**
The car will be repaired tomorrow.
Gestern ist der Wagen **repariert worden.**
The car was repaired yesterday.

In main clauses the auxiliary infinitive **werden** and the auxiliary past participle **worden** stand in final position, preceded directly by the past participle of the main verb.

(b) Ich weiß nicht, ob der Wagen **repariert worden ist.**
I don't know whether the car has been repaired.
Ich weiß nicht, ob der Wagen **repariert werden kann.**
I don't know whether the car can be repaired.

In dependent clauses the finite verb stands in its usual final position.

87. Substitutes for the Passive

In general, the passive is less frequent in German than in English. It is avoided by the use of various substitute constructions.

(a) **Man** plus Active Verb

PASSIVE	ACTIVE
Hier **wird** Deutsch **gesprochen.** *German is spoken here.*	Hier **spricht man** Deutsch. *German is spoken here.*
Die Türen werden jetzt **geschlossen.** *The doors are being closed now.*	**Man schließt** jetzt **die Türen.** *The doors are being closed now.*
Es ist gestern **getan worden.** *It was done yesterday.*	**Man hat es** gestern **getan.** *It was done yesterday.*

The passive is often replaced by an active verb with the indefinite subject **man,** especially when no agent or instrument is expressed.

(b) **Sein . . . zu** plus Infinitive

Er **ist nicht zu erreichen.**
(instead of) Er **kann nicht erreicht werden.**
He can't be reached.

Nichts **war zu machen.**
(instead of) Nichts **konnte gemacht werden.**
Nothing could be done.
Viele Burgen **waren zu sehen.**
(instead of) Viele Burgen **konnten gesehen werden.**
Many fortresses could be seen.

A passive construction combined with a modal auxiliary (especially **können**) may be replaced by a form of **sein** plus **zu** plus active infinitive.

(c) **Sich lassen** plus Infinitive

Das **läßt sich nicht machen.**
(instead of) Das **kann nicht gemacht werden.**
That can't be done.
Dieses Problem **läßt sich** leicht **lösen.**
(instead of) Dieses Problem **kann** leicht **gelöst werden.**
This problem can be solved easily.

The verb **sich lassen** plus active infinitive may be substituted for a passive construction usually involving the modal **können.**[1]

(d) Reflexive Verbs

Das **versteht sich** von selbst.
(instead of) Das **wird** von selbst **verstanden.**
That's understood. (*That goes without saying.*)
Das **lernt sich** schnell.
(instead of) Das **kann** schnell **gelernt werden.**
That can be learned quickly.

A reflexive verb is sometimes preferred to a passive construction.

---

[1] Note the passive meaning of the infinitive after nonreflexive **lassen:**

Er **wird** seinen Reifen **flicken.**
He'll repair his tire.

Er **läßt** seinen Reifen **flicken.**
He's having his tire repaired.

IV. ÜBUNGEN

A. *Setzen Sie die folgenden Sätze ins Imperfekt!*

1. Ich werde von einem Freunde begleitet.
2. Sie wird von ihrer Tante erzogen.
3. Die zerstörten Häuser werden wieder aufgebaut.
4. Wie wird das gemacht?
5. Wir werden gut bedient.
6. Diese Wahrheit wird oft vergessen.
7. Er wird zum Präsidenten gewählt.
8. Er wird oft geehrt.
9. Die Aufnahmen werden von Ilse gemacht.
10. Das Buch wird ihm empfohlen.

B. *Setzen Sie die Sätze in Übung A ins Perfekt!*

C. *Antworten Sie mit „ja" und gebrauchen Sie das Perfekt!*

BEISPIEL: Wurde er von seinen Eltern gelobt?
Ja, er ist von seinen Eltern gelobt worden.

1. Wurde er ins Krankenhaus gebracht?
2. Wurde er von Doktor Jung behandelt?
3. Wurde er operiert?
4. Wurden seine Freunde benachrichtigt?
5. Wurde er oft von seinen Freunden besucht?
6. Wurde er geheilt?
7. Wurde er letzte Woche entlassen?
8. Wurde er von seiner Frau abgeholt?

D. *Wiederholen Sie Übung C, indem Sie die Antworten mit* **Ich weiß nicht, ob** *beginnen!*

BEISPIEL: Wurde er von seinen Eltern gelobt?
Ich weiß nicht, ob er von seinen Eltern gelobt worden ist.

E. *Setzen Sie die folgenden Sätze ins Passiv!*

BEISPIEL: Mein Vater liest die Abendzeitung.
Die Abendzeitung wird von meinem Vater gelesen.

1. Ein junger Arzt behandelt Herbert.
2. Eine neue Sängerin spielt die Hauptrolle.
3. Viele Leute besuchen die Ausstellung.
4. Seine Freunde lieben ihn.
5. Meine Schwester schrieb beide Briefe.
6. Der Arzt beruhigte den Kranken.
7. Herbert schickte alle diese Pakete.
8. Die Zeitungen verbreiten die Nachricht.
9. Otto repariert den Reifen.
10. Diese Sängerin wird drei Lieder singen.
11. Wann werden Ihre Eltern das Haus verkaufen?

F. *Ändern Sie die passiven Sätze in aktive um, indem Sie* **man** *gebrauchen!*

BEISPIEL: Er ist vergessen worden.
Man hat ihn vergessen.

1. Das wird oft gesagt.
2. Das Haus wird neu angestrichen.
3. Bei uns wird Englisch gesprochen.
4. Das kann sehr schnell gemacht werden.
5. Der Dieb ist in der Nähe der Bank beobachtet worden.
6. Der Reifen muß sofort geflickt werden.
7. Alle Kinder werden nach Hause geschickt werden.
8. Ist ihr geholfen worden?
9. Wurde ihm für seine Arbeit gedankt?
10. Sind Sie richtig beraten worden?

G. *Beantworten Sie die folgenden Fragen dem Beispiel entsprechend!*

BEISPIEL: Kann man dieses Lied oft im Radio hören?
Ja, dieses Lied ist oft im Radio zu hören.

1. Kann man den Arzt sprechen?
2. Soll das Lied sehr schnell gesungen werden?
3. Müssen diese Briefe noch heute geschrieben werden?
4. Kann man dieses Buch in allen Buchhandlungen kaufen?
5. Kann man es ohne große Mühe lesen?
6. Sieht man viele Ruinen am Rhein?
7. Sieht man den See von diesem Fenster aus?

H. *Ersetzen Sie das Passiv durch eine Form von* **sich lassen**!

BEISPIEL: Das Fenster konnte nicht geöffnet werden.
Das Fenster ließ sich nicht öffnen.

1. Dieses Kleid kann nur trocken gereinigt werden.
2. Der Motor konnte nicht in Gang gebracht werden.
3. Das Problem konnte endlich gelöst werden.
4. Diese Suppe kann auch kalt gegessen werden.
5. Dieses Gedicht kann nicht so leicht gelesen werden.
6. So ein Fehler kann leicht gemacht werden.
7. Diese Meinung kann nur schwer vertreten werden.

I. *Ersetzen Sie das Passiv durch die reflexive Form des Verbs!*

BEISPIEL: Die Tür wurde geöffnet.
Die Tür öffnete sich.

1. Die Sache wird bald aufgeklärt werden.
2. Die Tür wurde hinter ihm geschlossen.
3. Die Lösung des Problems wird bald gefunden.
4. Alles ist endlich aufgeklärt worden.
5. Die Nachricht wurde in der ganzen Stadt verbreitet.
6. Die politische Lage ist durch diesen Zwischenfall verschlimmert worden.

J. *Gebrauchen Sie sechs der Nützlichen Ausdrücke in ganzen Sätzen!*

K. *Sagen Sie zuerst und schreiben Sie danach auf deutsch!*

1. Herbert wanted to go to Vienna.
2. His trip to Germany had been planned by his father, but Herbert had planned this tr p to Vienna himself.
3. But now he was sick and had to be treated by a doctor.
4. There was nothing to be done.
5. It goes without saying that he wasn't happy about it.
6. The flight tickets were already paid for and the hotel room was reserved.
7. Unfortunately Herbert had to stay in bed for four or five days.
8. Ilse visited him and was glad that he was being treated by a good doctor.

9. Mrs. Lenz had called Dr. Jung after she was told that Dr. Roberts couldn't be reached.
10. Herbert read a book that had been recommended to him by a friend.

Aufsatz

Sie erhalten die Nachricht, daß einer Ihrer Freunde mit Fieber zu Bett liegt. Sie rufen ihn an, aber die Mutter, die den Anruf annimmt, erklärt Ihnen, daß Ihr Freund eben schläft. Sie gibt Ihnen jedoch Auskunft über sein Befinden. Schreiben Sie das Gespräch mit der Mutter nieder! Sie möchten zum Beispiel wissen,

(1) seit wann Ihr Freund zu Bett liegt;
(2) ob die Krankheit eine Erkältung oder etwas anderes ist und wie lange sie voraussichtlich dauern wird;
(3) von welchem Arzt Ihr Freund behandelt wird und was für eine Medizin er einnehmen muß;
(4) ob Sie ihn besuchen dürfen und ob Sie etwas für ihn tun können. — Sie hoffen, daß Ihr Freund bis übermorgen wieder gesund ist, weil Sie vorhaben, mit ihm zu einem Fußballspiel zu gehen.

Participial Constructions;
Extended Adjective;
Infinitive Phrases.

Lektion 18

I. GESPRÄCH: Überraschende Nachricht

HERBERT: Frau Lenz, ich muß meine Sachen packen.

FRAU LENZ: Wozu denn? Sie haben es doch nicht eilig. Laut Ihrer Flugkarte brauchen Sie erst am zwölften September abzureisen.

HERBERT: Ja, das schon, aber ich fahre vorher noch eine Woche weg.

FRAU LENZ: Herbert! Gefällt es Ihnen nicht mehr bei uns?

HERBERT: Oh doch! Aber ich möchte zum Schluß noch Berlin sehen.

FRAU LENZ: Ach so. Das ist etwas anderes. Das kann ich Ihnen offen gestanden nicht übelnehmen. Berlin sollte man gesehen haben. — Was hat Sie plötzlich zu diesem Entschluß geführt?

Surprising News

HERBERT: Mrs. Lenz, I have to pack my things.

MRS. LENZ: What for? You aren't in any hurry. According to your flight ticket, you needn't leave until the twelfth of September.

HERBERT: That's true, but I'm going away for a week before then.

MRS. LENZ: Herbert! Don't you like it here with us anymore?

HERBERT: Oh, indeed I do. But I'd like to see Berlin before I leave.

MRS. LENZ: Oh. That's different. Frankly, I can't hold that against you. Berlin has to be seen. What made you decide suddenly?

HERBERT: Der eben angekommene Brief.
FRAU LENZ: Von Ihrem Vater. Das habe ich gesehen.
HERBERT: Mein Vater schreibt, daß er nach Deutschland kommt. Er hat geschäftlich in Berlin zu tun.
FRAU LENZ: Das ist allerdings eine Überraschung!
HERBERT: Ich soll ihn am Montag in Berlin treffen.
FRAU LENZ: Wirklich? Er kommt doch hoffentlich auch nach Frankfurt.
HERBERT: Aber gewiß. Wir fliegen zusammen nach New York zurück, aber vorher will er Sie hier besuchen.
FRAU LENZ: Meine Güte! Ich kann es kaum glauben. Mein Mann wird sich auch sehr freuen. Stellen Sie sich vor! Unser längst erhofftes Wiedersehen mit Ihrem Vater wird endlich wahr! — Aber warum hat er uns nicht geschrieben?
HERBERT: Er hat Sie überraschen wollen. Er schreibt, er hätte die Absicht, Sie aus Berlin telefonisch anzurufen.
FRAU LENZ: Na, ich bin froh, daß Sie mich auf diese Überraschung vorbereitet haben.

HERBERT: The letter that just arrived.
MRS. LENZ: From your father. I saw that.
HERBERT: My father writes that he's coming to Germany. He has to be in Berlin on business.
MRS. LENZ: Well, that's a surprise!
HERBERT: I'm supposed to meet him in Berlin Monday.
MRS. LENZ: Really? I hope he's also coming to Frankfurt.
HERBERT: Oh certainly. We'll fly back to New York together, but before that he wants to visit you here.
MRS. LENZ: My goodness! I can scarcely believe it. My husband will also be very happy. Imagine! Seeing your father again, just as we've been hoping for so long, is at last going to come true. But why didn't he write to us?
HERBERT: He wanted to surprise you. He writes that he intends to telephone you from Berlin.
MRS. LENZ: I'm glad you prepared me for this surprise.

HERBERT:	Für mich war es auch eine ganz unerwartete Nachricht. — Doch nun muß ich gleich zum Reisebüro, um die Flugkarte zu bestellen.
FRAU LENZ:	Der Abschied wird uns schwer fallen.
HERBERT:	Ich wäre gerne länger geblieben, aber ich muß Mitte September wieder auf die Universität.
FRAU LENZ:	Ilse wird Sie auch sehr vermissen.
HERBERT:	Wir werden uns schreiben. — Und wir werden uns wiedersehen.
FRAU LENZ:	Ach, Sie kommen nächstes Jahr wieder?
HERBERT:	Nein. Ilse kommt als Austauschstudentin nach Amerika.

HERBERT:	For me, too, it was completely unexpected news. But now I must go at once to the travel bureau to order the flight ticket.
MRS. LENZ:	Saying good-by will be hard.
HERBERT:	I would have liked to stay longer, but I have to go back to the University in the middle of September.
MRS. LENZ:	Ilse will also miss you very much.
HERBERT:	We'll write to each other. — And we'll see each other again.
MRS. LENZ:	Oh, you're coming back next year?
HERBERT:	No. Ilse is coming to America as an exchange student.

Fragen

Antworten Sie auf deutsch!

1. Wann wird Herbert nach Amerika zurückfliegen?
2. Was möchte er vor seinem Rückflug noch sehen?
3. Warum nimmt Frau Lenz es ihm nicht übel, daß er nach Berlin fahren will?
4. Welche überraschende Nachricht steht in dem Brief, den Herbert von seinem Vater erhalten hat?
5. Warum muß Herberts Vater nach Berlin reisen?
6. Weshalb hat er Frau Lenz nichts von dieser Reise geschrieben?
7. Fährt Herbert mit dem Flugzeug oder mit der Bahn nach Berlin?
8. Wann muß Herbert wieder auf die Universität?
9. Wie werden Herbert und Ilse in Verbindung bleiben?
10. Wo werden Herbert und Ilse sich wiedersehen?

Konversation

Fragen Sie Ihren Nachbar,

1. ob er Freunde hat, die ihn oft anrufen! [Ihr Nachbar muß jede Frage beantworten.]
2. wann er zum letzten Mal von seinem Vater einen Brief bekommen hat!
3. ob und warum er als Austauschstudent nach Deutschland gehen möchte!
4. ob er in einer großen oder in einer kleinen deutschen Stadt wohnen würde!
5. ob und warum er Berlin besuchen möchte!
6. ob er in Deutschland Verwandte oder Freunde hat, die er besuchen möchte!
7. wie viele Wochen oder Monate er in Deutschland verbringen möchte!
8. wie lange er vor einer Ferienfahrt zu packen beginnt!
9. wie man heutzutage am schnellsten über den Atlantik reist!
10. wohin er geht, um sich eine Flugkarte zu bestellen!

II. NÜTZLICHE AUSDRÜCKE

das schon	*that's true*
eilig	*hurried*
es eilig haben	*to be in a hurry*
jemand etwas übel nehmen	*to hold something against somebody*
fallen	*to fall*
einem schwer fallen	*to be (emotionally) difficult for somebody*
Es fällt mir schwer.	*It's difficult for me.*
einem leicht fallen	*to be (emotionally) easy for somebody*
Es fällt ihm leicht.	*It's easy for him.*
gestehen	*to admit, confess*
offen gestanden	*frankly, frankly speaking*
Mitte September	*in the middle of September*
in der Mitte der Woche, des Monats	*in the middle of the week, the month*
wahr	*true*
wahr werden	*to come true, become real*
zum Schluß	*at the end; in conclusion*
zu tun haben	*to have something to do*
Er hat geschäftlich zu tun.	*He has business to take care of.*
Er hat amtlich zu tun.	*He has official business (in an office of government).*

III. GRAMMATIK

88. Present Participle

INFINITIVE		PRESENT PARTICIPLE	
spielen	*to play*	**spielend**	*playing*
lächeln	*to smile*	**lächelnd**	*smiling*
hungern	*to be hungry*	**hungernd**	*going hungry*

The present participle is formed by adding **-d** to the infinitive.

89. Uses of Present and Past Participles[1]

(a) As Adjective

Das war eine **überraschende** Nachricht.
That was a surprising bit of news.
Ich habe mein **verlorenes** Buch endlich wieder gefunden.
I've finally found my lost book again.
Die Nachricht war sehr **überraschend.**
The news was very surprising.
Das Kind saß **weinend** auf der Treppe.
The child sat weeping on the stair.

The present and past participles may be used as adjectives, with appropriate adjective endings when preceding a noun.[2]

(b) As Noun-Adjective

Die Sterbende hat ihre Kinder nicht mehr erkannt.
The dying woman no longer recognized her children.
Viele Reisende kommen jedes Jahr nach Deutschland.
Many travelers come to Germany every year.
Der Gerettete konnte seine Dankbarkeit kaum aussprechen.
The man who was saved could scarcely express his gratitude.

The present and past participles may be used as noun-adjectives, with appropriate adjective endings.[3]

Note the following list of common participial noun-adjectives:

die Anwesenden (pl.)	*those present, the audience*
der Angestellte	*the employee*
der Bekannte	*the acquaintance*
der Gefangene	*the prisoner*

---

[1] The main use of the past participle is in the formation of compound tenses. (See Lektionen 2, 3, 13, 14, 17.)

[2] After a verb of motion, German uses the past participle where English uses the present participle:

Die Kinder kamen **gelaufen.**
The children came running.

[3] See Lektion 9, Section 52, for case endings of noun-adjectives.

der Geliebte	*the beloved*
der Reisende	*the traveler*
der Vorsitzende	*the chairman*

(c) In Set Phrases

Offen gestanden bin ich etwas enttäuscht.
Frankly speaking, I am somewhat disappointed
Genau betrachtet ist die Lage gar nicht so schlimm.
On close examination, the situation isn't really so bad.
Vom Westen kommend, hat man die beste Aussicht.
Coming from the west, one has the best view.

As in English, some participles may be used in set phrases.

(d) As Extended Adjective

Der **eben angekommene** Brief ist von meinem Vater.
The letter that just arrived is from my father.
Dies ist eine **auch Sie betreffende** Nachricht.
This is news that concerns you, too.

Participles used as adjectives before a noun may themselves have modifiers, which immediately precede them.[1] Compare the following examples:

ein **vergessener** Dichter
a forgotten poet
ein **längst vergessener** Dichter
a long forgotten poet
ein **seit vielen Jahren vergessener** Dichter
a poet who has been forgotten for many years

Note: Extended adjectives are a striking and typical feature of formal, especially scientific and scholarly, German. In conversation, they may occur in short expressions but are usually replaced by relative clauses:

Eine **auch Sie betreffende** Nachricht. . . .
Eine Nachricht, **die auch Sie betrifft. . . .**

---

[1] Descriptive adjectives may also be "extended," that is, have modifying elements:
Dieser **fast in der ganzen Welt bekannte** Roman ist von Günter Grass.
This novel, which is known almost throughout the world, is by Günter Grass.

90. Infinitive Phrases

(a) Er hatte vergessen **zu schreiben.**
He had forgotten to write.
Er hatte vergessen, den Brief **zu schreiben.**
He had forgotten to write the letter.
Er scheint den Brief **vergessen zu haben.**
He seems to have forgotten the letter.

Most verbs are linked to dependent infinitives by the preposition **zu.** (Compare the English use of *to.*)

Note: After certain verbs, the infinitive is used without **zu:**

Er **hörte** seine Schwester ein Lied **singen.**
He heard his sister sing a song.
Ich **sah** ihn über die Straße **gehen.**
I saw him crossing the street.

The most common verbs followed directly by an infinitive are:[1]

fühlen	*to feel*	**lassen**	*to let, permit*
helfen	*to help*	**sehen**	*to see*
hören	*to hear*	**spüren**	*to feel*

(b) Er ist zum Reisebüro gegangen, **um** sich eine Flugkarte **zu besorgen.**
He went to the travel bureau (in order) to get a flight ticket.
Er wollte nicht nach Amerika zurück, **ohne** Berlin **gesehen zu haben.**
He didn't want to return to America without having seen Berlin.
Er ist nach Berlin gefahren, **anstatt** in Frankfurt **zu bleiben.**
He went to Berlin instead of remaining in Frankfurt.

---

[1] Other verbs directly linked to a dependent infinitive are, of course, the modals, as well as **werden** as auxiliary for the future tense. Remember that **fühlen, hören, lassen, sehen, spüren,** like modals, form a "double infinitive" in compound tenses (see Lektion 4, Section 21):

Er hat ihn **kommen sehen.** *He saw him coming.*

The expressions **um zu, ohne zu,** and **anstatt (statt) zu** are used with an infinitive.[1]

IV. ÜBUNGEN

A. *Ersetzen Sie die Relativsätze durch Partizipien!*

BEISPIEL: Dies ist eine Arbeit, die sehr anstrengt.
Dies ist eine sehr anstrengende Arbeit.

1. Die Geschichte, die nun folgt, ist sehr interessant.
2. Dies ist kein neues Problem für einen Menschen, der denkt.
3. Die Kinder, die spielten, ließen sich nicht stören.
4. Dies war eine Nachricht, die sehr enttäuschte.
5. Der Dichter, der anwesend war, wurde im Laufe des Abends zweimal geehrt.
6. Der Sänger, der jetzt auftritt, ist ein weltberühmter Tenor.
7. Er wartet gespannt auf den Teil, der nun kommt.
8. Die Tiere, die in Europa vorkommen, sind mit wenigen Ausnahmen auch in Amerika bekannt.

B. *Ersetzen Sie die Relativsätze durch Partizipien!*

BEISPIEL: Dies ist ein Buch, das eben veröffentlicht worden ist.
Dies ist ein eben veröffentlichtes Buch.

1. Er hat die Flugkarte, die er verloren hatte, wieder gefunden.
2. Die Postkarte, die eben angekommen ist, ist von seiner Mutter.
3. Er kauft nur Artikel, die schon gebraucht worden sind.
4. Der Soldat, der verwundet war, starb am nächsten Morgen.
5. Er stand vor seinem Haus, das abgebrannt war.

---

[1] Note the position of **zu** with the infinitive of a separable verb:

Er beschloß, sofort zurück**zu**kehren.
He decided to return right away.
Sie kam herein, ohne sich vor**zu**stellen.
She came in without introducing herself.

6. „Faust“ ist ein Stück, das oft gespielt wird.
7. Der Teppich, der gereinigt worden ist, sieht wie neu aus.
8. Sie sprach von ihrem Vater, der kürzlich verstorben ist.
9. Er ist ein Gast, der gern gesehen wird.
10. Der Mann, der schwarz gekleidet ist, ist der Schiedsrichter.

C. *Ersetzen Sie das Attribut durch einen Relativsatz!*

BEISPIEL: Er hat seinen vor einem halben Jahr gekauften Hut noch nie getragen.
Er hat seinen Hut, den er vor einem halben Jahr gekauft hat, noch nie getragen.

1. Die über den Berg führende Straße ist kürzer.
2. Wernher von Braun ist ein auf der ganzen Welt bekannter Forscher.
3. Die aus vielen Filmen bekannte Schauspielerin ist gestern abend in unserem Theater aufgetreten.
4. Im Unterhaltungsprogramm war ein überall mit großem Erfolg auftretendes Trio.
5. Die meisten der im Krieg zerstörten Städte sind wieder aufgebaut worden.
6. Dies ist die am schwersten zu beantwortende Frage.

D. *Verbinden Sie die Satzpaare den Beispielen entsprechend!*

BEISPIELE: Ich sah ihn. Er ging über die Straße.
Ich sah ihn über die Straße gehen.

Er bat seine Schwester. Sie half ihm.
Er bat seine Schwester, ihm zu helfen.

1. Er faßte den Entschluß. Er rauchte nie mehr.
2. Ich hörte sie. Sie arbeitete in der Küche.
3. Sie denkt nie daran. Sie schreibt ihren Freunden.
4. Sie waren alle damit einverstanden. Sie verschoben die Reise.
5. Gestern sah ich sie. Sie rauchte auf der Straße.
6. Dürfte ich Sie bitten? Füllen Sie dieses Formular aus!
7. Es war seine Pflicht. Er warnte uns.
8. Ich half ihm. Er übersetzte den Brief.

9. Es wird mir ein Vergnügen sein. Ich treffe Sie dort.
10. Er hatte die Absicht. Er kehrte noch am selben Tage zurück.

E. *Beantworten Sie die Fragen den Beispielen entsprechend! Gebrauchen Sie die angegebenen Wörter in Ihren Antworten!*

BEISPIELE: Hat er sich verabschiedet? (weggehen, ohne)
Er ist weggegangen, ohne sich zu verabschieden.

Hat sein Vater ihm geholfen? (kommen, um)
Sein Vater ist gekommen, um ihm zu helfen.

1. Hat er Briefe geschrieben? (ins Kino gehen, anstatt)
2. Hat er Ilse eingeladen? (anrufen, um)
3. Ist er nach München gefahren? (zu Hause bleiben, anstatt)
4. Hat er seine Fahrkarte mitgenommen? (zum Bahnhof gehen, ohne)
5. Hat er das Zimmer vorausbestellt? (das Hotel anrufen, um)
6. Hat er Einkäufe gemacht? (ausgehen, um)
7. Hat er viel Geld ausgegeben? (Einkäufe machen, ohne)
8. Hat er die Geschenke mit der Post geschickt? (ein Paket packen, um)
9. Hat er das berühmte Museum besucht? (heimkehren, ohne)
10. Hat er das Fahrrad genommen? (zu Fuß gehen, anstatt)

F. *Gebrauchen Sie sechs der Nützlichen Ausdrücke in ganzen Sätzen!*

G. *Sagen Sie zuerst und schreiben Sie danach auf deutsch!*

1. When Herbert came home, he found a letter that had just arrived.
2. He learned that his father had to be in Berlin on business next week.
3. Instead of staying in Frankfurt, Herbert went to Berlin in order to meet his father there.
4. He wanted to go to Berlin without giving Mrs. Lenz the news about his father.
5. Mrs. Lenz came into the room while he was reading the letter and he tried to hide it.

6. But Mrs. Lenz saw the letter, and his father's unexpected visit to Germany didn't remain a secret anymore.
7. She was glad to know that Herbert's father would not return to New York without first coming to Frankfurt.
8. Their long expected reunion was at last going to come true.
9. Herbert's new German friends were sorry that he was leaving them.
10. There was another surprising bit of news. Ilse was preparing to fly across the Atlantic as an exchange student.
11. Herbert said good-by to his friends, but he promised to write them many letters.

Aufsatz

Sie sind vor einer Woche mit dem Flugzeug aus Deutschland zurückgekehrt. Nun schreiben Sie einem deutschen Freunde einen Brief, in dem Sie ihm von Ihrer Rückreise und Ihrer Ankunft zu Hause berichten. In Ihrem Brief schreiben Sie zum Beispiel:

(1) über den Flug, über das Wetter während des Fluges und ob das Flugzeug bei der Ankunft in Amerika Verspätung hatte;
(2) ob man im Flugzeug Deutsch oder Englisch oder beide Sprachen gesprochen hat;
(3) über die Mahlzeiten, die während des Fluges serviert wurden;
(4) ob ein Film gezeigt wurde oder ob Sie geschlafen oder etwas gelesen haben;
(5) von wem Sie bei der Ankunft am Flughafen empfangen wurden;
(6) wie Sie vom Flughafen nach Hause gefahren sind;
(7) ob Sie glücklich waren, Ihre Eltern, Geschwister und alten Freunde wiederzusehen.

Appendix

91. Syllabication

German words are divided at the end of a line according to units of sound (**Sprechsilben**).

a. A syllable normally begins with a consonant; thus, division occurs before a consonant: **ge-ben, Au-gen, schwei-ze-risch, Li-te-ra-tur.**
b. In a cluster of two or more consonants, the division occurs before the last consonant: **ir-ren, wer-den, Ge-dan-ken, Erb-se.**
c. The combinations **ch, sch, ß, ph,** and **st** are never divided: **ma-chen, wün-schen, hei-ßen, Philoso-phie, Fen-ster, er-ste.**
d. The combination **ck** is divided into **k-k: pak-ken.**
e. Compounds, including words with common prefixes and suffixes, are divided according to components: **Hals-tuch, Park-platz, Aus-druck, her-ein, be-sprechen, Häus-chen.**

92. Punctuation

German punctuation is basically similar to English. Note the following major differences:

(a) The comma is used to set off all dependent clauses, including infinitive clauses that have modifiers:

Der Brief, **den er schrieb,** war voller Fehler.
Ich würde es Ihnen sagen, **wenn ich es wüßte.**
Sie vergaß, **die Fenster zu schließen.**

Note: Simple infinitive phrases are not set off by commas: Es begann **zu regnen.**

(b) Exclamation points are normally used after imperatives: **Folgen Sie mir!**

(c) Quotations are preceded by a colon, and the first quotation mark is written on the line: **Er sagte: „Ich habe genug davon.“**

(d) In numerals, German uses the comma where English uses the period:

1,35 (eins Komma drei fünf) *1.35 (one point three five)*

Spacing alone sets off thousands:

943 185 762 *943,185,762*

The period indicates that a numeral is an ordinal:

der 4. Juli (der vierte Juli) *July 4th*

93. Summary of Word Order

(a) Verb Position

1. Normal Word Order

In normal word order (used in main clauses), the subject stands first, followed by the finite verb and the rest of the predicate. The nonfinite forms of the verb (infinitive and past participle) always stand at the end of a main clause:

Herbert fährt heute nach München.
Herbert is going to Munich today.
Er will Deutschland **besuchen.**
He wants to visit Germany.
Otto ist selten ins Kino **gegangen.**
Otto seldom went to the movies.

Note: When there are two infinitives (double infinitive), the infinitive of the main verb stands last, preceded by the infinitive of the dependent verb:

Er wird Deutschland **besuchen können.**
He will be able to visit Germany.
Er hat Deutschland **besuchen wollen.**
He wanted to visit Germany.

2. Inverted Word Order

In inverted word order (used in main clauses), one element of the predicate stands first, followed by the finite verb, the subject, and the rest of the predicate:

Heute **fährt Herbert** nach München.
Today Herbert is going to Munich.
Diesen Herrn **kenne ich** nicht.
I don't know this gentleman.
Ohne Reisepaß **kann Herbert** seine Reiseschecks nicht **umwechseln.**
Without his passport Herbert cannot exchange his travelers checks.

Note that, as in normal word order, the finite verb stands in second position.

3. Interrogative Word Order

In questions the finite verb precedes the subject, as in English:

Hat sie kein Geld?
Does she have no money?
Mit wem **hat er** gesprochen?
With whom did he speak?

If an interrogative word is used as the subject of the question, the finite verb immediately follows the subject, as in English:

Wer hat diesen Brief geschrieben?
Who wrote this letter?

4. Dependent Word Order

In dependent word order (used in dependent clauses) the finite verb stands at the end of the dependent clause:

Ich höre, daß Herbert heute nach München **fährt.**
I hear Herbert is going to Munich today.
Hier ist die Frau, die uns **helfen will.**
Here's the woman who wants to help us.
Ich weiß nicht, ob er ins Kino **gegangen ist.**
I don't know whether he has gone to the movies.

In a compound tense the infinitive or past participle precedes the finite verb. Observe, however, that a double infinitive always stands last in a clause and the finite verb immediately precedes:

Wir verstehen, warum Herbert nur Deutsch **hat sprechen wollen.**
We understand why Herbert wanted to speak only German.

5. Omission of **wenn, ob, daß**

Wenn

When the dependent conjunction **wenn** is omitted in a conditional clause, the finite form of the verb stands first:

Wenn er hier **wäre,** würden wir es ihm geben.
Wäre er hier, so würden wir es ihm geben.
If he were here, we would give it to him.

Wenn ich das gewußt **hätte,** wäre ich sofort gekommen.
Hätte ich das gewußt, so wäre ich sofort gekommen.
If I had known that, I'd have come immediately.

Ob (in **als ob**)

When the dependent conjunction **ob** is omitted, the finite verb immediately follows **als:**

Er tat, als ob er krank **wäre.**
Er tat, als **wäre** er krank.
He acted as though he were ill.

Er sah uns an, als ob er uns nicht verstanden **hätte.**
Er sah uns an, als **hätte** er uns nicht verstanden.
He looked at us as though he had not understood us.

Daß

When the dependent conjunction **daß** is omitted, the dependent clause has the word order of a main clause, that is, normal or inverted:

Sie behauptet, daß **sie** uns gestern **gesehen hätte.**
Sie behauptet, **sie hätte** uns gestern **gesehen.**
Sie behauptet, gestern **hätte sie** uns **gesehen.**
She claims she saw us yesterday.

(b) Direct and Indirect Objects

1. Two Nouns

An indirect object precedes a direct object when both are nouns. English may or may not follow this word order:

Otto hat **seinem Freund deutsche Zigaretten** gegeben.
Otto gave his friend German cigarettes. (Otto gave German cigarettes to his friend.)

2. Two Pronouns

A direct pronoun object precedes an indirect pronoun object, as in English:

Otto hat **sie ihm** gegeben.
Otto gave them to him.

3. Pronoun and Noun

A pronoun object precedes a noun object, as in English:

Otto hat **sie seinem Freund** gegeben.
Otto gave them to his friend.
Otto hat **ihm deutsche Zigaretten** gegeben.
Otto gave him German cigarettes.

(c) Pronoun Objects Preceding the Subject

A pronoun object normally precedes a noun subject or a polysyllabic pronoun subject in:

1. Questions

Wie hat **ihm der Arzt** geholfen?[1]
How did the doctor help him?
Hat **ihn der Vater** getadelt?
Did his father criticize him?

2. Inverted Word Order

Heute hat **sich unser Lehrer** furchtbar geärgert.
Today our teacher became terribly angry.
Leider hat **ihn niemand** gesehen.[2]
Unfortunately nobody saw him.

[1] But: Wie hat **er ihm** geholfen?
[2] But: Leider hat **sie ihn** gesehen.

3. Dependent Clauses

Es schien, als ob **sich** die beiden freundlich begrüßt hätten.
It seemed as if the two had greeted each other in a friendly way.
Wenn **es mir** die Eltern nicht verbieten, komme ich gerne.
If my parents don't forbid it, I'll be glad to come.

(d) Adverbial Expressions of Time, Manner, Place

Adverbial expressions of time and manner precede adverbial expressions of place:

Er ist **gestern in die Stadt** gegangen.
He went downtown yesterday.
Er ist **mit dem Fahrrad in die Stadt** gefahren.
He went downtown on his bicycle.
Er ist **gestern mit dem Fahrrad in die Stadt** gefahren.
He went downtown yesterday on his bicycle.

(e) Position of **nicht**

1. **Nicht** usually precedes the word it modifies.

a. an infinitive

Ich konnte meine Reiseschecks **nicht umwechseln.**
I couldn't exchange my travelers checks.

b. a past participle

Er ist gestern abend **nicht gekommen.**
He didn't come last night.

c. a predicate noun

Es ist **nicht meine Schwester** gewesen.
It wasn't my sister.

d. a predicate adjective or adverb

Das Wetter war letzte Woche **nicht heiß.**
The weather wasn't hot last week.
Sie hat **nicht lange** gesungen.
She didn't sing very long.

e. a prepositional phrase

Er war **nicht im Wohnzimmer.**
He wasn't in the living room.

f. a separable prefix standing at the end of a clause

Er geht heute **nicht aus.**
He isn't going out today.

g. any sentence element emphatically denied

Er ist **nicht gestern,** sondern vorgestern angekommen.
He did not arrive yesterday but the day before yesterday.

2. **Nicht** negating an entire main clause stands at the end of the clause if the verb is in the present or simple past:

Die Sonne scheint heute **nicht.**
The sun isn't shining today.
Er verstand mich **nicht.**
He didn't understand me.

Nicht negating an entire dependent clause precedes the verb in the present and simple past:

Wir bleiben zu Hause, da die Sonne heute **nicht** scheint.

94. Auxiliary Verbs

	INFINITIVE	
haben	**sein**	**werden**
	PAST PARTICIPLE	
gehabt	gewesen	geworden
	PRESENT INDICATIVE	
ich habe	ich bin	ich werde
du hast	du bist	du wirst
er hat	er ist	er wird
wir haben	wir sind	wir werden
ihr habt	ihr seid	ihr werdet
sie haben	sie sind	sie werden
	SIMPLE PAST	
ich hatte	ich war	ich wurde
du hattest	du warst	du wurdest
er hatte	er war	er wurde
wir hatten	wir waren	wir wurden
ihr hattet	ihr wart	ihr wurdet
sie hatten	sie waren	sie wurden

FUTURE INDICATIVE

ich werde haben	ich werde sein	ich werde werden
du wirst haben	du wirst sein	du wirst werden
er wird haben	er wird sein	er wird werden
wir werden haben	wir werden sein	wir werden werden
ihr werdet haben	ihr werdet sein	ihr werdet werden
sie werden haben	sie werden sein	sie werden werden

COMPOUND PAST

ich habe gehabt	ich bin gewesen	ich bin geworden
du hast gehabt	du bist gewesen	du bist geworden
er hat gehabt	er ist gewesen	er ist geworden
wir haben gehabt	wir sind gewesen	wir sind geworden
ihr habt gehabt	ihr seid gewesen	ihr seid geworden
sie haben gehabt	sie sind gewesen	sie sind geworden

PAST PERFECT

ich hatte gehabt	ich war gewesen	ich war geworden
du hattest gehabt	du warst gewesen	du warst geworden
er hatte gehabt	er war gewesen	er war geworden
wir hatten gehabt	wir waren gewesen	wir waren geworden
ihr hattet gehabt	ihr wart gewesen	ihr wart geworden
sie hatten gehabt	sie waren gewesen	sie waren geworden

FUTURE PERFECT

ich werde gehabt haben	ich werde gewesen sein
du wirst gehabt haben	du wirst gewesen sein
er wird gehabt haben	er wird gewesen sein
wir werden gehabt haben	wir werden gewesen sein
ihr werdet gehabt haben	ihr werdet gewesen sein
sie werden gehabt haben	sie werden gewesen sein

ich werde geworden sein
du wirst geworden sein
er wird geworden sein
wir werden geworden sein
ihr werdet geworden sein
sie werden geworden sein

PRESENT SUBJUNCTIVE I

ich habe	ich sei	ich werde
du habest	du seiest	du werdest
er habe	er sei	er werde
wir haben	wir seien	wir werden
ihr habet	ihr seiet	ihr werdet
sie haben	sie seien	sie werden

PRESENT SUBJUNCTIVE II

ich hätte	ich wäre	ich würde
du hättest	du wärest	du würdest
er hätte	er wäre	er würde
wir hätten	wir wären	wir würden
ihr hättet	ihr wäret	ihr würdet
sie hätten	sie wären	sie würden

PAST SUBJUNCTIVE I

ich habe gehabt	ich sei gewesen	ich sei geworden
du habest gehabt	du seiest gewesen	du seiest geworden
er habe gehabt	er sei gewesen	er sei geworden
wir haben gehabt	wir seien gewesen	wir seien geworden
ihr habet gehabt	ihr seiet gewesen	ihr seiet geworden
sie haben gehabt	sie seien gewesen	sie seien geworden

PAST SUBJUNCTIVE II

ich hätte gehabt	ich wäre gewesen	ich wäre geworden
du hättest gehabt	du wärest gewesen	du wärest geworden
er hätte gehabt	er wäre gewesen	er wäre geworden
wir hätten gehabt	wir wären gewesen	wir wären geworden
ihr hättet gehabt	ihr wäret gewesen	ihr wäret geworden
sie hätten gehabt	sie wären gewesen	sie wären geworden

FUTURE SUBJUNCTIVE

ich werde haben	ich werde sein	ich werde werden
du werdest haben	du werdest sein	du werdest werden
er werde haben	er werde sein	er werde werden
wir werden haben	wir werden sein	wir werden werden
ihr werdet haben	ihr werdet sein	ihr werdet werden
sie werden haben	sie werden sein	sie werden werden

CONDITIONAL

ich würde haben	ich würde sein	ich würde werden
du würdest haben	du würdest sein	du würdest werden
er würde haben	er würde sein	er würde werden
wir würden haben	wir würden sein	wir würden werden
ihr würdet haben	ihr würdet sein	ihr würdet werden
sie würden haben	sie würden sein	sie würden werden

IMPERATIVE

habe!	sei!	werde!
habt!	seid!	werdet!
haben Sie!	seien Sie!	werden Sie!

95. Modal Auxiliaries

dürfen	können	mögen	müssen	sollen	wollen
		PRESENT INDICATIVE			
ich darf	kann	mag	muß	soll	will
du darfst	kannst	magst	mußt	sollst	willst
er darf	kann	mag	muß	soll	will
wir dürfen	können	mögen	müssen	sollen	wollen
ihr dürft	könnt	mögt	müßt	sollt	wollt
sie dürfen	können	mögen	müssen	sollen	wollen
		SIMPLE PAST			
ich durfte	konnte	mochte	mußte	sollte	wollte
du durftest	konntest	mochtest	mußtest	solltest	wolltest
er durfte	konnte	mochte	mußte	sollte	wollte
wir durften	konnten	mochten	mußten	sollten	wollten
ihr durftet	konntet	mochtet	mußtet	solltet	wolltet
sie durften	konnten	mochten	mußten	sollten	wollten

FUTURE INDICATIVE

ich werde dürfen (können mögen, müssen, sollen, wollen), etc.

COMPOUND PAST

ich habe gedurft (gekonnt, gemocht, gemußt, gesollt, gewollt), etc.

PAST PERFECT

ich hatte gedurft (gekonnt, gemocht, gemußt, gesollt, gewollt), etc.

FUTURE PERFECT

ich werde gedurft haben (gekonnt haben, gemocht haben, gemußt haben, gesollt haben, gewollt haben), etc.

PRESENT SUBJUNCTIVE I

dürfen	können	mögen	müssen	sollen	wollen
ich dürfe	könne	möge	müsse	solle	wolle
du dürfest	könnest	mögest	müssest	sollest	wollest
er dürfe	könne	möge	müsse	solle	wolle
wir dürfen	können	mögen	müssen	sollen	wollen
ihr dürfet	könnet	möget	müsset	sollet	wollet
sie dürfen	können	mögen	müssen	sollen	wollen

PRESENT SUBJUNCTIVE II

ich dürfte (könnte, möchte, müßte, sollte, wollte), etc.

PAST SUBJUNCTIVE I

ich habe gedurft (gekonnt, gemocht, gemußt, gesollt, gewollt), etc.

PAST SUBJUNCTIVE II

ich hätte gedurft (gekonnt, gemocht, gemußt, gesollt, gewollt), etc.

FUTURE SUBJUNCTIVE

ich werde dürfen (können, mögen, müssen, sollen, wollen), etc.

CONDITIONAL

ich würde dürfen (können, mögen, müssen, sollen, wollen), etc.

96. Weak (Regular) and Strong (Irregular) Verbs

ACTIVE

INFINITIVE

kaufen	**fahren**
PRESENT PARTICIPLE	
kaufend	fahrend
PAST PARTICIPLE	
gekauft	gefahren
PRESENT INDICATIVE	
ich kaufe	ich fahre
du kaufst	du fährst
er kauft	er fährt
wir kaufen	wir fahren
ihr kauft	ihr fahrt
sie kaufen	sie fahren
SIMPLE PAST	
ich kaufte	ich fuhr
du kauftest	du fuhrst
er kaufte	er fuhr
wir kauften	wir fuhren
ihr kauftet	ihr fuhrt
sie kauften	sie fuhren
FUTURE INDICATIVE	
ich werde kaufen	ich werde fahren
du wirst kaufen	du wirst fahren
er wird kaufen	er wird fahren
wir werden kaufen	wir werden fahren
ihr werdet kaufen	ihr werdet fahren
sie werden kaufen	sie werden fahren

COMPOUND PAST

ich habe gekauft	ich bin gefahren
du hast gekauft	du bist gefahren
er hat gekauft	er ist gefahren
wir haben gekauft	wir sind gefahren
ihr habt gekauft	ihr seid gefahren
sie haben gekauft	sie sind gefahren

PAST PERFECT

ich hatte gekauft	ich war gefahren
du hattest gekauft	du warst gefahren
er hatte gekauft	er war gefahren
wir hatten gekauft	wir waren gefahren
ihr hattet gekauft	ihr wart gefahren
sie hatten gekauft	sie waren gefahren

FUTURE PERFECT

ich werde gekauft haben	ich werde gefahren sein
du wirst gekauft haben	du wirst gefahren sein
er wird gekauft haben	er wird gefahren sein
wir werden gekauft haben	wir werden gefahren sein
ihr werdet gekauft haben	ihr werdet gefahren sein
sie werden gekauft haben	sie werden gefahren sein

PRESENT SUBJUNCTIVE I

ich kaufe	ich fahre
du kaufest	du fahrest
er kaufe	er fahre
wir kaufen	wir fahren
ihr kaufet	ihr fahret
sie kaufen	sie fahren

PRESENT SUBJUNCTIVE II

ich kaufte	ich führe
du kauftest	du führest
er kaufte	er führe
wir kauften	wir führen
ihr kauftet	ihr führet
sie kauften	sie führen

IMPERATIVE

kaufe!	fahre!
kauft!	fahrt!
kaufen Sie!	fahren Sie!

PAST SUBJUNCTIVE I

ich habe gekauft	ich sei gefahren
du habest gekauft	du seiest gefahren
er habe gekauft	er sei gefahren
wir haben gekauft	wir seien gefahren
ihr habet gekauft	ihr seiet gefahren
sie haben gekauft	sie seien gefahren

PAST SUBJUNCTIVE II

ich hätte gekauft	ich wäre gefahren
du hättest gekauft	du wärest gefahren
er hätte gekauft	er wäre gefahren
wir hätten gekauft	wir wären gefahren
ihr hättet gekauft	ihr wäret gefahren
sie hätten gekauft	sie wären gefahren

FUTURE SUBJUNCTIVE

ich werde kaufen	ich werde fahren
du werdest kaufen	du werdest fahren
er werde kaufen	er werde fahren
wir werden kaufen	wir werden fahren
ihr werdet kaufen	ihr werdet fahren
sie werden kaufen	sie werden fahren

CONDITIONAL

ich würde kaufen	ich würde fahren
du würdest kaufen	du würdest fahren
er würde kaufen	er würde fahren
wir würden kaufen	wir würden fahren
ihr würdet kaufen	ihr würdet fahren
sie würden kaufen	sie würden fahren

PASSIVE

INFINITIVE

geliebt werden	**gesehen werden**

PRESENT INDICATIVE

ich werde geliebt	ich werde gesehen
du wirst geliebt	du wirst gesehen
er wird geliebt	er wird gesehen
wir werden geliebt	wir werden gesehen
ihr werdet geliebt	ihr werdet gesehen
sie werden geliebt	sie werden gesehen

SIMPLE PAST

ich wurde geliebt	ich wurde gesehen
du wurdest geliebt	du wurdest gesehen
er wurde geliebt	er wurde gesehen
wir wurden geliebt	wir wurden gesehen
ihr wurdet geliebt	ihr wurdet gesehen
sie wurden geliebt	sie wurden gesehen

FUTURE INDICATIVE

ich werde geliebt werden	ich werde gesehen werden
du wirst geliebt werden	du wirst gesehen werden
er wird geliebt werden	er wird gesehen werden
wir werden geliebt werden	wir werden gesehen werden
ihr werdet geliebt werden	ihr werdet gesehen werden
sie werden geliebt werden	sie werden gesehen werden

COMPOUND PAST

ich bin geliebt worden	ich bin gesehen worden
du bist geliebt worden	du bist gesehen worden
er ist geliebt worden	er ist gesehen worden
wir sind geliebt worden	wir sind gesehen worden
ihr seid geliebt worden	ihr seid gesehen worden
sie sind geliebt worden	sie sind gesehen worden

PAST PERFECT

ich war geliebt worden	ich war gesehen worden
du warst geliebt worden	du warst gesehen worden
er war geliebt worden	er war gesehen worden
wir waren geliebt worden	wir waren gesehen worden
ihr wart geliebt worden	ihr wart gesehen worden
sie waren geliebt worden	sie waren gesehen worden

FUTURE PERFECT

ich werde geliebt worden sein	ich werde gesehen worden sein
du wirst geliebt worden sein	du wirst gesehen worden sein
er wird geliebt worden sein	er wird gesehen worden sein
wir werden geliebt worden sein	wir werden gesehen worden sein
ihr werdet geliebt worden sein	ihr werdet gesehen worden sein
sie werden geliebt worden sein	sie werden gesehen worden sein

PRESENT SUBJUNCTIVE I

ich werde geliebt	ich werde gesehen
du werdest geliebt	du werdest gesehen
er werde geliebt, etc.	er werde gesehen, etc.

PRESENT SUBJUNCTIVE II

ich würde geliebt	ich würde gesehen
du würdest geliebt	du würdest gesehen
er würde geliebt, etc.	er würde gesehen, etc.

PAST SUBJUNCTIVE I

ich sei geliebt worden	ich sei gesehen worden
du seiest geliebt worden	du seiest gesehen worden
er sei geliebt worden, etc.	er sei gesehen worden, etc.

PAST SUBJUNCTIVE II

ich wäre geliebt worden	ich wäre gesehen worden
du wärest geliebt worden	du wärest gesehen worden
er wäre geliebt worden, etc.	er wäre gesehen worden, etc.

CONDITIONAL

ich würde geliebt werden	ich würde gesehen werden
du würdest geliebt werden	du würdest gesehen werden
er würde geliebt werden, etc.	er würde gesehen werden, etc.

97. Reflexive Verbs

sich fürchten	**sich helfen**
PRESENT INDICATIVE	
ich fürchte mich	ich helfe mir
du fürchtest dich	du hilfst dir
er fürchtet sich	er hilft sich
wir fürchten uns	wir helfen uns
ihr fürchtet euch	ihr helft euch
sie fürchten sich	sie helfen sich

For the formation of other tenses, follow the conjugations on pages 259-261.

98. Irregular Verbs

INFINITIVE	SIMPLE PAST	PAST PART.	3RD SG. PRES.
backen (*bake*)	(buk) backte	gebacken	bäckt
befehlen (*command*)	befahl	befohlen	befiehlt
befleißen, sich (*apply oneself*)	befliß	beflissen	
beginnen (*begin*)	begann	begonnen	
beißen (*bite*)	biß	gebissen	

INFINITIVE	SIMPLE PAST	PAST PART.	3RD SG. PRES.
bergen (*hide*)	barg	geborgen	birgt
bersten (*burst*)	barst	ist geborsten	birstet
betrügen (*deceive*)	betrog	betrogen	
beweisen (*prove*)	bewies	bewiesen	
biegen (*bend*)	bog	gebogen	
bieten (*offer*)	bot	geboten	
binden (*bind*)	band	gebunden	
bitten (*beg, request*)	bat	gebeten	
blasen (*blow*)	blies	geblasen	bläst
bleiben (*remain, stay*)	blieb	ist geblieben	
bleichen (*bleach*)	blich	geblichen	
braten (*roast*)	briet	gebraten	brät
brechen (*break*)	brach	gebrochen	bricht
brennen (*burn*)	brannte	gebrannt	
bringen (*bring, take*)	brachte	gebracht	
denken (*think*)	dachte	gedacht	
dreschen (*thrash*)	drosch	gedroschen	drischt
dringen (*penetrate*)	drang	ist gedrungen	
empfangen (*receive*)	empfing	empfangen	empfängt
erlöschen (*go out, become extinct* [*light, flame*])	erlosch	ist erloschen	
erscheinen (*appear*)	erschien	ist erschienen	
erschrecken (*be startled*)	erschrak	ist erschrocken	erschrickt
essen (*eat*)	aß	gegessen	ißt
fahren (*drive, travel*)	fuhr	(ist) gefahren	fährt
fallen (*fall*)	fiel	ist gefallen	fällt
fangen (*catch*)	fing	gefangen	fängt
fechten (*fence; fight*)	focht	gefochten	ficht
finden (*find*)	fand	gefunden	
flechten (*plait, braid*)	flocht	geflochten	flicht
fliegen (*fly*)	flog	(ist) geflogen	
fliehen (*flee*)	floh	ist geflohen	
fließen (*flow*)	floß	ist geflossen	
fressen (*eat*)	fraß	gefressen	frißt
frieren (*be cold; freeze*)	fror	gefroren	
gären (*ferment*)	gor gärte	ist gegoren (gegärt)	
gebären (*give birth to*)	gebar	geboren	gebiert
geben (*give*)	gab	gegeben	gibt
gedeihen (*thrive*)	gedieh	ist gediehen	

INFINITIVE	SIMPLE PAST	PAST PART.	3RD SG. PRES.
gefallen (*please*)	gefiel	gefallen	gefällt
gehen (*go*)	ging	ist gegangen	
gelingen (*succeed*)	gelang	ist gelungen	
gelten (*be worth, be considered*)	galt	gegolten	gilt
genesen (*recover*)	genas	ist genesen	
genießen (*enjoy*)	genoß	genossen	
geschehen (*happen*)	geschah	ist geschehen	geschieht
gestehen (*confess*)	gestand	gestanden	
gewinnen (*win*)	gewann	gewonnen	
gießen (*pour*)	goß	gegossen	
gleichen (*resemble*)	glich	geglichen	
gleiten (*slide, slip*)	glitt	ist geglitten	
glimmen (*glow*)	glomm	geglommen	
graben (*dig*)	grub	gegraben	gräbt
greifen (*grasp, grip*)	griff	gegriffen	
haben (*have*)	hatte	gehabt	hat
halten (*hold; stop*)	hielt	gehalten	hält
hängen (*hang*)	hing	gehangen	hängt
hauen (*beat; hew*)	hieb	gehauen	
heben (*lift, raise*)	hob	gehoben	
heißen (*be called*)	hieß	geheißen	
helfen (*help*)	half	geholfen	hilft
kennen (*know*)	kannte	gekannt	
klimmen (*climb*)	klomm	ist geklommen	
klingen (*sound, tinkle*)	klang	geklungen	
kneifen (*pinch*)	kniff	gekniffen	
kommen (*come*)	kam	ist gekommen	
kriechen (*creep, crawl*)	kroch	ist gekrochen	
laden (*load*)	lud	geladen	lädt
lassen (*let; cause*)	ließ	gelassen	läßt
laufen (*run*)	lief	ist gelaufen	läuft
leiden (*suffer*)	litt	gelitten	
leihen (*lend*)	lieh	geliehen	
lesen (*read*)	las	gelesen	liest
liegen (*lie, be lying*)	lag	gelegen	
lügen (*tell a lie*)	log	gelogen	
mahlen (*grind*)	mahlte	gemahlen	
meiden (*avoid*)	mied	gemieden	
melken (*milk*)	molk (melkte)	gemolken (gemelkt)	

INFINITIVE	SIMPLE PAST	PAST PART.	3RD SG. PRES.
messen (*measure*)	maß	gemessen	mißt
nehmen (*take*)	nahm	genommen	nimmt
nennen (*name, call*)	nannte	genannt	
pfeifen (*whistle*)	pfiff	gepfiffen	
preisen (*praise*)	pries	gepriesen	
quellen (*gush forth*)	quoll	ist gequollen	quillt
raten (*advise; guess*)	riet	geraten	rät
reiben (*rub*)	rieb	gerieben	
reißen (*tear, rend*)	riß	gerissen	
reiten (*ride horseback*)	ritt	(ist) geritten	
rennen (*run*)	rannte	ist gerannt	
riechen (*smell*)	roch	gerochen	
ringen (*struggle, wrestle*)	rang	gerungen	
rinnen (*trickle*)	rann	ist geronnen	
rufen (*call*)	rief	gerufen	
salzen (*salt*)	salzte	gesalzen (gesalzt)	
saufen (*drink*)	soff	gesoffen	
saugen (*suck*)	sog (saugte)	gesogen (gesaugt)	
schaffen (*create*)	schuf	geschaffen	
scheiden (*part*)	schied	geschieden	
scheinen (*shine; seem*)	schien	geschienen	
schelten (*scold*)	schalt	gescholten	schilt
scheren (*shear*)	schor	geschoren	
schieben (*push*)	schob	geschoben	
schießen (*shoot*)	schoß	geschossen	
schlafen (*sleep*)	schlief	geschlafen	schläft
schlagen (*beat, hit, strike*)	schlug	geschlagen	schlägt
schleichen (*sneak*)	schlich	ist geschlichen	
schleifen (*sharpen*)	schliff	geschliffen	
schließen (*close*)	schloß	geschlossen	
schlingen (*sling*)	schlang	geschlungen	
schmeißen (*throw*)	schmiß	geschmissen	
schmelzen (*melt*)	schmolz	(ist) geschmolzen	schmilzt
schneiden (*cut*)	schnitt	geschnitten	
schreiben (*write*)	schrieb	geschrieben	
schreien (*shout, scream*)	schrie	geschrie(e)n	
schreiten (*stride*)	schritt	ist geschritten	
schweigen (*be silent*)	schwieg	geschwiegen	

INFINITIVE	SIMPLE PAST	PAST PART.	3RD SG. PRES.
schwellen (*swell*)	schwoll	ist geschwollen	schwillt
schwimmen (*swim*)	schwamm	(ist) geschwommen	
schwinden (*dwindle*)	schwand	ist geschwunden	
schwingen (*swing*)	schwang	geschwungen	
schwören (*swear*)	schwor (schwörte)	geschworen (geschwört)	
sehen (*see*)	sah	gesehen	sieht
sein (*be*)	war	ist gewesen	ist
senden (*send*)	sandte (sendete)	gesandt (gesendet)	
sieden (*boil, seethe*)	sott (siedete)	gesotten (gesiedet)	
singen (*sing*)	sang	gesungen	
sinken (*sink*)	sank	ist gesunken	
sinnen (*meditate*)	sann	gesonnen	
sitzen (*sit*)	saß	gesessen	
speien (*spit*)	spie	gespie(e)n	
spinnen (*spin*)	spann	gesponnen	
sprechen (*speak*)	sprach	gesprochen	spricht
sprießen (*sprout*)	sproß	ist gesprossen	
springen (*jump*)	sprang	ist gesprungen	
stechen (*prick, sting*)	stach	gestochen	sticht
stehen (*stand*)	stand	gestanden	
stehlen (*steal*)	stahl	gestohlen	stiehlt
steigen (*climb, ascend*)	stieg	ist gestiegen	
sterben (*die*)	starb	ist gestorben	stirbt
stinken (*stink*)	stank	gestunken	
stoßen (*push*)	stieß	gestoßen	stößt
streichen (*stroke; paint*)	strich	gestrichen	
streiten (*fight, quarrel*)	stritt	gestritten	
tragen (*carry; wear*)	trug	getragen	trägt
treffen (*meet; hit*)	traf	getroffen	trifft
treiben (*drive*)	trieb	getrieben	
treten (*kick; step*)	trat	(ist) getreten	tritt
trinken (*drink*)	trank	getrunken	
tun (*do*)	tat	getan	
verbergen (*hide*)	verbarg	verborgen	verbirgt
verbieten (*forbid*)	verbot	verboten	
verderben (*spoil*)	verdarb	verdorben	verdirbt

INFINITIVE	SIMPLE PAST	PAST PART.	3RD SG. PRES.
vergessen (*forget*)	vergaß	vergessen	vergißt
verlieren (*lose*)	verlor	verloren	
vermeiden (*avoid*)	vermied	vermieden	
vermögen (*be able*)	vermochte	vermocht	vermag
verzeihen (*forgive; excuse*)	verzieh	verziehen	
wachsen (*grow*)	wuchs	ist gewachsen	wächst
waschen (*wash*)	wusch	gewaschen	wäscht
weben (*weave*)	wob (webte)	gewoben (gewebt)	
weisen (*show, point to*)	wies	gewiesen	
wenden (*turn*)	wandte (wendete)	gewandt (gewendet)	
werben (*vie, compete*)	warb	geworben	wirbt
werden (*become, get*)	wurde	ist geworden	wird
werfen (*throw*)	warf	geworfen	wirft
wiegen (*weigh*)	wog	gewogen	
winden (*wind*)	wand	gewunden	
wissen (*know*)	wußte	gewußt	weiß
ziehen (*pull; go, march*)	zog	(ist) gezogen	
zwingen (*force*)	zwang	gezwungen	

99. Personal Pronouns

SINGULAR

NOM.	ich	du	er	sie	es	man
GEN.	(meiner)	(deiner)	(seiner)	(ihrer)	(seiner)	—
DAT.	mir	dir	ihm	ihr	ihm	einem
ACC.	mich	dich	ihn	sie	es	einen

PLURAL

NOM.	wir	ihr	sie	Sie
GEN.	(unserer)	(euerer)	(ihrer)	(Ihrer)
DAT.	uns	euch	ihnen	Ihnen
ACC.	uns	euch	sie	Sie

100. Interrogative Pronouns wer and was

NOM.	wer	was
GEN.	wessen	—
DAT.	wem	—
ACC.	wen	was

101. Declension of der and dieser

SINGULAR					
der	die	das	dieser	diese	dieses
des	der	des	dieses	dieser	dieses
dem	der	dem	diesem	dieser	diesem
den	die	das	diesen	diese	dieses

PLURAL (ALL GENDERS)	
die	diese
der	dieser
den	diesen
die	diese

102. Declension of der and welcher as Relative Pronouns

SINGULAR					
der	die	das	welcher	welche	welches
dessen	deren	dessen	—	—	—
dem	der	dem	welchem	welcher	welchem
den	die	das	welchen	welche	welches

PLURAL (ALL GENDERS)	
die	welche
deren	—
denen	welchen
die	welche

103. Der-Words

dieser	*this*	mancher	*many a*
jeder	*each, every* (plural: alle)	solcher	*such a*
jener	*that*	welcher	*which, what*

104. Declension of Ein-Words

SINGULAR			PLURAL (ALL GENDERS)
ein	eine	ein	keine
eines	einer	eines	keiner
einem	einer	einem	keinen
einen	eine	ein	keine

105. Declension of Ein-Words Used as Pronouns (declined like der)

SINGULAR			PLURAL (ALL GENDERS)
einer	eine	eines	keine
eines	einer	eines	keiner
einem	einer	einem	keinen
einen	eine	eines	keine

106. Ein-Words

ein	*a, an*	unser	*our*
kein	*not a, no*	euer	*your*
mein	*my*	ihr	*their*
dein	*your*	Ihr	*your* (conventional)
sein	*his, its*		
ihr	*her, its*		
sein	*its, his, her*		

107. Strong Adjective Endings (Not Preceded by Der- or Ein-Word)

SINGULAR		
gut**er** Kaffee	heiß**e** Suppe	kalt**es** Wasser
gut**en** Kaffees	heiß**er** Suppe	kalt**en** Wassers
gut**em** Kaffee	heiß**er** Suppe	kalt**em** Wasser
gut**en** Kaffee	heiß**e** Suppe	kalt**es** Wasser

PLURAL

gut**e** Männer (Frauen, Kinder)
gut**er** Männer (Frauen, Kinder)
gut**en** Männern (Frauen, Kindern)
gut**e** Männer (Frauen, Kinder)

108. Weak Adjective Endings (After Der-Word)

SINGULAR		
der groß**e** Mann	die schön**e** Frau	das klein**e** Kind
des groß**en** Mannes	der schön**en** Frau	des klein**en** Kindes
dem groß**en** Mann	der schön**en** Frau	dem klein**en** Kind
den groß**en** Mann	die schön**e** Frau	das klein**e** Kind

PLURAL

die gut**en** Männer (Frauen, Kinder)
der gut**en** Männer (Frauen, Kinder)
den gut**en** Männern (Frauen, Kindern)
die gut**en** Männer (Frauen, Kinder)

109. Adjective Endings After Ein-Words

SINGULAR

ein groß**er** Mann	eine schön**e** Frau	ein klein**es** Kind
eines groß**en** Mannes	einer schön**en** Frau	eines klein**en** Kindes
einem groß**en** Mann	einer schön**en** Frau	einem klein**en** Kind
einen groß**en** Mann	eine schön**e** Frau	ein klein**es** Kind

PLURAL

keine gut**en** Männer (Frauen, Kinder)
keiner gut**en** Männer (Frauen, Kinder)
keinen gut**en** Männern (Frauen, Kindern)
keine gut**en** Männer (Frauen, Kinder)

110. Prepositions Used with the Genitive

anstatt, statt	*instead of*	diesseits	*this side of*
trotz	*in spite of*	jenseits	*that side of*
um . . . willen	*for the sake of*	oberhalb	*above*
während	*during*	unterhalb	*below*
wegen	*because of*	innerhalb	*within*
		außerhalb	*outside of*

111. Prepositions Used with the Dative Only

aus	*out of*	mit	*with*
außer	*besides, except*	nach	*after, to, according to*
bei	*near, at (someone's house)*	seit	*since, for (temporal)*
		von	*from, by*
entgegen	*toward*	zu	*to*
gegenüber	*opposite, toward*		

112. Prepositions Used with the Accusative Only

durch	*through, by means of*	ohne	*without*
für	*for*	um	*around, at (time)*
gegen	*against*	wider	*against*

113. Prepositions Used with the Dative or Accusative

an	*on, at, to*	über	*over, above, via*
auf	*on, upon*	unter	*under, among*
hinter	*behind*	vor	*before, in front of*
in	*in, into*	zwischen	*between*
neben	*beside, next to*		

114. Numerals

	CARDINALS	ORDINALS
0	null	
1	eins	der, die, das erste
2	zwei	zweite
3	drei	dritte
4	vier	vierte
5	fünf	fünfte
6	sechs	sechste
7	sieben	sieb(en)te
8	acht	achte
9	neun	neunte
10	zehn	zehnte
11	elf	elfte
12	zwölf	zwölfte
13	dreizehn	dreizehnte
14	vierzehn	vierzehnte
15	fünfzehn	fünfzehnte
16	sechzehn	sechzehnte
17	siebzehn	siebzehnte
18	achtzehn	achtzehnte
19	neunzehn	neunzehnte
20	zwanzig	zwanzigste
21	einundzwanzig	einundzwanzigste
22	zweiundzwanzig	zweiundzwanzigste
30	dreißig	dreißigste
40	vierzig	vierzigste
50	fünfzig	fünfzigste
60	sechzig	sechzigste
70	siebzig	siebzigste
80	achtzig	achtzigste
90	neunzig	neunzigste
100	hundert	hundertste
101	hunderteins	hunderterste
121	hunderteinundzwanzig	hunderteinundzwanzigste
200	zweihundert	zweihundertste
1000	tausend	tausendste

eine Million	*one million*
zwei Millionen	*two million*
eine Milliarde	*one billion*
eine Billion	*1000 billions*

Vocabularies

The vocabulary is complete except for some obvious cognates and a few common pronouns, prepositions, and similar basic words. Genitive endings are given only for nouns forming their genitive in **-(e)n** or **-(e)ns.** Principal parts are listed for irregular verbs. Separable prefixes are hyphenated. A dash stands for the key word.

ab: — und zu now and then
ab-biegen, bog ab, abgebogen to turn
ab-brennen, brannte ab, abgebrannt to burn down
der **Abend, -e** evening; **am —** in the evening; **der bunte —** variety show
abend: heute — tonight; **gestern —** last night
das **Abendessen, -** dinner
die **Abendzeitung, -en** evening paper
aber but
ab-fahren (fährt ab), fuhr ab, ist abgefahren to leave
die **Abfahrt, -en** departure
abhängig dependent
ab-holen to get, call for
ab-legen to take (*an exam*)
ab-nehmen (nimmt ab), nahm ab, abgenommen to take off
die **Abreise, -n** departure
ab-reisen to leave
der **Abschied, -e** departure, parting; **— nehmen** to take leave
die **Absicht, -en** intention
ab-steigen, stieg ab, ist abgestiegen to descend, get off
ab-stellen to turn off
die **Abwesenheit, -en** absence
die **Adresse, -n** address
ähnlich similar
die **Ahnung, -en** idea
alkoholfrei nonalcoholic
all all; **alle zwei Jahre** every two years
allein alone
allerdings indeed, however
alles everything
allzu (far) too
die **Alpen** Alps
als when, as; than; **— ob** as if
also therefore; so
alt old
das **Alter** age
das **Altertum, ⸚er** antiquity
altmodisch old-fashioned
(das) **Amerika** America
der **Amerikaner, -** American
amerikanisch American
amtlich official, ministerial
amüsant amusing
sich amüsieren
ander- other, different; **etwas anderes** something different; **niemand anders** nobody else; **unter anderem** among other things
andermal: ein — some other time
ändern to change
an-fangen (fängt an), fing an, angefangen to begin
angegeben given
die **Angelegenheit, -en** situation, business
angenehm pleasant, agreeable
der **Angestellte, -n, -n** employee
die **Angst, ⸚e** anxiety, worry, fear; **— haben vor** to be afraid of; **— machen** to frighten
an-halten (hält an), hielt an, angehalten to stop
sich an-hören to listen to
an-kommen, kam an, ist angekommen to arrive
die **Ankunft, ⸚e** arrival
an-nehmen (nimmt an), nahm an, angenommen to accept, receive
der **Anruf, -e** telephone call
an-rufen, rief an, angerufen to telephone
sich an-schaffen to buy, get
(sich) an-schauen to look at, watch
anschließend subsequent
(sich) an-sehen (sieht an), sah an, angesehen to look at
die **Ansicht, -en** view, opinion
anstatt, anstelle instead of
an-stellen to turn on
an-stoßen (stößt an), stieß an, angestoßen to clink glasses
an-streichen, strich an, angestrichen to paint
an-strengen to require an effort; **sich —** to make an effort
die **Anstrengung, -en** effort
die **Antwort, -en** answer
antworten to answer

anwesend present
die **Anwesenden** (*pl.*) audience, those present
an-ziehen, zog an, angezogen to dress; **sich —** to get dressed
der **Anzug, ⸚e** suit
der **Apfelkuchen, -** apple cake
der **Apparat, -e** apparatus, set
die **Arbeit, -en** work
arbeiten to work
der **Arbeiter, -** worker
die **Arbeiterin, -nen** (woman) worker
der **Arbeitstag, -e** workday
der **Arbeitsschluß** end of the work period
der **Architekt, -en** architect
ärgern to annoy; **sich —** to be angry, annoyed
arm poor
die **Art, -en** kind, sort, type
der **Arzt, ⸚e** doctor, physician
atmen to breathe
auch also, too
auf-bauen to build up
auf-bewahren to keep, reserve, save
der **Aufenthalt, -e** stay, sojourn
auf-fallen (fällt auf), fiel auf, ist aufgefallen to strike, astonish
die **Aufgabe, -n** exercise, assignment
der **Aufgang, ⸚e** rise, ascent
auf-gehen, ging auf, ist aufgegangen to rise, open
aufgeregt excited
auf-hängen to hang up
auf-hören to stop
auf-klären to clear up, explain
auf-machen to open
aufmerksam attentive; **ich mache Sie — auf** I call your attention to
die **Aufnahme, -n** photograph, picture; **eine — machen** to take a picture
auf-passen to pay attention
der **Aufsatz, ⸚e** composition
auf-stehen, stand auf, ist aufgestanden to get up, stand up
auf-treten (tritt auf), trat auf, ist aufgetreten to appear, come forward

das **Auge, -n** eye
der **Augenblick, -e** moment
augenblicklich at the moment
aus-brechen (bricht aus), brach aus, ist ausgebrochen to break out
der **Ausdruck, ⸚e** expression
aus-drücken to express
der **Ausflug, ⸚e** excursion, trip; **einen — machen** to take a trip
das **Ausflugsziel, -e** destination
aus-füllen to fill out, complete
der **Ausgang, ⸚e** exit
aus-geben (gibt aus), gab aus, ausgegeben to spend
aus-gehen, ging aus, ist ausgegangen to go out
ausgezeichnet excellent
aus-kommen, kam aus, ist ausgekommen (mit) to get along (with)
die **Auskunft, ⸚e** information
die **Auslage, -n** display
der **Ausländer, -** foreigner
ausländisch foreign
aus-leeren to empty
aus-machen to matter; **das macht nichts aus** that doesn't matter
die **Ausnahme, -n** exception
sich aus-ruhen to rest
aus-sehen (sieht aus), sah aus, ausgesehen to appear, look
außer except
äußerst extremely, very
die **Aussicht, -en** view
aus-sprechen (spricht aus), sprach aus, ausgesprochen to express
aus-steigen, stieg aus, ist ausgestiegen to get out
aus-stellen to display, exhibit
die **Ausstellung, -en** display, exhibition
aus-suchen to select
der **Austauschstudent, -en, -en** exchange student
die **Austauschstudentin, -nen** (female) exchange student
ausverkauft sold out
die **Auswahl, -en** selection, choice
das **Ausweispapier, -e** identification paper

sich ausziehen, zog aus, ausgezogen to undress
das **Auto, –s** auto
die **Autobahn, –en** autobahn, superhighway
das **Autofahren** driving
der **Autor, –en** author

das **Bad, ¨–er** bath, bathroom
Bad Homburg *spa near Frankfurt*
die **Bahn, –en** railroad; **mit der —** by train
bald soon
der **Balkon, –e** balcony
der **Balkonplatz, ¨–e** balcony seat
der **Ball, ¨–e** ball
der **Band, ¨–e** volume
die **Bank, ¨–e** bench
die **Bank, –en** bank
der **Bankbeamte, –n, –n** bank official, teller
der **Bankier, –s** banker
(das) **Bayern** Bavaria
der **Beamte, –n, –n** clerk, official
beantworten to answer
die **Bedeutung, –en** meaning
bedienen to serve
die **Bedienung** service
sich beeilen to hurry
beeinflussen to influence
sich befassen to concern oneself
der **Befehl, –e** command, order
befehlen (befiehlt), befahl, befohlen to command, order
sich befinden, befand, befunden to be; to feel
das **Befinden** state of health
befürchten to fear, be afraid
begegnen to meet
begehen, beging, begangen to commit
beginnen, begann, begonnen to begin
begleiten to accompany
begreifen, begriff, begriffen to understand, grasp
begrüßen to greet
behandeln to treat
behaupten to claim
beide both
beiseite aside
das **Beispiel, –e** example; **zum —** for example
bekannt known, well-known
der **Bekannte, –n, –n** acquaintance
bekannt-machen to introduce; to announce
bekommen, bekam, bekommen to get, receive
belästigen to bother, annoy
beliebt popular
die **Beliebtheit** popularity
bemerken to notice
benachrichtigen to inform
sich benehmen (benimmt), benahm, benommen to behave
benutzen to use
das **Benzin** gasoline
beobachten to observe
die **Beobachtung, –en** observation
beraten to advise; **sich — lassen** to take advice
bereits already
der **Berg, –e** mountain
bergab downhill
bergauf uphill
der **Bericht, –e** report
berichten to report
der **Beruf, –e** profession
beruhigen to calm; **sich —** to calm oneself
berühmt famous
berühren to touch
bescheiden modest
die **Bescheinigung, –en** receipt
beschließen, beschloß, beschlossen to decide
beschreiben, beschrieb, beschrieben to describe
besetzt occupied
besichtigen to see, look at, visit
besitzen, besaß, besessen to possess
besonders especially
besorgen to get; to take care of
besorgt anxious, worried
die **Besorgung, –en** taking care; shopping
besprechen (bespricht), besprach, besprochen to discuss
besser better

bestehen, bestand, bestanden to endure; to pass (*an examination*); **— auf** to insist on; **— aus** to consist of
bestellen to order
bestimmt certain(ly), definite(ly)
bestürzt upset
der **Besuch, –e** visit
besuchen to visit
betrachten to look at, observe
betreffen (betrifft), betraf, betroffen to concern
der **Betrieb, –e** workshop, factory; activity; **dort ist —** there's something going on there
das **Bett, –en** bed
bevor before
(sich) bewegen to move
die **Bewegung, –en** movement
beweisen, bewies, bewiesen to prove
bezahlen to pay
bezweifeln to doubt
das **Bier, –e** beer
der **Biergeruch, ¨e** smell of beer
der **Bierkrug, ¨e** beer mug
das **Bild, –er** picture
bilden to form
billig inexpensive, cheap
bis until, up to
bißchen: ein — a little
bitte please; **— schön** please; you are welcome
bitten, bat, gebeten to beg, request; **— um** to ask for
blau blue
blauweiß blue and white
bleiben, blieb, ist geblieben to remain, stay
der **Blick, –e** glance; **auf den ersten —** at first sight
blitzen: es blitzt it's lightening
die **Blume, –n** flower
der **Boden, ¨** floor
die **Bohnensuppe, –n** bean soup
Bonn *city on the Rhine, capital of the Federal Republic of Germany*
das **Boot, –e** boat
brauchen to need
braun brown
brav well-behaved, upright
brennen, brannte, gebrannt to burn
der **Brief, –e** letter
die **Brille, –n** (pair of) glasses
bringen, brachte, gebracht to bring, take along
der **Bruder, ¨** brother
der **Brunnen, –** fountain
das **Buch, ¨er** book
der **Bücherladen, ¨** bookstore
die **Buchhandlung, –en** bookstore
das **Büchlein, –** little book, booklet
bunt many-colored; **ein bunter Abend** a variety show
die **Burg, –en** fortress, castle
das **Büro, –s** office

der **Chef, –s** boss
die **Chemie** chemistry
der **Christ, –en, –en** Christian
das **Christentum** Christianity
der **Cowboy, –s** cowboy

da there; since; **— unten** down there
dabei at the same time
das **Dach, ¨er** roof
dafür for it; therefore
dagegen against it; on the other hand
daher from there; therefore
dahin there; **bis —** until then
damals then, at that time
die **Dame, –n** lady
damit with it, with them; so that, in order that
dämmern to dawn; to get dark
der **Dampfer, –** steamer, steamboat
danach afterward
der **Dank** thanks, gratitude
dankbar grateful
die **Dankbarkeit** gratitude
danken to thank; **danke!** thank you!
dann then
daran in it, of it, on it
die **Darbietung, –en** performance, presentation
Darmstadt *city south of Frankfurt*
der **Darsteller, –** performer, actor
darüber about it, concerning it

daß that
das **Datum, Daten** date
die **Dauer** duration, length
dauern to last; to take (time)
davon about that, from that
das **Deck, –e** deck
die **Decke, –n** cover; ceiling
deinetwegen as far as you're concerned
denken, dachte, gedacht to think; **— an** to think of; **sich —** to imagine
denn for, because; *as a particle used to strengthen a question*
deswegen for that reason, therefore
deutlich clear
(das) **Deutsch** German; **auf deutsch** in German
der **Deutsche, –n, –n** German
(das) **Deutschland** Germany
der **Deutschlehrer, –** German teacher
der **Deutschprofessor, –en** German professor
der **Dezember** December
der **Dichter, –** poet, writer
dick fat, thick
der **Dieb, –e** thief
dienen to serve
diesmal this time
diesseits on this side
das **Ding, –e** thing; object
der **Diplomat, –en, –en** diplomat
die **Distanz, –en** distance
doch however, on the contrary; after all, surely
die **Dollarnote, –n** dollar bill
donnern to thunder
das **Dorf, ¨–er** village
dort there
Dortmund *city in the Ruhr area, northwest Germany*
der **Dortmunder, –** man from Dortmund
das **Drama, Dramen** drama
der **Dramatiker, –** playwright, dramatist
draußen outside
drehen to turn
die **Drogistin, –nen** (female) pharmacist
drohen to threaten
drüben: da — over there
der **Duft, ¨–e** scent, aroma, odor
dumm stupid, foolish
dunkel dark
durch through
durch-fallen (fällt durch), fiel durch, ist durchgefallen to fail (an exam)
durch-kommen, kam durch, ist durchgekommen to get through, pass
durchschauen to see through
dürfen (darf), durfte, gedurft to be allowed to
Dürrenmatt, Friedrich *Swiss playwright (b. 1921)*
der **Durst** thirst; **— haben** to be thirsty
durstig thirsty
das **Düsenflugzeug, –e** jet plane
das **Dutzend, –e** dozen

eben flat, even; just (now)
ebenfalls likewise
die **Ecke, –n** corner
ehe before
ehren to honor
ehrlich honest
das **Ei, –er** egg
eigen own
eigentlich in fact, really
das **Eigentum, ¨–er** property
eilig hurried; **ich habe es —** **I'm** in a hurry
einander one another
sich ein-bilden to imagine
der **Eindruck, ¨–e** impression
einfach simple
die **Einfahrt, –en** entrance
ein-fallen (fällt ein), fiel ein, ist eingefallen to occur (to someone); **es fällt mir ein** it occurs to me
der **Eingang, ¨–e** entrance
einige several
der **Einkauf, ¨–e** purchase; **Einkäufe machen** to shop
ein-kaufen to shop, go shopping
ein-laden (lädt ein), lud ein, eingeladen to invite

die **Einladung, –en** invitation
ein-lösen to cash
einmal once, one time
ein-nehmen (nimmt ein), nahm ein, eingenommen to take (in)
ein-schlafen (schläft ein), schlief ein, ist eingeschlafen to fall asleep
ein-sehen (sieht ein), sah ein, eingesehen to understand, see
die **Einspritzung, –en** injection
ein-steigen, stieg ein, ist eingestiegen to get aboard, get in
ein-stellen to put in; **das Radio —** to tune in the radio
ein-treten (tritt ein), trat ein, ist eingetreten to step in, enter
einverstanden agreed
der **Einwohner, –** inhabitant
einzig only, single
das **Eis** ice; ice cream
die **Eltern** parents
der **Empfang, ⸚e** reception
empfangen (empfängt), empfing, empfangen to receive
der **Empfangschef, –s** head clerk (*in a hotel*)
empfehlen (empfiehlt) empfahl, empfohlen to recommend; **sich —** to take leave
empfindlich sensitive, touchy
das **Ende, –n** end; **zu —** over, at an end
enden to end
endlich finally, at last
die **Endprüfung, –en** final examination
eng narrow, tight
englisch English
der **Englischlehrer, –** English teacher
entfernen to remove
entgegen toward
entgehen, entging, ist entgangen to escape
entlang along
entlassen (entläßt), entließ, entlassen to dismiss
der **Entschluß, ⸚sse** decision; **einen — fassen** to decide
entschuldigen to excuse; **sich —** to apologize
die **Entschuldigung, –en** excuse; **um — bitten** to apologize, beg pardon
sich entspannen to relax
entsprechend according to; corresponding to
entstehen, entstand, entstanden to begin, arise
enttäuschen to disappoint
entwickeln to develop
das **Entwickeln** development, developing
entziffern to decipher
entzückend delightful
sich erbarmen to have mercy
die **Erbse, –n** pea
das **Erdgeschoß, –sse** ground floor, first floor
erfahren (erfährt), erfuhr, erfahren to experience; to learn
der **Erfolg, –e** success
erfrischend refreshing
die **Erfrischung, –en** refreshment
ergänzen to complete
erhalten (erhält), erhielt, erhalten to receive, get
erhoffen to expect, hope for
erhöhen to raise, increase
erinnern to remind; **sich — an** to remember
sich erkälten to catch cold
die **Erkältung, –en** cold
erkennen, erkannte, erkannt (an) to recognize (by)
erklären to explain
sich erkundigen to inquire
erlauben to permit, allow
das **Erlebnis, –se** experience
erledigen to settle, take care of
erreichen to reach
erscheinen, erschien, ist erschienen to appear
erschrecken (erschrickt), erschrak, ist erschrocken to be frightened
ersetzen to replace
erst first; only, not until
der **Erwachsene, –n, –n** adult
erwähnen to mention
erwarten to await, expect
erzählen to tell, relate

erziehen, erzog, erzogen to rear, educate
erzielen to get, obtain
essen (ißt), aß, gegessen to eat
etwa about, approximately
etwas something; somewhat; **so —** something like that
das **Examen, –** examination
das **Experiment, –e** experiment

das **Fach, ⸚er** subject
die **Fahne, –n** banner, flag
fahren (fährt), fuhr, (ist) gefahren to go, travel, ride; to drive
der **Fahrer, –** driver; cyclist
die **Fahrkarte, –n** ticket
das **Fahrrad, ⸚er** bicycle
der **Fahrstuhl, ⸚e** elevator
die **Fahrt, –en** ride
der **Fall, ⸚e** fall
fallen (fällt), fiel, ist gefallen to fall; **— lassen** to drop; **es fällt mir schwer** it is difficult for me
falls in case
falsch wrong, false; **etwas — machen** to do something wrong
die **Familie, –n** family
die **Farbe, –n** color
der **Farbendruck, –e** color print
farbig colorful
fassen to hold, grasp; **einen Entschluß —** to decide
fast almost
der **Februar** February
fehlen to be missing; **was fehlt Ihnen?** what's wrong (with you)?
der **Fehler, –** mistake, error
die **Feier, –n** celebration
feiern to celebrate
fein fine
der **Feind, –e** enemy
der **Felsen, –** rock, cliff
das **Fenster, –** window
die **Ferienfahrt, –en** vacation trip
der **Ferienplan, ⸚e** vacation plan
die **Ferienreise, –n** vacation trip
der **Fernsehapparat, –e** television set
fern-sehen (sieht fern), sah fern, ferngesehen to watch television
das **Fernsehen** television; **im —** on television
das **Fernsehprogramm, –e** television program
fertig finished; **— werden** to finish
die **Festlichkeit, –en** festivity
das **Feuer, –** fire
das **Fieber** fever, temperature
der **Fieberkranke, –n, –n** man ill with a fever
der **Film, –e** film, motion picture
filmen to film
finden, fand, gefunden to find; to think of
der **Finger, –** finger
die **Flagge, –n** flag
die **Flasche, –n** bottle
das **Fleisch** meat
fleißig diligent
flicken to repair, mend
das **Flickzeug, –e** repair equipment
fliegen, flog, ist geflogen to fly
flimmern to flicker
flüchtig, fleeting, hasty, hurried
der **Flug, ⸚e** flight
der **Flughafen, ⸚e** airport
die **Flugkarte, –n** flight ticket
das **Flugzeug, –e** airplane
der **Fluß, ⸚sse** river
die **Flüssigkeit, –en** liquid
folgen to follow; to obey
folgend following
die **Form, –en** form
das **Formular, –e** form, blank
der **Forscher, –** researcher, scientist
fort away; **in einem —** continuously
fort-bleiben, blieb fort, ist fortgeblieben to stay away
fort-gehen, ging fort, ist fortgegangen to go away
der **Fotoapparat, –e** camera
das **Fotogeschäft, –e** camera shop
die **Fotografie, –n** photograph
die **Frage, –n** question
fragen to ask; **— nach** to ask for, inquire about
französisch French
die **Frau, –en** woman, wife
das **Fräulein, –** miss
frei free; **im Freien** outdoors
die **Freiheit, –en** freedom, liberty

freilich of course, certainly
fremd foreign
die **Freude, –n** joy; **— haben an** to be happy with
sich freuen to be pleased, glad; **sich — auf** to look forward to; **sich — über** to be glad about
der **Freund, –e** friend
die **Freundin, –nen** friend
freundlich friendly
der **Friede, –ns, –n** peace
frieren, fror, gefroren to freeze; **mich friert** I'm cold
frisch fresh
froh (über) glad, merry, happy (about)
die **Frucht, ⸚e** fruit
früh early; **früher** earlier; formerly
das **Frühjahrssemester, –** spring semester
der **Frühling, –e** spring
das **Frühstück, –e** breakfast
(sich) fühlen to feel
führen to lead; **eine Pension —** to run a boardinghouse; **ein Gespräch —** to have a conversation
füllen to fill
der **Funke, –ns, –n** spark
die **Furcht** fear
furchtbar terrible, fearful
fürchten to fear, dread; **sich — vor** to be afraid of
der **Fuß, ⸚e** foot; **zu — gehen** to go on foot
der **Fußball** football, soccer
der **Fußballkampf, ⸚e** football (soccer) game
das **Fußballspiel, –e** football (soccer) game
Füssen *town in the Bavarian Alps*
der **Fußgänger, –** pedestrian

der **Gang, ⸚e** trip; gear; **in — bringen** to start, set going
ganz complete(ly), quite
gar: — nicht not at all
die **Garage, –n** garage
Garmisch *popular resort in the Bavarian Alps*
der **Garten, ⸚** garden
die **Gartenwirtschaft, –en** open-air restaurant
der **Gast, ⸚e** guest
die **Gastgeberin, –nen** hostess
das **Gebäck, –e** pastry, baked goods
das **Gebäude, –** building
geben (gibt), gab, gegeben to give; **es gibt** there is, there are
das **Gebiet, –e** area
gebildet educated
das **Gebirge, –** mountains
gebrauchen to use
die **Geburt, –en** birth
der **Geburtstag, –e** birthday
das **Geburtstagsgeschenk, –e** birthday present
der **Gedanke, –ns, –n** thought
das **Gedicht, –e** poem
die **Geduld** patience
geeignet suitable, fit
gefallen (gefällt), gefiel, hat gefallen to please; **das gefällt mir** I like that
der **Gefallen, –** favor
der **Gefangene, –n, –n** prisoner
gefaßt prepared; **sich — machen auf** to prepare oneself for something
gegen against, toward
die **Gegend, –en** area, region
gegenseitig one another; reciprocal
gegenüber opposite
gegenwärtig present, right now
gehen, ging, ist gegangen to go; **es geht mir gut** I'm well
gehorchen to obey
gehören to belong
geläufig fluent
gelb yellow
das **Geld, –er** money
die **Gelegenheit, –en** opportunity
der **Geliebte, –n, –n** beloved
gelingen, gelang, ist gelungen to succeed; **es gelingt mir** I succeed
das **Gemälde, –** painting
gemütlich congenial; leisurely
genau exact
genug enough

genügen to be sufficient, suffice
das **Gepäck** baggage
gerade straight; **— aus** straight ahead
gern(e) gladly; **ich habe es —** I like it; **ich rauche —** I like to smoke
der **Geruch, ⸚e** odor
geschäftlich relating to business
der **Geschäftsmann, ⸚er** businessman
das **Geschäftsviertel, -** business district
geschehen (geschieht), geschah, ist geschehen to happen
das **Geschenk, –e** present, gift
die **Geschichte, –n** story, history
die **Geschwister** brothers and sisters
die **Gesellschaft, –en** company; party; **— leisten** to keep company, accompany
das **Gesicht, –er** face
gespannt eager, intent
das **Gespräch, –e** conversation; dialog
gestehen, gestand, gestanden to admit, confess; **offen gestanden** frankly speaking
gestern yesterday; **— abend** last night
gesund healthy, healthful
das **Getränk, –e** beverage
das **Gewicht, –e** weight
gewinnen, gewann, gewonnen to win
gewiß certain
das **Gewissen** conscience
das **Gewitter, -** thunderstorm
gewöhnlich usual(ly)
das **Glas, ⸚er** glass
der **Glaube, –ns, –n** belief
glauben to believe, think
gleich same, even; indifferent; immediately
gleichen to be like, look like
gleichzeitig simultaneous
gleiten, glitt, ist geglitten to glide
das **Glück** (good) luck; **— haben** to be lucky, happy; **zum —** fortunately
glücklich happy; lucky
glücklicherweise fortunately
Goethe, Johann Wolfgang von *German poet, dramatist, novelist, and philosopher (1749-1832)*
der **Gott, ⸚er** god
Grass, Günter *German novelist (b. 1927)*
gratulieren to congratulate
greifen, griff, gegriffen to seize
die **Grenze, –n** border
groß large, big
die **Großeltern** grandparents
der **Großvater, ⸚** grandfather
die **Gruppe, –n** group
gut good; well; **jemand — leiden können** to like somebody
die **Güte** goodness

das **Haar, –e** hair
haben (hat), hatte, gehabt to have; to own
hageln to hail
halb half; **ein halbes Jahr** half a year
die **Hälfte, –n** half
die **Halle, –n** hall, lobby
die **Halsentzündung, –en** sore throat
das **Halstuch, ⸚er** scarf
halten (hält), hielt, gehalten to hold, stop; **— von** to think of; **einen Vortrag —** to give a lecture
die **Haltestelle, –n** stop
die **Hand, ⸚e** hand; **die — geben** to shake hands; **die Hände voll haben** to have one's hands full
sich handeln um to deal with, concern
der **Handschuh, –e** glove
hängen, hing, gehangen to hang, be hanging
der **Haufen, -** heap
das **Hauptfach, ⸚er** major subject
das **Hauptgebäude, -** main building
die **Hauptrolle, –n** leading part
die **Hauptstraße, –n** main street, main road
das **Haus, ⸚er** house; **nach Hause** home; **zu Hause** at home
der **Hausarzt, ⸚e** family doctor
der **Hausschlüssel, -** house key
das **Heft, –e** notebook, pamphlet
heilen to cure; (*with* **sein**) to get well

heim homeward
die **Heimatstadt, ⸚e** home town
heim-kehren to return home
heiraten to marry
heiß hot
heißen, hieß, geheißen to be called; **d.h. (das heißt)** that is; **ich heiße** my name is
helfen (hilft), half, geholfen to help
der **Helfer, –** helper
der **Herbst** fall, autumn
herein in
herein-kommen, kam herein, ist hereingekommen to come in, enter
der **Herr, –n, –en** gentleman
das **Herrenartikelgeschäft, –e** men's wear store
herrlich wonderful, glorious
herum around
das **Herz, –ens, –en** heart
heute today; **— abend** this evening, tonight
heutzutage nowadays
hier here
die **Hilfe, –n** help
das **Himalayagebirge** the Himalayas
hinauf-gehen, ging hinauf, ist hinaufgegangen to go up
hinein in
hin-gehen, ging hin, ist hingegangen to go (there)
hinten in the back, in the rear
hinter behind
das **Hinterhaus, ⸚er** rear building
das **Hinterrad, ⸚er** rear wheel
hinunter-gehen, ging hinunter, ist hinuntergegangen to go down
die **Hitze** heat
hoch high
das **Hochhaus, ⸚er** high-rise building
höchst extremely, very
hoffen to hope
hoffentlich I hope
die **Hoffnung, –en** hope, expectation; **sich Hoffnungen machen** to have hopes
die **Höhe, –n** height
der **Höhepunkt, –e** high point, climax
der **Holländer, –** Dutchman
die **Holländerin, –nen** Dutchwoman
holländisch Dutch
das **Holz, ⸚er** wood
hören to hear; **Radio —** to listen to the radio
das **Hotel, –s** hotel
das **Hotelzimmer, –** hotel room
hübsch attractive, pretty
der **Hügel, –** hill
der **Hund, –e** dog
der **Hunger** hunger; **— haben** to be hungry
hungern to be hungry, starve
hungrig hungry
husten to cough
der **Hut, ⸚e** hat
hüten to watch, guard; **das Bett —** to be confined to bed

die **Idee, –n** idea
immer always; **— noch** still
immerhin nevertheless
indem while, by (doing)
der **Indianer, –** Indian
der **Inhalt** contents
die **Inschrift, –en** inscription
interessant interesting
das **Interesse, –n** interest; **— haben für** to be interested in
sich interessieren (für) to be interested (in)
inzwischen in the meantime
irgend: irgendein any, some; **— jemand** someone, anyone; **irgendwo** somewhere
sich irren to err, make a mistake
der **Irrtum, ⸚er** error
(das) **Italien** Italy

ja yes; indeed; *as a particle lends emphasis or suggests surprise*
das **Jahr, –e** year
jahrelang for years
die **Jahreszeit, –en** season
das **Jahrhundert, –e** century
der **Januar** January
je ever; **— nach** according to
jedenfalls in any case, however
jeder every
jemals ever

jemand somebody
jenseits on the far side of
jetzt now
jung young
der **Junge, –n, –n** boy, youth
der **Juni** June
der **Juli** July

der **Kaffee** coffee
kalt cold
die **Kamera, –s** camera
der **Kampf, ⸚e** fight; game
die **Kapelle, –n** band
das **Kapitel, –** chapter
kaputt ruined, broken
die **Karte, –n** card, ticket
das **Kartenspiel, –e** card game
die **Kartoffel, –n** potato
der **Käse** cheese
die **Kasse, –n** cashier's; box office
kaufen to buy
kaum scarcely, hardly
kein not a, not any, no
keiner nobody
keineswegs by no means, not at all
die **Kellnerin, –nen** bar maid, waitress
kennen, kannte, gekannt to know
kennen-lernen to meet
das **Kilogramm, –e** kilogram (*2.2 pounds*)
der **Kilometer, –** kilometer (*0.62 mile*)
das **Kind, –er** child
die **Kindervorstellung, –en** children's performance
das **Kindlein, –** little child
das **Kino, –s** motion-picture theater
die **Kirche, –n** church
der **Klang, ⸚e** sound
klar clear, obvious
das **Klassenzimmer, –** classroom
klatschen to applaud
das **Klavier, –e** piano
das **Kleid, –er** dress
sich kleiden to dress
klein small, little
das **Kleingeld** (small) change
die **Kleinstadt, ⸚e** small town
klingeln to ring
klingen, klang, geklungen to sound
klopfen to knock
der **Knopf, ⸚e** button
die **Köchin, –nen** cook
das **Kolleg: ins — gehen** to attend lectures
Köln Cologne
der **Komiker, –** comedian
komisch comical, funny
kommen, kam, ist gekommen to come
die **Komödie, –n** comedy
der **Komparativ** comparative degree
die **Konditorei, –en** café, pastry shop
der **König, –e** king
die **Königin, –nen** queen
das **Königsschloß, ⸚sser** royal castle
das **Königtum, ⸚er** kingdom
der **Konjunktiv** subjunctive
können (kann), konnte, gekonnt can, to be able to
die **Konversation, –en** conversation
das **Konzert, –e** concert
der **Kopf, ⸚e** head
das **Kopfweh** headache
korrekt correct, proper
kostbar expensive
kosten to cost
die **Kosten** costs, expenses
das **Kostüm, –e** costume, uniform
krachen to crackle
kräftig strong, powerful
krank ill, sick
der **Kranke, –n, –n** sick person, patient
der **Krankenbesuch, –e** sick call
das **Krankenhaus, ⸚er** hospital
die **Krankheit, –en** illness
die **Krawatte, –n** tie
die **Kreuzung, –en** crossing, intersection
das **Kreuzworträtsel, –** crossword puzzle
der **Krieg, –e** war
kriegen to get
das **Kriminalstück, –e** detective story
kritisch critical
der **Kuchen, –** cake
der **Kugelschreiber, –** ball-point pen
kühl cool
der **Künstler, –** artist
kurz short

kürzlich recent(ly)

die **Laborantin, –nen** lab assistant
lächeln to smile
lachen to laugh
der **Laden, ¨** store
die **Lage, –n** situation, location
das **Land, ¨er** country
landen to land
die **Landkarte, –n** map
die **Landebahn, –en** landing strip
lang long; **schon lange** for a long time
die **Länge, –n** length, duration
langsam slow
langweilen to bore
der **Lärm, –e** noise
lassen, ließ, gelassen to let, permit; to leave; **etwas tun —** to have something done
der **Lauf, ¨e** course; gait, running
laufen (läuft), lief, ist gelaufen to run; **ein Film läuft** a film is showing
laut loud; according to
läuten to ring
leben to live
das **Leben** life
die **Lederhosen** leather shorts
die **Ledertasche, –n** leather bag
leer empty
legen to lay, put, place; **sich —** to lie down
lehren to teach
der **Lehrer, –** teacher
die **Lehrerin, –nen** teacher
leicht light; easy
leid painful, disagreeable; **es tut mir —** I am sorry
leiden, litt, gelitten (an) to suffer (from); **jemand gut — können** to like somebody
leider unfortunately
leise soft
sich leisten to afford; **Gesellschaft —** to keep company, accompany
die **Lektion, –en** lesson
die **Lektüre, –n** reading
lernen to learn
lesen (liest), las, gelesen to read
der **Leser, –** reader
letzt- last
die **Leute** *pl.* people
lieb dear
die **Liebe** love
lieben to like, love
liebenswürdig kind, amiable
lieber rather; **ich habe (mag) das —** I prefer that; **ich tue das —** I prefer doing that
liebst- dearest; **ich habe das am liebsten** I like that best
das **Lied, –er** song
liegen, lag, gelegen to lie, recline
links to the left
der **Liter, –** liter (*1.06 quarts*)
das **Lob** praise
loben to praise
das **Lokal, –e** place; inn, tavern
die **Loreley** *a siren in German legend who lured sailors onto a cliff on the Rhine river;* Loreley Rock
los loose; **was ist —?** what's going on? what's the matter?
lösen to solve
los-lassen (läßt los), ließ los, losgelassen to let go, set free
die **Lösung, –en** solution
der **Löwe, –n, –n** lion
die **Luft, ¨e** air
die **Luftpost** air mail
lügen to lie
die **Lust, ¨e** desire; **— haben, etwas zu tun** to want to do something; **— haben nach etwas** to feel like having something
lustig gay, cheerful
das **Lustspiel, –e** comedy

machen to make, do; **Einkäufe —** to shop; **etwas falsch —** to do something the wrong way; **Freude —** to please; **eine Reise —** to take a trip; **einen Spaziergang —** to take a walk; **sich gefaßt — auf** to prepare oneself for; **sich Hoffnungen —** to have hopes; **sich Sorgen — um** to worry about; **sich ein Vergnügen aus etwas —** to take pleasure in something
das **Mädchen, –** girl, miss

die **Mahlzeit, –en** meal
Mainz *city on the Rhine, west of Frankfurt*
das **Mal, –e** time; **zum ersten —** for the first time
mal sometime
malen to paint
der **Maler, –** painter
die **Malerin, –nen** painter
man one, you, they
manchmal occasionally
der **Mann, ⸚er** man, husband
die **Mannschaft, –en** team
der **Mantel, ⸚** overcoat
das **Märchenschloß, ⸚sser** fairy-tale castle
die **Mark** mark (*about $0.25*)
marschieren to march
das **Maschinengewehr, –e** machine gun
das **Matterhorn** *famous mountain peak in southern Switzerland*
die **Medizin, –en** medicine, drug
mehrere several
meinen to mean; to mean to say
meinetwegen as far as I'm concerned
die **Meinung, –en** opinion; **der — sein, die — vertreten** to be of the opinion
meist most
meistens for the most part, mostly
der **Meister, –** master
der **Mensch, –en, –en** man, human being
die **Miene, –n** facial expression
die **Milliarde, –n** billion
das **Mineralwasser** mineral water
die **Minute, –n** minute
mißverstehen, mißverstand, mißverstanden to misunderstand
mit-bringen, brachte mit, mitgebracht to bring along
miteinander with one another
mit-fahren, (fährt mit), fuhr mit, ist mitgefahren to go along
das **Mitglied, –er** member
mit-nehmen (nimmt mit), nahm mit, mitgenommen to take along
der **Mittag, –e** noon
das **Mittagessen, –** lunch
die **Mitte** middle; **— April** in the middle of April
mit-teilen to inform, tell
der **Mittelpunkt, ⸚e** middle, center
mittelschwer medium heavy
mitten (in) in the middle (of)
die **Mitternacht** midnight
der **Mittwoch** Wednesday
mögen (mag), mochte, gemocht to like, care for, like to; may
möglich possible
die **Möglichkeit, –en** possibility
der **Monat, –e** month
der **Montag, –e** Monday
das **Moos, –e** moss
der **Morgen, –** morning; **morgen** tomorrow; **heute morgen** this morning; **morgens** in the morning, mornings
der **Motor, –en** motor, engine
müde tired, weary
die **Müdigkeit** tiredness
die **Mühe, –n** effort; difficulty
mühelos easy, effortless
die **Münchnerin, –nen** woman from Munich
das **Museum, Museen** museum
die **Musik** music; band
musikalisch musical, musically talented
der **Musiker, –** musician
die **Musikerin, –nen** musician
müssen (muß), mußte, gemußt must, to have to
die **Mutter, ⸚** mother

nach after; to; according to
der **Nachbar, –n** neighbor
nachdem after
nachher afterward
der **Nachmittag, –e** afternoon; **heute nachmittag** this afternoon
die **Nachricht, –en** news
die **Nachrichtensendung, –en** news broadcast
nächst– next
die **Nacht, ⸚e** night; **nachts** at night
der **Nachttisch, –e** bedside table
nach-zählen to count again
nah(e) near

die **Nähe** closeness, vicinity
sich nähern to approach
der **Name, -ns, -n** name
natürlich natural; of course
die **Naturwissenschaft, -en** natural science
nebenan close by
nebeneinander one next to the other
das **Nebenfach, ⸚er** minor subject
der **Nebensatz, ⸚e** dependent clause
die **Nebenstraße, -n** byroad
nehmen (nimmt), nahm, genommen to take
nennen, nannte, genannt to name
nett nice
neu new
neugierig curious
das **Neujahr** New Year
neulich recently
Neuschwanstein *famous castle near Füssen, Bavaria*
nichts nothing
nie never; **noch —** never yet, not ever
nieder-schreiben, schrieb nieder, niedergeschrieben to write (down)
niedrig low
niemand nobody
noch still, yet; **— ein** another; **— einmal** once more; **— nicht** not yet
nötig necessary
nun now
nur only
nützlich useful

ob whether; **als —** as if
oben above; up, upstairs
ober- upper
Oberammergau *village in the Bavarian Alps, famous for its passion plays*
oberflächlich superficial
oberhalb above
obgleich although
obschon although
obwohl although
oder or
der **Ofen, ⸚** stove
offen open; **— gestanden** frankly speaking
der **Offizier, -e** officer
öffnen to open
oft often; **so —** as often as
öfter several times, frequently
ohne without; **— daß** without
das **Öl, -e** oil
der **Ölstand, ⸚e** oil level
der **Onkel, -** uncle
der **Opel** *German car*
die **Oper, -n** opera
die **Operation, -en** operation
operieren to operate
das **Orchester, -** orchestra
der **Ort, ⸚er** place
(das) **Österreich** Austria

paar: ein — a few
das **Paar, -e** pair, couple
das **Päckchen, -** pack
packen to pack
das **Packpapier, -e** wrapping paper
das **Paket, -e** package, parcel
die **Panne, -n** breakdown, puncture
die **Papiertüte, -n** paper bag
der **Park, -s** park
parken to park
das **Parkett, -e** orchestra (*in a theater, etc.*)
der **Parkplatz, ⸚e** parking lot
das **Partizip, -s, -ien** participle
passen to be suitable; to fit
passend appropriate; correct
passieren to pass, go by; (*with* **sein**) to occur, happen
das **Passionsspiel, -e** passion play
die **Paßkontrolle** passport control
die **Pause, -n** intermission, half time
das **Pech** bad luck
das **Pedal, -e** pedal; **in die Pedale treten** to pedal
die **Pension, -en** boardinghouse
das **Perfekt** compound past, perfect tense
die **Person, -en** person
das **Personalpronomen, -** personal pronoun
die **Pfeife, -n** pipe; whistle
das **Pferd, -e** horse

die **Pflicht, –en** duty
die **Pille, –n** pill
das **Plakat, –e** poster, bill
der **Plan, ⸚e** plan
der **Platz, ⸚e** place; seat; square; **— nehmen** to sit down
die **Platzanweiserin, –nen** usher(ette)
plaudern to chat, converse
plötzlich sudden
das **Plusquamperfekt** past perfect
politisch political
der **Portier, –s** doorman
das **Porto, –s** postage
die **Post** post office; mail; **mit der — schicken** to mail
die **Postkarte, –n** postcard
der **Postschalter, –** post-office counter
das **Präsens** present tense
die **Präsensform, –en** form of the present
der **Präsident, –en, –en** president
der **Preis, –e** price; prize
der **Prinz, –en, –en** prince
die **Prinzessin, –nen** princess
das **Problem, –e** problem
das **Programm, –e** program
das **Pronomen, –** pronoun
Prost Here's to you! To your health!
prüfen to check, test
die **Prüfung, –en** examination
der **Pudel, –** poodle
der **Pullover, –s** sweater
die **Pumpe, –n** pump
der **Punkt, –e** point, dot; **um Punkt acht** at eight exactly
pünktlich punctual

das **Rad, ⸚er** wheel; bicycle
rad-fahren (fährt rad), fuhr rad, ist radgefahren to ride a bicycle
der **Radfahrer, –** cyclist
das **Radio, –s** radio; **— hören** to listen to the radio; **im —** on the radio
der **Radioapparat, –e** radio (set)
raten (rät), riet, geraten to advise
der **Rauch** smoke
rauchen to smoke
rechnen to calculate, reckon; **— mit** to count on
recht right; quite; **— haben** to be right; **er weiß es nicht —** he's not too sure
rechts on the right
der **Rechtsanwalt, ⸚e** lawyer, attorney
rechtzeitig on time
die **Rede, –n** speech, discourse; **die — von etwas sein** to be a question of, be about something
reden to talk
der **Redner, –** speaker
die **Regel, –n** rule
regnen to rain
reich rich, wealthy
der **Reichtum, ⸚er** wealth
der **Reifen, –** tire; hoop
die **Reifenpanne, –n** puncture, blowout
die **Reihe, –n** row; **an der — sein** to be up
reinigen to clean
die **Reise, –n** trip; **eine — machen** to take a trip
das **Reisebüro, –s** travel agency
reisen to travel
der **Reisende, –n, –n** tourist, traveler
der **Reisepaß, ⸚sse** passport
die **Reisetasche, –n** flight bag, traveling bag
reiten, ritt, ist geritten to ride
die **Reklame, –n** advertisement, commercial
der **Relativsatz, ⸚e** relative clause
rennen, rannte, ist gerannt to run
reparieren to repair
die **Republik, –en** republic
die **Reserve, –n** reserve, substitute
das **Reserverad, ⸚er** spare tire
reservieren to reserve
die **Residenzstadt, ⸚e** royal residence, capital
der **Respekt** respect; **— haben vor** to respect
der **Rest, –e** rest, remainder
das **Restaurant, –s** restaurant
das **Resultat, –e** result
retten to save, rescue
der **Rhein** Rhine
die **Rheinfahrt, –en** trip on the Rhine
die **Rheinreise, –n** trip on the Rhine

der **Rheindampfer, -** Rhine steamer, Rhine boat
richtig correct, right; real
die **Richtung, -en** direction
der **Ritt, -e** ride
rollen to roll
der **Roman, -e** novel
Romulus *Romulus (Augustulus), last Roman emperor;* **— der Große** *comedy by Friedrich Dürrenmatt*
die **Rose, -n** rose
rot red
der **Rückflug, ⸚e** return flight
die **Rückkehr** return
die **Rückreise, -n** return trip
rufen, rief, gerufen to call
das **Rugbyspiel, -e** rugby game
der **Ruhetag, -e** day of rest
die **Ruine, -n** ruin
rund round
der **Rundfunk** radio, broadcasting
die **Rundschau** panorama; review

die **Sache, -n** thing
die **Sage, -n** legend, saga
sagen to say, tell
der **Samstag** Saturday
der **Sänger, -** singer
die **Sängerin, -nen** singer
der **Satellit, -en, -en** satellite
der **Satz, ⸚e** sentence, clause
das **Satzpaar, -e** pair of sentences
der **Satzteil, -e** phrase
sauber clean
die **Schachtel, -n** box; package
schade too bad, unfortunate; **es ist —** it's a pity
schaden to harm
der **Schalter, -** window, booth
sich schämen to be ashamed
der **Schatten, -** shadow
schätzen to value; to appreciate
schauen to look, see
das **Schaufenster, -** display window, show window
der **Schauspieler, -** actor
die **Schauspielerin, -nen** actress
der **Scheck, -s** check
der **Schein, -e** shine; appearance
scheinen, schien, geschienen to seem; to shine
die **Scheune, -n** barn
schicken to send
schieben, schob, geschoben to push, shove
der **Schiedsrichter, -** referee, umpire
das **Schiff, -e** ship
der **Schiffskapitän, -e** captain of a ship
schildern to describe
Schiller, Friedrich von *German dramatist and poet (1759-1805)*
schlafen (schläft), schlief, geschlafen to sleep
die **Schlange, -n** snake; **— stehen** to stand in line
der **Schlauch, ⸚e** inner tube; hose
schlecht bad
schließen, schloß, geschlossen to close
schlimm bad
das **Schloß, ⸚sser** castle
der **Schluck, ⸚e** sip, mouthful
schlucken to swallow
der **Schluß, ⸚sse** conclusion, end; **zum —** at the end, in conclusion
der **Schlüssel, -** key
schmecken to taste; to taste good
der **Schmerz, -en** pain
der **Schnee** snow; **es gibt —** it's going to snow
schneiden, schnitt, geschnitten to cut
schneidig smart, dashing
schneien to snow
schnell fast
das **Schnürchen, -** string, cord; **wie am — gehen** to go like clockwork
schon already; (*as intensifying particle*) indeed, no doubt
schön beautiful; all right, good, fine, O.K.
die **Schönheit, -en** beauty
schreiben, schrieb, geschrieben to write
der **Schreibtisch, -e** desk, writing table
der **Schuh, -e** shoe
die **Schulaufgabe, -n** lesson, homework
schuld guilty

schulden to owe
die **Schule, –n** school
der **Schüler, –** student, pupil
der **Schutzmann, ⸗er** policeman
schwarz black; **schwarzgekleidet** (dressed) in black
schweigen, schwieg, geschwiegen to keep silent
die **Schweiz** Switzerland
der **Schweizer, –** Swiss
die **Schweizerin, –nen** Swiss woman
schweizerisch Swiss
schwer heavy, difficult; **es fällt mir —** it's difficult for me
die **Schwester, –n** sister
schwierig difficult
die **Schwierigkeit, –en** difficulty
schwimmen, schwamm, (ist) geschwommen to swim
der **See, –n** lake
sehen (sieht), sah, gesehen to see
sehr very; very much
seit since; **— zwei Jahren** for the last two years
seitdem since
die **Seite, –n** page, side
die **seitenlinie, –n** sideline
Selb– same
selber self; myself, himself, etc.
selbst self; myself, himself, etc.; even
selbstverständlich obvious, of course
selten seldom
das **Semester, –** semester
die **Semesterprüfung, -en** semester examination
senden, sandte, gesandt to send
der **Sender, –** (radio) station; (TV) channel
die **Sendung, –en** program (*on radio or TV*); shipment
servieren to serve
setzen to put, set; **sich —** to sit down
sicher sure; safe
die **Sicherheit, –en** certainty
singen, sang, gesungen to sing
sinken, sank, (ist) gesunken to sink
der **Sinn** thought; mind; **etwas im — haben** to have something in mind; to plan; **in den — kommen** to occur
der **Sitz, –e** seat
sitzen, saß, gesessen to sit
die **Skiausrüstung, –en** skiing equipment
so . . . wie as . . . as
sobald as soon as
sofort immediately
sogar even
der **Sohn, ⸗e** son
so lange as long as
solch such
der **Soldat, –en, –en** soldier
sollen (soll), sollte, gesollt to be supposed to, to be to; shall, should; to be said to
der **Sommer, –** summer
die **Sommerferien** *pl.* summer vacation
der **Sommertag, –e** summer day
sondern but (rather, on the contrary)
die **Sonne, –n** sun
der **Sonnenaufgang, ⸗e** sunrise
der **Sonntag, –e** Sunday; **sonntags** on Sunday
sonst otherwise
die **Sorge, –n** worry, anxiety; **sich Sorgen machen um** to worry about
sowie as well as
(das) **Spanien** Spain
spannend exciting
sparsam economical, thrifty
der **Spaß, ⸗sse** joke; **— beiseite** all joking aside
spät late; **wie — ist es?** what time is it?
spazieren-gehen, ging spazieren, ist spazierengegangen to take a walk, go for a walk
der **Spaziergang, ⸗e** walk; **einen — machen** to take a walk
der **Speisesaal, –säle** dining room
der **Spezialist, –en, –en** specialist
das **Spiel, –e** play, game
spielen to play; to act; to be shown, be given
der **Spieler, –** player

die **Spielerin, –nen** player
der **Sport, –e** sport
sportlich sporting, athletic
der **Sportplatz, ⸚e** arena, stadium
die **Sprache, –n** language
sprechen (spricht), sprach, gesprochen to speak
springen, sprang, ist gesprungen to jump
spüren to feel
der **Staat, –en** state
die **Stadt, ⸚e** city
das **Stadion, Stadien** stadium
der **Stadtteil, –e** section (of a city)
das **Stadtzentrum** center of a city
stammen to come from, originate
der **Stammtisch, –e** club table
stark strong, severe, heavy
statt instead of
statt-finden, fand statt, stattgefunden to take place
stecken to put, stick
stehen, stand, gestanden to stand; to be printed, be written
stehen-bleiben, blieb stehen, ist stehengeblieben to stop
stehen-lassen (läßt stehen), ließ stehen, stehengelassen to leave
stehlen (stiehlt), stahl, gestohlen to steal
steigen, stieg, ist gestiegen to climb; **ins Examen —** to take an examination
stellen to put, place
der **Stellvertreter, –** substitute, deputy
sterben (stirbt), starb, ist gestorben to die
das **Steuer, –** steering wheel
stimmen to agree; to vote; **es stimmt** that's right, true
die **Stimmung, –en** mood, atmosphere
der **Stock, Stockwerke** story, floor
das **Stockwerk, –e** story, floor
stolz auf proud of
der **Stolz** pride
stoppen to stop
stören to disturb
stoßen (stößt), stieß, gestoßen to push, toss; to kick
die **Strafe, –n** punishment, (violation) ticket
die **Straße, –n** street
die **Straßenbahn, –en** streetcar
das **Straßenbahngeleise, –** streetcar track
die **Straßenecke, –n** street corner
die **Straßenkreuzung, –en** street intersection
die **Strecke, –n** stretch, way, road
streiten, stritt, gestritten to quarrel
streng strict, severe
das **Stück, –e** piece; presentation, drama
der **Student, –en, –en** student
die **Studentin, –nen** student
der **Studentenverein, –e** student club
die **Studienkollegin, –nen** fellow student
studieren to study
das **Studium** studies, studying
der **Stuhl, ⸚e** chair
die **Stunde, –n** hour
Stuttgart *city on the Neckar river in southwestern Germany*
das **Substantiv, –e** noun
suchen to look for
der **Süden** south
der **Superlativ** superlative degree
die **Suppe, –n** soup
die **Süßigkeit, –en** candy, sweets

tadeln to criticize
die **Tafel, –n** board, plate, panel; notice
der **Tag, –e** day
die **Tageszeit, –en** time of day
die **Tagung, –en** meeting, convention
das **Tal, ⸚er** valley
der **Tank, –e** tank
tanken to get gasoline
die **Tankstelle, –n** gasoline station
der **Tankwart, –e** gas-station attendant
die **Tante, –n** aunt
tanzen to dance
der **Tänzer, –** dancer
die **Tasche, –n** pocket
das **Taschentuch, ⸚er** handkerchief
die **Tasse, –n** cup
die **Tat, –en** act, deed
die **Tatsache, –n** fact

tatsächlich as a matter of fact, indeed; real
tauschen change, exchange
tausend thousand
die **Taxe, –n** taxi
der **Tee** tea
die **Teegesellschaft, –en** tea (party)
der **Teil, –e** part
teilen to divide; to share
teil-nehmen (nimmt teil), nahm teil, teilgenommen (an) to take part (in), participate
telefonisch by telephone
der **Teller, –** plate
der **Tenor, ⸚e** tenor
der **Teppich, –e** carpet
die **Terrasse** terrace, observation deck
teuer expensive
das **Theater, –** theater
die **Theaterkasse, –n** box office
das **Theaterstück, –e** play
tief deep
das **Tier, –e** animal
die **Tinte, –n** ink
der **Tisch, –e** table; **sich zu — setzen** to sit down at the table (*for a meal*)
die **Tischplatte, –n** table top
der **Titel, –** title
todkrank deathly ill
das **Tor, –e** gate; (*in soccer*) goal
die **Torte, –n** torte, fancy cake
der **Torwart, –e** goalie
tot dead
tot-schlagen (schlägt tot), schlug tot, totgeschlagen to strike dead, kill
tragen (trägt), trug, getragen to carry; to wear
die **Tragödie, -n** tragedy
trauen to trust
die **Trauer** mourning
das **Trauerspiel, –e** tragedy
traurig sad
treffen (trifft), traf, getroffen to meet; **es gut —** to be lucky
die **Treppe, –n** staircase; **eine — hoch** one flight up, on the second floor
treten (tritt), trat, ist getreten to step, go; **in die Pedale —** to pedal
treu loyal, faithful
die **Treue** loyalty, faithfulness
trinken, trank, getrunken to drink
das **Trinkgeld, –er** tip, gratuity
trocken dry
trotz in spite of
trotzdem although; nevertheless
tüchtig capable, sturdy
tun, tat, getan to do
die **Tür, –en** door
die **Türkei** Turkey
der **Turnverein, –e** athletic club

übel bad; sick; **mir ist —** I'm sick
übel-nehmen (nimmt übel), nahm übel, übelgenommen to hold against
über over, above; via, by way of
überall everywhere
überhaupt on the whole, at all; **— nicht** not at all
überlegen superior
übermorgen day after tomorrow
übernachten to stay overnight
überraschen to surprise
die **Überraschung, –en** surprise
überreden to convince, persuade
übersetzen to translate
über-ziehen, zog über, übergezogen to pull over
übrigens incidentally
die **Übung, –en** exercise
die **Uhr, –en** time; watch, clock; o'clock; **um wieviel —?** at what time?
um around; at; **um . . . zu** in order to, to
um-ändern to change
umarmen to embrace
um-drehen to turn around
umher-schauen to look around
der **Umstand, ⸚e** circumstance; *pl.* formalities
um-wechseln to exchange
der **Umweg, –e** detour, roundabout way
unbegreiflich incomprehensible
unbekannt unknown
unerwartet unexpected
der **Unfall, ⸚e** accident
ungesund unhealthful, unhealthy

ungewöhnlich unusual
das **Unglück, -e** misfortune; accident
unglücklich unhappy; unlucky
unhöflich impolite
die **Universität, -en** university
unklar unclear
das **Unkraut, ¨-er** weed
unmöglich impossible
unpraktisch impractical
unrecht wrong; **— haben** to be wrong
unsicher insecure, uncertain
der **Unsinn** nonsense
unter under; beneath
unterbrechen (unterbricht), unterbrach, unterbrochen to interrupt
unter-bringen, brachte unter, untergebracht to house, shelter
unterhalb below
sich unterhalten (unterhält), unterhielt, unterhalten to converse; to enjoy oneself
das **Unterhaltungsprogramm, -e** variety show
die **Unterkunft, ¨-e** lodging
unternehmen (unternimmt), unternahm, unternommen to undertake
der **Unterschied, -e** difference
unterwegs on the way
unverständlich incomprehensible
usw. = und so weiter and so on

der **Vater, ¨-** father
die **Verabredung, -en** appointment
sich verabschieden to take leave
die **Veranstaltung, -en** arrangement; **die sportliche —** sport event
verbieten, verbot, verboten to prohibit
verbinden, verband, verbunden to join, unite
die **Verbindung, -en** connection, contact; fraternity
verboten forbidden, prohibited
das **Verbot, -e** prohibition
(sich) verbreiten to spread
verbringen, verbrachte, verbracht to spend (*time*)
vereinigen to unite
der **Verein, -e** club
der **Verfasser, -** author
vergehen, verging, ist vergangen to pass
vergessen (vergißt), vergaß, vergessen to forget
das **Vergnügen, -** pleasure; **sich ein — aus etwas machen** to take pleasure in something
verheiratet married
verkaufen to sell
der **Verkehr** traffic
das **Verkehrszeichen, -** traffic signal
verlassen (verläßt), verließ, verlassen to leave, depart from; **sich — auf** to rely on
verlegen embarrassed
die **Verletzung, -en** injury
verlieren, verlor, verloren to lose
vermeiden, vermied, vermieden to avoid
vermissen to miss
vermögen (vermag), vermochte, vermocht to be able to
vermutlich presumably, probably
vernünftig intelligent
veröffentlichen to publish
verpacken to pack up
verreisen to leave (for a trip)
die **Versammlung, -en** meeting
verschieben, verschob, verschoben to postpone
verschieden various, different
verschlimmern to make worse
versehen (versieht), versah, versehen to provide, supply
die **Verspätung, -en** delay; **— haben** to be late
versprechen (verspricht), versprach, versprochen to promise
verstehen, verstand, verstanden to understand; **es versteht sich** that's understood
verstorben deceased
der **Versuch, -e** attempt, experiment
versuchen to attempt, try
verteidigen to defend
vertreten (vertritt), vertrat, vertreten to represent; **die Meinung —** to be of the opinion
verwandt related
der **Verwandte, -n, -n** relative
verwenden to use
verwunden to wound, injure

die **Verzeihung** pardon; **um — bitten** to beg pardon, apologize
verzollen to declare (at customs)
der **Vetter, –n** nephew
viel much; **viele** many
vielleicht perhaps
das **Volk, ⸚er** people, nation
voll full; **voller** full of
vor before, in front of; ago; **er hat etwas —** he intends to do something, he has something in mind; **es kommt mir —** it seems to me
voraus-bestellen to reserve, order in advance
voraussichtlich presumably, probably
vorbei past
vorbei-gehen, ging vorbei, ist vorbeigegangen to pass
vor-bereiten to prepare
die **Vorderseite, –n** front, facade
vorerst first of all
vor-haben to plan, have in mind
der **Vorhang, ⸚e** curtain
vorher before, previously
vorig– previous; last
vor-kommen, kam vor, ist vorgekommen to occur; to exist; to appear, seem
der **Vormittag, –e** forenoon, morning; **am —** in the morning
vorne up front
der **Vorschlag, ⸚e** proposal, suggestion
vor-schlagen (schlägt vor), schlug vor, vorgeschlagen to suggest
vorsichtig careful, cautious
der **Vorsitzende, –n, –n** chairman
die **Vorstadt, ⸚e** suburb; outskirts
vor-stellen to introduce; **sich** (*acc.*) **—** to introduce oneself; **sich** (*dat.*) **—** to imagine
die **Vorstellung, –en** performance; conception
der **Vorteil, –e** advantage
der **Vortrag, ⸚e** lecture
das **Vorwort** preface
vor-ziehen, zog vor, vorgezogen to prefer

wach awake
wachsen (wächst), wuchs, ist gewachsen to grow
der **Wagen, –** automobile, car
wählen to elect
wahr true; **— werden** to come true, become real; **nicht —?** isn't that right?
während while; during
die **Wahrheit, –en** truth
wahrscheinlich probably, apparently
die **Wahrscheinlichkeit, –en** probability
der **Wald, ⸚er** woods, forest
die **Wand, ⸚e** wall
wandern to wander; to be (go) on an outing
wann when
das **Warenhaus, ⸚er** store
warnen to warn
warten to wait; **— auf** to wait for
warum why
was what; **— für ein** what kind of a
waschen (wäscht), wusch, gewaschen to wash
das **Wasser** water
wechseln to change
der **Wecker, –** alarm clock
weder . . . noch neither . . . nor
der **Weg, –e** way, road, route
weg away
wegen because of
weg-gehen, ging weg, ist weggegangen to go away
weg-werfen (wirft weg), warf weg, weggeworfen to throw away
weh: (sich) — tun to hurt (oneself)
wehen to blow
Weihnachten Christmas
weil because
Weimar *city in central Germany, today in East Germany*
der **Weinberg, –e** vineyard
weinen to weep
weit far, distant; **bei weitem** by far; **und so weiter (usw.)** and so on, etc.

weiter further, additional; *verbal prefix expressing continuation*
weiter-gehen, ging weiter, ist weitergegangen to go on
weiter-regnen to keep on raining
welcher, welche, welches which
die **Weltanschauung, -en** philosophy of life
weltberühmt world-famous
der **Weltkrieg, -e** world war
der **Weltmeister, -** world champion
wem whom, to whom
wen whom
wenden, wandte, gewandt to turn
wenig little, few; **weniger** less, fewer
wenn when, whenever, if; **wenn . . . auch** even if
werden (wird), wurde, ist geworden to become
das **Werk, -e** work
das **Werkzeug, -e** tool
weshalb why
wessen whose
der **Westen** west
das **Wetter** weather
der **Wetterbericht, -e** weather report
wichtig important
wider against
widerstehen, widerstand, widerstanden to resist
wie how, as; **— bitte?** I beg your pardon, I didn't understand
wieder again
der **Wiederaufbau** rebuilding, reconstruction
wiederholen to repeat
wieder-holen, holte wieder, wiedergeholt to get again
wieder-kommen, kam wieder, ist wiedergekommen to come again
wieder-sehen (sieht wieder), sah wieder, wiedergesehen to see again
das **Wiedersehen** reunion; **(auf) —!** good-by, so long
wiegen, wog, gewogen to weigh
Wien Vienna
wild wild
der **Wille, -ns, -n** will
willen: um . . . — for the sake of
willkommen welcome
der **Wind, -e** wind
winken to signal, wave
der **Winter, -** winter
der **Winterartikel, -** winter article
wirklich real(ly), truly
das **Wirtshaus, ⸚er** tavern
wissen (weiß), wußte, gewußt to know; **ich weiß es nicht recht** I'm not too sure
wo where
die **Woche, -n** week
woher from where
wohl well; probably; **mir ist —** I'm well
wohnen to live, dwell
wohnhaft in residence, dwelling
die **Wohnung, -en** apartment
das **Wohnviertel, -** residential section
wollen (will), wollte, gewollt to want (to); to be about to, intend to; to claim
womit with what, with which
womöglich wherever possible, if possible
das **Wort, -e** *or* **⸚er** word
das **Wörterbuch, ⸚er** dictionary
worüber about what
wozu what for
sich wundern to be astonished; **es wundert mich** I am surprised
wünschen to wish, want

die **Zahl, -en** number, figure
das **Zahlwort, ⸚er** number, numeral
zähmen to tame
der **Zahnarzt, ⸚e** dentist
das **Zahnweh** toothache
zeigen to show
die **Zeit, -en** time; **die ganze —** all the time
die **Zeitangabe, -n** time, stating the time
zeitig on time
die **Zeitschrift, -en** periodical
die **Zeitung, -en** newspaper
zerstören to destroy
der **Zettel, -** sheet of paper

das **Zeugnis, –se** report card, transcript of grades
ziehen, zog, gezogen to pull; (*with* **sein**) to move, go
das **Ziel, –e** goal, purpose
ziemlich rather
die **Zigarette, –n** cigarette
das **Zimmer, –** room
das **Zollamt, ⸚er** customs office
der **Zollbeamte, –n, –n** customs officer
die **Zollkontrolle, –n** customs inspection
der **Zucker** sugar
zuerst at first, first
zufrieden satisfied, pleased
der **Zug, ⸚e** train
der **Zuhörer, –** listener
die **Zukunft** future
zuletzt at last, last
zurück back, returned
zurück-fliegen, flog zurück, ist zurückgeflogen to fly back
zurück-kehren to return
zurück-kommen, kam zurück, ist zurückgekommen to come back
zusammen together
zusammen-kommen, kam zusammen, ist zusammengekommen to come together, get together
die **Zusammenkunft, ⸚e** meeting, reunion
die **Zusammensetzung, –en** compound, composition
zusammen-stürzen to collapse
der **Zuschauer, –** spectator
der **Zustand, ⸚e** condition
zwar as a matter of fact, to be sure
der **Zweck, –e** purpose
der **Zweifel, –** doubt
zweifellos undoubtedly
zweifeln to doubt
zweimal twice
zwischen between
das **Zwischenexamen, –** periodic examination
der **Zwischenfall, ⸚** incident

ENGLISH-GERMAN

able: be — können
about über; von; ungefähr
accompany begleiten
across über
act spielen; **— as if** tun als ob
actor der Schauspieler, –; der Darsteller, –
address die Adresse, –n
afraid: be — of Angst haben vor, sich fürchten vor
after nach; nachdem
afternoon der Nachmittag, –e; **this —** heute nachmittag
ago vor
all alle; **in —** im Ganzen; insgesamt
airplane das Flugzeug, –e
airport der Flughafen, ¨–
almost beinahe
along entlang
already schon
also auch
although obgleich; obwohl
always immer
amazed: be — sich wundern
America (das) Amerika
American der Amerikaner, –
American amerikanisch
annoyed: be — sich ärgern
another noch ein
answer antworten; beantworten
apple cake der Apfelkuchen, –
arrest verhaften
arrive an-kommen
article der Artikel, –
as als; **— if** als ob
ask fragen; **— for something** um etwas bitten
athletic athletisch; **— club** der Turnverein, –e
Atlantic der Atlantik
attend besuchen
attendant (*at a gas station*) der Tankwart, –e
attention die Aufmerksamkeit, –en; **I call your — to** ich mache Sie aufmerksam auf (+ *acc.*); **I call to your — that** Ich mache Sie darauf aufmerksam, daß
August der August
autobahn die Autobahn, –en

bad schlecht; schlimm; **too —** schade
balcony der Balkon, –e
ball der Ball, ¨–e
band die Kapelle, –n
bank die Bank, –en; (*of a river*) das Ufer, –
Bavaria (das) Bayern
because weil; da; denn
bed das Bett, –en; **in —** im Bett
before vor; vorher; bevor
begin beginnen, an-fangen
behind hinter
belong gehören
best-known bekanntest–
better besser; **like —** lieber haben
bicycle das Fahrrad, ¨er; **— excursion** der Ausflug mit dem Fahrrad
big groß
bike das Rad, ¨–er; das Fahrrad, ¨–er
birthday der Geburtstag, –e; **— present** das Geburtstagsgeschenk, –e
bit: — of news die Nachricht, –en
blow blasen, wehen; **— up** auf-blasen, auf-pumpen
boardinghouse die Pension, –en
book das Buch, ¨–er
bookstore der Bücherladen, ¨–
boring langweilig
borrow sich (*dat.*) leihen
both beide
box die Kiste, –n; die Schachtel, –n
boy der Junge, –n, –n
bring bringen
brother der Bruder, ¨–
build bauen
building das Gebäude, –
business: on — geschäftlich
but aber
buy kaufen

call rufen, an-rufen
camera shop das Fotogeschäft, –e
can können
car der Wagen, –; das Auto, –s
card die Karte, –n
castle das Schloß, ¨–sser; die Burg, –en

catch fangen; **— cold** sich (*acc.*) erkälten
cause verursachen
cheap billig
chemistry die Chemie
city die Stadt, ¨e
claim behaupten
class die Klasse, –n
clever klug
club der Verein, –e; **athletic —** der Turnverein, –e
cold kalt; **I am —** mich friert; mir ist kalt; **catch —** sich (*acc.*) erkälten
color print der Farbdruck, –e
come kommen; **— back** zurück-kommen; **— in** herein-kommen; **— together** zusammen-kommen
commercial die Reklame, –n
cool kühl
couple das Paar, –e
course: of — natürlich, selbstverständlich
criminal der Verbrecher, –
cup die Tasse, –n
curtain der Vorhang, ¨e

daughter die Tochter, ¨
day der Tag, –e
December der Dezember
decipher entziffern
deck das Deck, –e; **on —** auf dem Deck
detective story die Kriminalgeschichte, –n; das Kriminalstück, –e
develop entwickeln; **for developing** zum Entwickeln
difference der Unterschied, –e; **make no —** nichts aus-machen
difficult schwer, schwierig
dining room das Eßzimmer, –; der Speisesaal, –säle
directly direkt
display window das Schaufenster, –
discuss besprechen
do tun, machen
doctor der Arzt, ¨e
dollar der Dollar, –s
drink trinken
drive fahren
during während

each jeder, jede, jedes
easy leicht
eighteen achtzehn
elsewhere anderswo
end das Ende, –n; **at the —** am Ende
evening der Abend, –e; **this —** heute abend
every jeder, jede, jedes
everything alles
examination die Prüfung, –en; das Examen, –; **final —** die Endprüfung, –en; **periodic —** das Zwischenexamen, –; **semester —** die Semesterprüfung, –en
except außer
exchange um-wechseln
exchange student der Austauschstudent, –en, -en; die Austauschstudentin, –nen
exciting erregend
excursion der Ausflug, ¨e
existence: be in — existieren
expected erwartet, erhofft
expensive teuer
explain erklären

fail (*an examination*) durch-fallen
family die Familie, –n
far fern; weit; **on the — side** jenseits
father der Vater, ¨
February der Februar
few wenige; **a —** einige
fill füllen
film der Film, –e
find finden
finish beenden, fertig-machen
first erst; zuerst
fix flicken, reparieren
flag die Fahne, –n
flight der Flug, ¨e; **— ticket** die Flugkarte, –n
fluently fließend, geläufig
fly fliegen
follow folgen
for für; seit
forget vergessen
formerly früher
forward: to look — to sich (*acc.*) freuen auf (+ *acc.*)
fraternity die Verbindung, –en
free frei

Frenchwoman die Französin, –nen
frequently oft
friend der Freund, –e; die Freundin, –nen
from aus
funny komisch; lustig

game das Spiel, –e; **soccer —** das Fußballspiel, –e
gas das Benzin; **— station** die Tankstelle, –n
German deutsch; **in —** auf deutsch; **—** (*language*) das Deutsch; (*person*) der Deutsche, –n, –n
Germany (das) Deutschland
get erhalten, bekommen; **— gas** tanken; **— together** zusammenkommen
give geben
glad: be — about sich (*acc.*) freuen über
go gehen; **— along** mit-gehen; **— to lectures** ins Kolleg gehen; **— up** auf-gehen
good gut; **good-by!** auf Wiedersehen! **to say good-by** sich (*acc.*) verabschieden
government die Regierung, –en
great groß

half halb; die Hälfte, –n
half time die Pause, –n; die Halbzeit, –en
handkerchief das Taschentuch, ⸚er
happen geschehen
happy glücklich; **be — about** sich (*acc.*) freuen über
have haben; **— in mind** vor-haben; **— something done** etwas tun lassen; **— to** müssen
hear hören
help helfen
here hier
hide verbergen
hill der Hügel, –
home: come — heim-kehren
hotel das Hotel, –s; **— room** das Hotelzimmer, –
house das Haus, ⸚er; **at our —** bei uns

how wie; **— do you do?** es freut mich, Sie kennenzulernen
however aber, jedoch; trotzdem

if wenn; **as —** als ob
ill krank
inquire about sich (*acc.*) erkundigen nach
inscription die Inschrift, –en
instead of anstatt
intend wollen, die Absicht haben
interested: be — in sich (*acc.*) interessieren für
interesting interessant
intermission die Pause, –n
into in
introduce vor-stellen
invite ein-laden
Italian der Italiener, –

January der Januar
just eben; gerade; nur

know (*a fact*) wissen; (*a person*) kennen; (*a language*) können

lady die Dame, –n
last letzt–
lazy faul
leading: the — actor der Hauptdarsteller, –
learn lernen; erfahren
leather glove der Lederhandschuh, –e
leather shorts die Lederhosen
leave lassen; verlassen; stehen-lassen
lecture der Vortrag, ⸚e; **give a —** einen Vortrag halten; **go to lectures** (*at a university*) ins Kolleg gehen
letter der Brief, –e
library die Bibliothek, –en
like mögen; gern haben; **I — it** es gefällt mir
listen horchen, zu-hören; **— to the radio** Radio hören
little klein; **a —** ein wenig
live leben; wohnen
living room das Wohnzimmer, –
long lang
look schauen; **— at** (sich) an-schauen, (sich) an-sehen; **— for** suchen; **— forward to** sich freuen auf (+ *acc.*)

lose verlieren
loud laut
low niedrig

mail schicken, mit der Post schicken
make machen; **— no difference** nichts aus-machen
man der Mann, ⸚er
many viele; **— a** mancher, manche, manches
mark die Mark
mathematics die Mathematik
meet begegnen, treffen; kennen-lernen
minute die Minute, –n
modern modern
Monday der Montag
money das Geld
month der Monat
more mehr
morning der Morgen, –; **this —** heute morgen
mother die Mutter, ⸚
mountain(s) das Gebirge, –
movies: go to the — ins Kino gehen
much viel
museum das Museum, Museen; **art —** das Kunstmuseum
must müssen
my mein

natural(ly) natürlich
need brauchen
nephew der Neffe, –n, –n
nevertheless dennoch, trotzdem
new neu
news die Nachricht, –en; **— broadcast** die Nachrichtensendung, –en
next nächst–
nice nett, sympathisch
night die Nacht, ⸚e; **last —** gestern abend
no nein; kein
nothing nichts
notice bemerken
now jetzt, nun
nowadays heutzutage

occur ein-fallen
official der Beamte, –n, –n
often oft
old alt; **— grads** alte Herren
one man
only nur; erst
opera die Oper, –n
orchestra das Parkett, –e
order bestellen; **in — to** um . . . zu
other ander–; **each other** einander

pair das Paar, –e
parents die Eltern (*pl.*)
parking lot der Parkplatz, ⸚e
party die Gesellschaft, –en
passport der Reisepaß, ⸚sse
pay zahlen, bezahlen; **— for** bezahlen
people die Leute (*pl.*)
performance die Vorstellung, –en
perhaps vielleicht
place das Lokal, –e
plan planen
play das Stück, –e; das Schauspiel, –e
play spielen; (*of movies*) laufen
player der Spieler, –
please bitte
police die Polizei
politics die Politik
poor schlecht; schlimm
prepare (*food*) zu-bereiten; (*for a trip*) sich bereit-machen
present das Geschenk, –e; **birthday —** das Geburtstagsgeschenk, –e
present vor-stellen
price der Preis, –e; **for that —** zu diesem Preis
probable wahrscheinlich
professor der Professor, –en
program das Programm, –e
promise versprechen
pump die Pumpe, –n
purchase der Einkauf, ⸚e

radio das Radio, –s; **— set** der Radioapparat, –e
rain der Regen; regnen; **it rains** es regnet
reach erreichen
read lesen
really wirklich
reception der Empfang, ⸚e
recommend empfehlen
refreshment die Erfrischung, –en
remain bleiben
remind erinnern an (+ *acc.*)

repair material das Flickzeug, –e
reply antworten, entgegnen
reserve reservieren, voraus-bestellen
restaurant das Restaurant, –s; das Gasthaus, ¨er
return zurück-kehren
reunion das Wiedersehen, –; die Zusammenkunft, ¨e
Rhine der Rhein; **— trip** die Rheinfahrt, –en
right das Recht, –e
river der Fluß, ¨sse
rob berauben
role die Rolle, –n
room das Zimmer, –; **hotel —** das Hotelzimmer, –
route der Weg, –e
ruin die Ruine, –n
run rennen, laufen; **— into somebody** jemand begegnen; **—** (*a boarding-house*) führen

safe sicher
salesgirl die Verkäuferin, -nen
say sagen; **it goes without saying** es versteht sich
scarf das Halstuch, ¨er
seat der Sitz, –e; der Sitzplatz, ¨e
secret das Geheimnis, –se
see sehen
seem scheinen; vor-kommen
select aus-wählen
selection die Auswahl, –en
sell verkaufen
September der September
serve servieren, bedienen
several mehrere
shake schütteln; **— hands with** die Hand geben
sharp: at eight — Punkt acht (Uhr)
shop der Laden, ¨
shop Einkäufe machen, ein-kaufen
short kurz
show die Vorstellung, –en
sick krank
simply einfach
since seit
sister-in-law die Schwägerin, –nen
sit sitzen
skyscraper der Wolkenkratzer, –
smart klug
snow der Schnee; schneien; **it snows** es schneit
soccer der Fußball
some einige
something etwas
sometimes manchmal
sorry: I am — es tut mir leid; ich bedauere
southeast of südöstlich von
speak sprechen
spend (*time*) verbringen; (*money*) aus-geben
spring der Frühling
stadium das Stadion
stay bleiben
steamer das Schiff, –e; der Dampfer, –
stop halten, an-halten; stehen-bleiben
store der Laden, ¨
story der Stock; das Stockwerk, –e
street die Straße, –n
student der Student, –en, –en; die Studentin, –nen
study lernen, studieren
succeed: I — es gelingt mir
such solcher, solche, solches
suddenly plötzlich
suggestion der Vorschlag, ¨e
summer der Sommer
Sunday der Sonntag
superior überlegen
supposed: to be — to sollen
surprise erstaunen, überraschen
surprising überraschend
sweater der Pullover, –

table der Tisch, –e; **special —** der Stammtisch, –e; **— top** die Tischplatte, –n
take bringen, nehmen; **— an exam** ins Examen steigen
talk sprechen, plaudern
tank der Tank, –e
tavern das Wirtshaus, ¨er
tea der Tee
team die Mannschaft, –en
television das Fernsehen; **— set** der Fernsehapparat, –e; **on —** im Fernsehen
tell sagen; **be told** erfahren, vernehmen
than als
that is das heißt (d.h.)

theater das Theater, –
then dann
there dort, da
thing das Ding, –e; die Sache, **–n**
think denken; glauben
thirsty durstig
three drei
through durch
thunderstorm das Gewitter, –
ticket die Karte, –n; die Eintrittskarte, –n; (*train and bus*) die Fahrkarte, –n; (*airplane*) die Flugkarte, –n
tie die Krawatte, –n
time die Zeit, –en; **have a good —** sich (*acc.*) amüsieren; **some other —** ein andermal
tire der Reifen, –
today heute
together zusammen
tomorrow morgen
too zu; auch
travel reisen
travelers check der Reisescheck, –s
treat behandeln
trip die Reise, –n; **take a —** eine Reise machen; **vacation —** die Ferienreise, –n
true wahr; **come —** wahr werden
try versuchen
two zwei

understand verstehen
unexpected unerwartet, unverhofft
unfortunately leider
unhappy unglücklich
university die Universität, –en
until bis
use der Gebrauch, ⸚e; die Verwendung, –en; **be able to make good — of** gut gebrauchen können
use gebrauchen, benutzen
useful nützlich
usually gewöhnlich

vacation die Ferien (*pl.*); der Urlaub, –e; **— trip** die Ferienreise, –n
valuable wertvoll
very sehr
via über (+ *acc.*)
Vienna (das) Wien
village das Dorf, ⸚er
vineyard der Weinberg, –e
visit der Besuch, –e; besuchen

wait warten; **— for** warten auf (+ *acc.*)
wall die Wand, ⸚e
want wollen; wünschen
war der Krieg, –e
waste verschwenden
watch sich (*dat.*) an-sehen
way der Weg, –e; **by — of** über (+ *acc.*)
week die Woche, –n
well gut; **I am —** es geht mir gut
what was; was für (ein)
wheel das Steuer
when wenn; als; wann
where wo; wohin
while während, als
whole ganz
whose wessen
wicked schlecht, bös
win gewinnen
wind der Wind
winter der Winter
with mit
without ohne
work die Arbeit, –en
wrap verpacken
write schreiben

year das Jahr, –e
yellow gelb
yesterday gestern
young jung

Index

(Numbers refer to pages)

Glossary

ABLAUT: Vowel variation (trinken, trank, getrunken) indicating distinctions in verb forms.

ACCUSATIVE CASE: The case primarily of the direct object.

ACTIVE: The form of the verb indicating that the subject acts.

ADJECTIVE: A word that modifies a noun or pronoun.

ADVERB: A word that modifies a verb, an adjective, or another adverb.

ATTRIBUTIVE ADJECTIVE: An adjective that precedes the noun it modifies.

AUXILIARY VERB: A verb that helps in the conjugation of another verb **(haben, sein, werden).**

CASE: The form of a noun, pronoun, article, or adjective indicating its function in a clause. German has four cases: nominative, genitive, dative, accusative.

CLAUSE: A group of words containing a subject and predicate. A main (independent) clause can stand alone; a subordinate (dependent) clause can function only as part of another clause.

COMPARISON: The change in the form of an adjective or adverb showing degrees of quality: positive **(schön),** comparative **(schöner),** superlative **(der, die, das schönste; am schönsten).**

CONJUGATION: The changes of form in verbs showing number, person, tense, mood, voice.

CONJUNCTION: A word used to connect words, phrases, or clauses. Coordinating conjunctions connect expressions of equal value. Subordinating conjunctions connect a subordinate clause with another clause.

DATIVE CASE: The case primarily of the indirect object.

DECLENSION: The change of form in nouns, pronouns, or adjectives indicating gender, number, and case.

DEFINITE ARTICLE: **der, die, das** (*the*).

DEMONSTRATIVE: Indicating or pointing out the person or thing referred to (*this, that, these, those*).

DER-WORDS: Words following the inflectional pattern of the definite article.

EIN-WORDS: Words following the inflectional pattern of the indefinite article in the singular, **kein** in the plural.

FINITE VERB: The verb form showing person, number, tense.

GENDER: The grammatical classification of nouns: masculine, feminine, neuter.

GENITIVE CASE: The case indicating primarily possession and origin.

IMPERATIVE: The mood of the verb expressing a command or directive.

INDEFINITE ARTICLE: **ein, eine, ein** (*a, an*).